DERRIDA

DERRIDA

Negotiating the Legacy

Edited by
MADELEINE FAGAN, LUDOVIC GLORIEUX,
INDIRA HAŠIMBEGOVIĆ AND MARIE SUETSUGU

EDINBURGH UNIVERSITY PRESS

© editorial material and organisation Madeleine Fagan, Ludovic Glorieux,
Indira Hašimbegović and Marie Suetsugu, 2007
© the chapters their several authors, 2007

Edinburgh University Press Ltd
22 George Square, Edinburgh

Typeset in Goudy Old Style by
Iolaire Typesetting, Newtonmore, and
printed and bound in Great Britain by
Cromwell Press, Trowbridge, Wilts

A CIP record for this book is available from the British Library

ISBN 978 0 7486 2546 8 (hardback)
ISBN 978 0 7486 2547 5 (paperback)

Contents

Acknowledgements

We would like to thank Nick Vaughan-Williams for his outstanding contribution and without whom this project would not have materialised. Special thanks also go to Jenny Edkins, Mike Foley and Maja Zehfuss for their guidance in the course of this project. We would like to thank the Department of International Politics at University of Wales, Aberystwyth for their accommodation of the Aberystwyth Post International Group (APIG) and their ongoing support. In particular, thanks to Elaine Lowe for her assistance and co-operation throughout the preparation of this volume. Many thanks to all the APIG members for their engagement and support. We also thank the *Millennium: Journal of International Studies* for allowing the previously published chapter by Richard Beardsworth to appear in this volume.

Introduction: Inheriting Deconstruction, Surviving Derrida

Ludovic Glorieux and Indira Hašimbegović

The death of Jacques Derrida on 8 October 2004 generated a wave of reactions and unleashed a unique attention to the event. The passing away of one of the most important philosophers of the twentieth century cannot go unnoticed. While life, and therefore death, was central to his thinking on responsibility, friendship, hospitality and politics, his actual death affects his 'work' in ways that deserve a certain assessment, a careful attention. This necessity to assess the event and its impact on what might be left behind, what we might garner from him, is instigated by the loss of Derrida and the infinite distance that now separates, more than ever before, the body from the name.

Beside the necessity to respond to Derrida's death directly, to begin thinking what his death might involve for the consideration of what he wrote and thought, the need to produce this volume was accentuated by the public obituaries following his death. It was a question of not allowing these to become definitive; to respond in order to defeat those biting epitaphs. Tinted by misunderstanding and ill-advised criticism, displaying a malignant wit and vicious satire, some journalists found the silence of the philosopher a weak point to exploit. Condemning his thought as 'obscurantism', of being 'murky', 'enigmatic' or self-contradictory, *The New York Times* and *The Economist* made remarkable efforts to denigrate his work, coming to the conclusion that '[h]e was a sincere and learned man, if a confused one' who 'vehemently resisted any attempt to clarify his ideas'.[1] Defining deconstruction as an esoteric approach, they were able to make all arguments, including anti-semitic claims, acceptable and justifiable; basically, that it is nothing but a catch-all term, undefined and thus suitable for Derrida's academic devotees.[2] Dissatisfied with such simplistic assertions and idle approaches, we believe that some reflection on the topic of Derrida's thought, affected in many ways by his death, is necessary. In short, we are under the impression that now *il nous regarde*: he is looking at us as well as being at our concern.[3] So, from one side we are being stared at from beyond the grave, and from the other we are looking back in an inquiring fashion. Thus, we wondered how to respond to this call that we feel it is imperative to answer.

In the aftermath of his death, a different relation with Derrida's work is established: he can no longer answer for his work, he is no longer there as a possible master of its destiny. None the less, there exits a palpable desire to orchestrate his account, to comprehend what Derrida the philosopher is all about and consequently, to homogenise what is already called his '*oeuvre*'. Now that there are so many voices being raised against his work, what could be Derrida's legacy? It is possible that, in his spirit, we cannot make a final assertion. We ought to leave a place for critique, to allow and be receptive to interpretations: in short to be sensitive to negotiation. In this atmosphere, we open this collection with a reflection on what it means to inherit and what deconstruction has to say about inheritance. Tracing through the issue of inheritance, and using the gestures of deconstruction, we would like to argue that deconstruction is, in fact, itself a way of inheriting. Taking this to its logical consequence, we shall be reaching beyond the topic of heritage: deconstruction as inheritance unfolds a different conception of time, a recurrence of the past that facilitates the possibility of a future. In this oscillation between life and death, the argument comes back to us, to our position where talking about inheritance situates us as survivors.

Finally, the very theme of survival opens up a different imagination of living, of being with others and with the death of others; it effectively provides crucial conclusions for our conception of the political as it means that it can no longer monopolise in an ontology of presence the subject of politics as one always present, unique, countable and undifferentiable.

The Unease of Inheriting

The gift of inheritance

Let us then start with a discussion on heritage: what does heritage mean in deconstructive sense – as opposed to a more straightforward, common version of it – and what may that in turn inspire? As survivors of Derrida, we occupy a position that is, we should say, uncomfortable. Standing beside the grave of the man and the philosopher, we find ourselves citing him and asking:

> what happens when a great thinker becomes silent, one whom we knew living, whom we read and reread, and also heard, one from whom we are

still awaiting a response, as such a response would help us not only to think otherwise but to read what we thought we had already read under his signature, a response that held everything in reserve, and so much more than we thought we had already recognized there?[4]

This arrangement that we cannot escape, this death that we cannot ignore positions us in a structure governed by loss. What organises our reaction, what informs our attention to the event is an act of disappearance, a noticeable absence. Paradoxically, it is because of this void that we are looking for something. Some kind of remainder, we are convinced through our presence here, will tie the knot between the two realms of death and life, with which we are both now intertwined and ill at ease. The two realms bind our life: one of outliving others – which is structured by the living memory of the dead (in us) – and the forthcoming death of others. Thus, as we outlive this one other, we start oscillating, interestingly enough, between the indeterminate poles of life and death, we are weaving a spirit that has yet to be defined – and disturbed by an activity, that which Derrida calls the art of the weaver, consisting of tying and untying knots, of complicating the very fabric of our present existence.[5]

In a systematic fashion then, one is looking for something that is passed over, a gift passed on to the circle of mourners. Animated by one question, we wonder relentlessly what is the heritage with which we are left? Some paper, some thing that will testify, to the satisfaction of all, what has been left – behind, before, between. In this frantic analysis of the remains of the dead, of his belongings and his possessions, in the hope of finding a homogeneous given, we are halted. Resistance to this inquiry is fusing from all sides; we are caught in our own game – in its tight and unimaginative rules of inheritance – unable to find what we came looking for, forgetting that it is for what and who is lost in the first place that we engaged in this search.

In this type of rescue mission we display a desire for an ontology of the *is* that seems infallible; to the satisfaction of many it gathers what it was looking for: a safe testament that allows the mourners to sit back and rest in peace. No doubt that there is, in a heritage, a gift. However, the idea of a gift as a given, of *a* given, present to us all is not enough: it is a one-dimensional vision of what inheriting can consist of as well as an infidelity to the loss that initiated this search. In other words, we cannot subordinate the absence of the lost one to our own existence when it is the latter that is at the very centre of our troubled inquiry. Can we marginalise what we have at heart, and what is at the heart of our concern, for the sake of straightfowardness, for our urge for a gift as a given? In respect to this absence and in regard to the position we inhabit, we are moved – and we can no longer rest. The realisation that not solely what presents itself to us ought to deserve our attention forces us to leave some place to the unpresentable. Because we have to share what we are – or the place we occupy – with the past, we are also vulnerable to it, to its returning, to its disturbance and to what it can do to the present and the future. As such we are set in movement: we move critically from past to future via a transcended present; we establish ties and knots between times that appeared irreconcilable: the past of the present and the unforeseen future, all at once in the existence of the heir. Inheritance gives us a different relation to the past as, in order to respect the absence, there always needs to be some place for it – in the present, and in the future. This key notion, where the heir is traversed by time, puts him in the position of survivor – not quite here, or there, not quite alive but pursued by the death of others that is taking (its) place. As we shall see later, the argument has moved from the dead to the living, from 'his' position (an other's) to ours (the 'we') and this is bearing interesting consequences on how we may think politics.

Deconstruction as inheritance

In order to formulate conceptually a structure of inheritance and to account for the movement that a heritage initiates we have a duty, as the discussion above demonstrates, to always remain faithful to the loss that is at its origin. What our form of heritage, what our desire for fidelity demands is to take into account, and always be accountable to, the deceased. In these terms, the argument goes, deconstruction is in itself a way of 'inheriting'. It echoes what the process of inheriting requires: unearthing, contesting, breaking, negotiating. In deconstruction we have more than the duty to repeat, to rehearse: it is more than mimicking. It consists of a capacity to re-affirm and re-invent what survives and what is left before us, considering that which is left not as a gift or as a given. There is no comfort or ease in the process and the act of inheriting, and instead of 'a secure comfort that we rather too quickly associate with this word [legatee], the heir must always respond to a sort of double injunction, a contradictory assignation'.[6] Technically speaking, inheriting as deconstruction is a double draw – a double injunction, to paraphrase Derrida. *On the one hand*, it consists of a vulnerability to the ghost of the other, to his remain that can always unpredictably hunt and disturb our present. We are concerned here with those inscriptions that cannot be straightforwardly decoded – that which is sent off beyond the present, whose spirit will reappear and we do not know how. The bet we are taking, of deferring our relation with the heritage in order to remain faithful to the dead other and his return, not now but later, coming from the past right in the future, is one with time, and the destabilisation we are forcing upon it. In Derrida's words:

> The legacy and the allegation, the legibility of the legend or inscription . . . [is], only put off until later or sent off elsewhere. This sending or putting off [renvoi] gestures towards the past of an inheritance only by remaining to come.[7]

We can never be sure of the path we are engaging on and what will be the outcome. We cannot know the full extent; we cannot measure the amplitude of the heritage at any time. So we are betting and taking a risk by considering a heritage under the conceptual framework of deconstruction.

On the other hand, it is a form of retrieval – and possibly then, a form of debt. Derrida formulates this in *De Quoi Demain* stating that we have to draw from our heritage the conceptual tools permitting us to challenge the limits imposed by that heritage in the first place.[8] Moreover, this type of interaction, incessant and tireless with our heritage, he insists, is the work of deconstruction. Drawing from the past, re-evaluating it with the purpose of trespassing its own limits. Hence, those draws demand a critical involvement of the survivor to assess and reflect upon the heterogeneity of what is left in its eternal deferral, of what has been done in so many ways, especially in details. One is not left to rest but is forced to respond to the call of a heritage that is not there, given and handed in. In this testament we are offered an edgy gift indeed, one that is not given, and one that is effectively complicating the very attempt at inheriting anything.

Hence, for that work of re-reading, deconstruction in itself is a way of inheriting: favouring a special arrangement with time, it conceives of inheritance and the work it requires as anachronistic. It is an attempt at outdoing, preceding the past in the name of that past for a future out of that past – that remains reliant on that past that is now the future of the present heirs.[9] It qualifies as a way of inheriting through its relation to time both following in the foot steps of what was done and breaking from it in its name, opening up from the past a never closed future.

POLITICS OF SURVIVING

Until now we have spoken about, in so many words, the death of the other (Derrida as a specific other). Our reflection has been uniquely tinted by his death. Turning our focus in the opposite direction we would understand that, while probing the challenging terrains of inheritance and legacy, we tend to position ourselves as survivors. The time has come, perhaps, to begin speaking about surviving itself. Deconstruction, as we proposed, is ultimately a way of inheriting: it demands a different relation to a reformulated notion of time via its resistance to the idea of heritage as a given. Allowing for a non-totalising relationship to the past through the idea of non-presence (ghost) and non-presentability, deconstruction as inheritance propels this past towards the future and displaces the rule of presence and present in terms of *is*. Moving one step further, deconstruction as inheritance opens a different conceptualisation of the relationship between living and dying by establishing the mode of surviving as a structural condition. We are insisting here on speaking about surviving, not simply living or *outliving* someone who passed away. Somebody may have died, and we may continue to live; but what seem to be two separate poles (life and death) gather in a rather close relationship in the structure of survival. Notice that it is not only the rapprochement between the two poles that our query is directed towards here. We are equally concerned by the premise of this discussion: someone has died, another one is lost. We wish to argue that our act of surviving can only happen between two: between life and death, between one and the other. Investigating these two, one after another and one with another, we shall pursue our initial thrust of deconstruction as inheritance that will lead us, eventually, to political conclusions. In this regard inheriting deconstruction as a way of inheriting does not give us definite formulas or political agendas. In fact, as the former section demonstrates, such a thing would go against the grain of any kind of deconstructive engagement. Thus, there is no such thing as a concrete, deconstructive answer of 'what is to be done?'. However, deconstruction as a way of inheriting establishes a relation to time and to death, which in turn allows for a possibility of a different grammar for ethico-political engagement. The repercussions of thinking on legacy, we argue, go as far as inspiring conceptual tools for thinking politics.

Formulating living in terms of surviving in a deconstructive sense bears a significant consequence; insisting upon the mode of survival as the originary form of living unveils the reliance of such a living upon death. Indeed, surviving is neither just dying nor just living but it happens in between the two,[10] and is thus unsubstitutable to the concept of living. In fact, surviving is precisely what comes to make problematic the idea of a category. To speak about surviving is to speak about trace and about ghost, about life haunted by that other, but that is only made possible as life through this haunting.

Taking this notion of surviving seriously we are led to think differently about the couple life–death and the relation between one and another's death. Conceptual tools arising from this thinking will be encountered throughout like the notion of disjointed time, the necessity of absence and the essential relation with the other. This reflection, however, is haunted by one term: *with*. The introduction of this term in this context is crucial. In both situations – life with death, and being one with another – the advent of this *with* into the argument will be disturbing and have further consequences. It will destabilise the modalities and temporal determinations, the taxonomies and the grammar of the political that counts on the separation of living and dying, on the separation of the 'One' and the 'other' and on the monopolisation of present tense as its only possible time. In that regard, what we propose here is that engaging with the concept and the problematic of inheritance in a deconstructive way leads us to speak about surviving as a unique formulation of living, which would in turn be a possible ground of political inspiration.

With one who is not present

In the exposition we established that living as surviving is necessarily a relation to a non-presence and non-presentability. Therefore, in its very formulation it must begin with an association with absence. This necessity of counting on that which is not present equally makes problematic any onto-temporal determination in terms of *is* (presence and present tense) in regard to politics and to being-together.

If we define our act of living as living-on, or surviving after death, it means that we define it in relation to the others who are dead. Perhaps long gone ones that we have never known. Or, perhaps, some other others that we have known. In any case, the very formulation of 'I' or 'we' in this structure that we inhabit is conditioned by some death. The ability to say 'I am here' happens on the condition that I can also say 'the other is not here'. This would be the first logical axiom of surviving, as it would make no sense to speak about it, had it not been for the assumption of the death and absence of the other. And here, perhaps, we begin to see how surviving occurs between the two – living and dying, and is not issued by either alone. Whatever happens between such two as living or dying, Derrida says, must maintain itself with some ghost. With that which *is* not.[11] Any act of living-on is reliant upon a non-presence, which is neither dead nor alive, but which makes possible the notion of living as living-on. Insofar as saying 'I am' is conditioned by the death of the others, then necessarily this formula must read as: 'I am *with* (ghosts)'. The rudimentary expression of presence and present tense – I am – is thus marked by absence and non-presence. The originary declaration of presence and its inevitable grammar are, all of a sudden, disturbed. The singular formulation of the 'one' that heralds its unique presence through the 'I am', is suddenly not so much alone – more than one. In the very place and moment 'one' begins by counting (itself first), we ought to realise that this counting is rendered possible only on the condition of there being more than just one. Not one plus one that results in two ones alike; but *with* the other and others who no longer (or not yet) are and whose absence makes one – 'one' of a longer series, two, three, etc. – possible. So the possibility of the sentence 'I am', of the perfect example of the grammatico-temporal assertion of present is displaced through the haunting by the past. What happens in this 'place' (which, it appears is no longer its proper place) and domain of present is the advent of the past through the appearance of the ghost. The future also comes into play, as we have mentioned in the previous section, as this ghost does not let itself be caught by the claims of present. It has to have a possibility of returning. 'The future', Derrida claims, 'can only be for the ghosts, and the past'.[12] The non-presence that is inscribed in the proper act and moment of living must necessarily transport this living (as a living-on) towards the future and, therefore, make problematic the idea of a single proper moment. Because it counts with the other who is not presentable, it cannot finish such a counting, and it must, in the now amply rehearsed terminology of Derrida, remain *à venir* – to come. According to him, this reliance upon living as surviving which in turn brings forth the haunting at the very centre of any attempt of onto-temporal assertion of *is* would mark a possibility of resistance to the formula of responsibility and justice (and hence necessarily politics) that may only answer to the claims of *is*, as:

> no ethics, no politics, whether revolutionary or not, seems possible and thinkable and just that does not recognize in its principle the respect for those others who are no longer or for those who are not yet there, presently living, whether they are already dead or not yet born. No justice [. . .] seems possible or thinkable without the principle of some responsibility, beyond all living present, within that which disjoins the living present, before the ghost of those who are not yet born or who are already dead.[13]

Because where there is one, there is not only one but more than one, this begins to entail the conception of time as *contretemps*,[14] and this in turn demands propelling the notion of justice and responsibility beyond the present. Or, put differently, by underscoring how the act of living in terms of surviving involves being-with those who are not present, Derrida demonstrated that the time of the political cannot abide to any single, proper moment determined in terms of present–presence, but must happen in time which cannot be equal to itself, in time that is out of joint. And as such, the categories of the political that simultaneously takes place in and overflows the present must count on the non-present and non-presence as well. In fact, the possibility of meaning of these categories is given precisely through this initial *with* before any formulation or association has yet taken place, in the very moment one ventures to say 'I' or 'we'.

Where there is one, there is always more than one

The second relation, the one involving the other and the death of the other, is conditioned by the couple life-death and equally marks the act of living. While this point comes after the preceding one, it would be absurd to consider it as subordinate. They both develop and share a vocabulary that implies their simultaneity in the vicinity of the concept of survival. In summarising the similar lexicon they both share, the act of living is already a living-*with* which reveals how the notion of 'one' as the only one the political can begin counting with, is problematic. Again, it appears, living as an act of 'one' who may say 'I am' is not possible without the counting on the other – 'I am *with*' – which again makes impossible the notion of justice and responsibility in terms of given symmetry. As we shall see, the other defines my living as a living-*with*, and I am from the beginning placed in the structure of responsibility and relation to the other. This issue of the death of the other arises in conjuncture with the idea of learning to live (here we could add to learn to live justly, rightly or politically). In other words, it concerns the act of living as an act – and this involves death; it involves being more than one where one is no longer one.

As we cannot get out of reach of the relation life–death and the dead himself, we have to detour our argument and start off with life. It is in Derrida's major work, *Specters of Marx*, that opens with a discussion about learning how to live, that Derrida argues that living as an act is not possible with the reliance upon the notion of life alone. Life, he maintains, must learn from something else than itself:

> To live is, by definition, not something one learns. Not from oneself. It is not learned from life, taught by life. Only from the other and by death. In any case from the other at the edge of life. At the internal border or the external border, it is a heterodidactics between life and death . . . If it –

learning to live – remains to be done, it can happen only between life and death. Neither in life nor in death alone.[15]

To learn to live is to live with a relation to death. Or rather, the signature of death in this context seems to be inscribed into the name of living itself. From the very beginning, then, my own relation to life, indeed, my relation to myself as myself, is established through this structure marked by death. I begin living only by surviving as I learn to live only through death. To learn to live cannot be reliant upon any notion of life-in-itself, but must rely upon the other: 'From the other and by death . . . from the other at the edge of life'. Out of the first part of this quote we gather that only the other can teach me how to live, how to perform the act in which I am already performing – living. But then, who is *at the edge of life*? The other at the threshold of his death, or the other at the edge of my life, where there is no more 'I' or 'one'? From the edge, the other teaches me how to live, engaged from the beginning in this act, which, it appears, can never be only mine, as it involves the other. If learning how to live involves death, then the only death which can make possible my learning to live is that of the other. While this death can never be appropriated – it is the other's singularity – it is the first and the only death I can possibly have a relation to. So in this regard, my relation to the other must begin with my possibility of surviving him. But surviving here requires to live with the death of the other rather than negating the existence and the being of the other. Living-on, in other words, in so far as it happens between life and death, must also belong to the other. By being the only relation to death that I have, the other in that sense bears my death.

To further engage with one's relation to the death of the other, let us pursue with the analysis of Blanchot's text, *The Moment of My Death*, Derrida recounts a dialogue:

One of the two, One of the Two says to the Other 'I am alive', and would thus be the one who has survived. But it is the other, the one who has survived, who responds to him: 'No you are dead'. And this is a colloquium, this is the dialogue between two witnesses who are moreover [*au demeurant*] the same, alive and dead, living-dead, and both of whom in abidance [*en demeurance*] claim or allege that one is alive, the other dead, as if life went only to an *I* and death to a *you*.[16]

They are the same, Derrida says, alive and dead. The possibility of surviving begins with the inclusion of the other, hence it must always happen *with* the other. This is not to say that one and the other are the same, one of the two alike: that would be re-introducing the idea of symmetry and exemplarity as the original condition. Instead, precisely because they are *not* the same, because the death of the other separates him from me, this act of surviving becomes significant and begins to operate with the notion of time and political categories of responsibility and justice that avoid the rule of *is*. My presence in terms of 'I am' is, in Blanchot's words, 'only presence at a distance, and this distance is absolute – that is, irreducible; that is, infinite'.[17] The other as the ultimate separation from me through his death, is the condition of my living, structures my living as surviving by including himself in it. The infinity and the absolute alterity of the other is precisely what induces dissymmetry and the impossibility of closure into the notion of living qua surviving and into the idea of 'one-self' or 'I'. To the extent that the other is included into my act of living through his death (and hence my death), which renders my living living-*with*, then this living-*with* is always with something infinite, something that does not give itself to a definition, conceptualisation or ontologisation. In the centre of the 'I' or 'one', as we have already rehearsed, there is then something that resists the grounding of this one, and gives the possibility for one another. In Blanchot's words:

> What calls me most radically into question? Not my relation to myself as finite or as the consciousness of being before death or for death, but my presence in the proximity of another who by dying removes himself definitively, to take upon myself another's death as the only death that concerns me, this is what puts me beside myself, this is the only separation that can open me, in its very impossibility, to the Openness of a community.[18]

Speaking about survival in this way disturbs the categories: life – that goes to an 'I' – and death – that goes to another (you). Because it happens between life and death, survival does not happen solely to the 'one' of the two, but always involves more than one. It begins involving more than one at the very threshold, at the very edge where there is no more one. Or perhaps, we could say, that as soon as there is more than one, there is no more just one. There is no time in which one is only one, given that the existence and the possibility of one is always conditioned by a *with*. What characterises the traditional political lexicon is precisely its concern with the formulas of who is who of politics, with how many there are (here, present). It begins by counting: one, two . . . all the ones alike. It begins with 'One' as the origin; one who is capable of saying: 'I am'.

Our reflection here was animated by the question of whether we could imagine politics that instead of counting with one first, counted with a *with*; instead of the original utterance 'I am' it allowed saying 'I am haunted'.[19] In other words, what interests us is whether it would be possible to attempt to imagine a kind of political thinking that counts with a trace, that speaks with the ghost and that takes seriously the notion of non-presence. This, of course, should not happen on account of displacing entirely the idea of counting, equality and sameness, because this would remove the possibility of response and action. Exemplary cannot be substituted by singular entirely, because it is at the same time the condition of the singular. Equally, we cannot think *with* without thinking 'one' as well. Thus, the concern is not with simply erasing the existing categories, but rather exploring whether it is possible to accentuate in our political thinking that the singular is also the condition of the exemplar and that the *with* is the condition of 'one'. The point would not be to dispense with a concept (and such a task will shortly be said to be impossible and absurd), but to inquire into the kind of thinking that is made possible from the exploration of the limit of the concept, of the *between*. Such thinking, Derrida argues, would necessarily be more attuned to the notion of justice in terms of *to-come*, as it would involve the other (as not being present and thus not subordinated to the rule of 'is') in its calculation. Counting (because counting is necessary) with and on the absence (which remains unaccountable for) would have to reorient the formulas of political thinking from the exclusive bedazzlement with presence–present towards the conception of time that is out of joint – *contretemps*. The time of this kind of politics would be the time of surviving, and yet 'time that only gives itself in its withdrawal'.[20] The time of surviving, because it must count with the unaccountable and infinitely other of the dead, must always be displaced from the present. But this, Derrida argues is a possibility as:

> 'without this *non-contemporaneity of the living present*, without that which secretly unhinges it, without this responsibility and this respect for justice concerning those *who are not there*, what sense would there be to ask the question 'where?', 'where tomorrow?', 'whither?'.[21]

This means that the openness of the horizon of political living can only ever make sense in relation to the possibility of absence and non-presence. It can only become meaningful and possible through the engagement with death – mine as well as the other's. Indeed, mine as that of the other.

IN THE SPIRIT OF NEGOTIATION

What we have demonstrated in those two last sections is that inheritance based on a central loss of absence, disturbs classical arrangements of time. Inspired by the movement of inheritance, we argued that we should conceive of inheritance as deconstruction in itself: the work of inheritance is deconstructive in nature. Animated by this conclusion, we pursued the argument concerning the time of inheritance that is indeed an intricate gift: one that situates the notion of heritage as well as one that places us in a position of survivors in that structure. And it is in the analysis of that placement (as survivors) that we opened up the discussion to the realm of politics. The aporetic relation between life and death and the unstable leaning of ours towards the death of others (as our own) propels the idea of politics towards a new grammar. It is a grammar that challenges the ontology of the 'is', one that demands an unforeseeable future, one that accepts living with ghost and, as we have seen, one that thus complicates the basic categories of life, death, individual and time of politics. While we have dwelled for a while on what we feel are the key issues of inheritance and legacy, it is time to turn towards an opening of this negotiation, to make it happen. Far from wanting to put a definitive sense to Derrida's legacy with our own conclusions, the upcoming chapters open up routes to this legacy with a desire for negotiation. Negotiation comes with a sense of battle, of confrontation and discussion that all the authors of the subsequent chapters evoke. They do not allow a type of legacy rest and sink within the reader but they challenge each other in an imaginative joust. And it is in that context that not only is the plurality of writers important, but also their interdisciplinarity. Derrida's impact was felt in different spheres of knowledge. Proposing various avenues for that heritage from the standpoint of only one discipline would have missed a double opportunity. This interdisciplinarity emphasises both the importance, in order to address the demands of such a legacy, of taking into account the diversity of Derrida's texts in their use and application regardless of the discipline they belong to, and also to profit from this variety of voices to inspire cross-fertilising ideas in those given disciplines. Academic boundaries should not, especially in this case, forbid such an attempt at multiplying views on Derrida's legacy and, as the different texts demonstrate, it is in the possibility of borrowing conceptual tools from literature, philosophy, politics . . . that some future development in those disciplines is made possible. Referring back to the previous section, it would be ill-advised now to foreclose the concept that inspires this volume, the one that looms over our relation with the dead, and thus with others, namely the in-between.

The in-between of academic disciplines has, indeed, much to offer and in the spirit of Derrida, we draw from this *entre-deux* to approach, from the oblique, his heritage. Hence, instead of trying to appropriate *a* Derrida to one discipline, the texts speak from unique perspectives for the benefit of the many.

The question that animates the first section, 'The future of deconstruction' is one that necessarily arises in any discussion or negotiation about legacy, namely one asking what the continued relevance of Derrida's thought is and what future may be reserved for it in the projects of philosophy and politics. While the entire negotiation of this volume is in many ways fuelled precisely by reflection upon this issue, and while this question equally functions as the incitation to this project itself, the focus of this section is more directly oriented towards the topic of the future – possible futures of deconstruction and deconstruction's own relation to the issue of the future.

Christopher Norris opens this discussion with a reflection upon the qualification of Derrida's thought within the discipline of philosophy, advocating against the unwarranted and polemical critique issued against Derrida from the camp of analytical philosophy. A deeper engagement with Derrida's philosophy, he argues, would reveal that the rigour of Derrida's method is far closer to that of the analytical tradition than is usually recognised, and if the misunderstandings and polemics could be overcome, Derrida's work would prove a contributing dimension to analytical thought. Richard Beardsworth's and Alex Thomson's contributions engage with the question of the relevancy of deconstruction for the critical project in relation to world politics and contemporary political issues. Recognising at length the significance of Derrida's thought, Richard Beardsworth enters the negotiation arguing that deconstruction today is characterised by theoretical hesitation and disengagement, due to its focus upon the notion of aporia and its refusal to determine the alterity. Rather than constituting an ultimate opening towards the otherness, such a refusal runs a serious risk of leaving alterity vulnerable to other reductive forces of determination. Therefore, Beardsworth argues, the project of critical philosophy in the future must be formulated in terms of an engagement at the level where the real is being constructed and determined, and so the significance of deconstruction in this project will depend upon its own ability to articulate its relation to the grounds of engagement with our historical actuality.

Taking up the pressing issue of Islam and democracy, Thomson also addresses the critique issued by Beardsworth regarding the shortcoming of deconstruction with regard to political engagement with our historical actuality. 'What distinguishes deconstruction from critical philosophy', he argues, 'is not a lack of attention to the here and now, but the construction of a double gesture which recognises that the urgency of the here and now may always obscure the vital question of the future'.[22] This engagement with the notion of aporia that in Thomson's chapter concentrates on Islam and the concept of democracy features also in Mick Dillon's chapter in terms of the aporia of justice as the undeconstructable messianic kernel of deconstruction. Dillon's contribution is concerned with the issue of the future and the messianic in Derrida's thought, which he juxtaposes to the 'talk of the times' about future in the contemporary political discourses, specifically that of the US Office of Force Transformation. Revealing the techno-teleological desire behind the conception of the future of the latter, Dillon demonstrates that the future in a deconstructive sense is reliant upon the aporetic and hence does not see its horizon in teleological terms. The future as a future that is not seen from the point of view of the 'end', in other words, is that of deconstruction. Here, we are dealing with the aporia as a source of political openness and as a place from which the promise of politics is sent off.

The chapters in the section entitled 'Interrupting the same', explore precisely the possibilities of the impossibility of closure (aporia), by examining the ways in which the notion of the aporetic, the paradoxical and the ambiguous is denied and resisted by traditional political discourses. As this violent denial necessarily entails a crisis of the same (because of the return of the other to and from the very centre), the authors of the chapters consider different ways in which such a crisis or constant encountering with ambiguity may be exploited as an opportunity for a different political imagery. Maja Zehfuss's concern is with the 'War on Terror' and the way its narrative is orchestrated by a certain notion of memory. Through her reading of Derrida, Zehfuss challenges the idea of temporal linearity, demonstrating how the work of memory involves the reversal of time and retroactive creation of the past. This ambiguity of time, she argues, can be exploited as '[i]t is not through doing the "right thing" as established by the past, but in facing the impossible decision and embracing the danger of the future that we may move towards the ethical'.

In continuation, Josef Ansorge's paper takes issue with the three major contemporary discourses in International Relations (IR), that of Kenneth Waltz, Francis Fukuyama and Samuel Huntington. Through a reading of *Politics of Friendship* he demonstrates how, despite their apparent differences, they all operate on the same conception of the political: one where the nature of the political is decided before the politics has even begun. This chapter alerts us to a serious feature in contemporary IR, namely that much of the debate within it is carried out on the same onto-political basis, which is both exclusionary and violent in its origins. Ansorge proposes that a different and less exclusionary thinking within IR would have to substitute the conception of friendship in terms of exemplar for the conception of friendship formulated in relation to the notion of singularity.

In his chapter, Dan Bulley examines the ways in which the deconstructive concept of decision may influence a different conception and formulation of foreign policy. Through reading the series *The West Wing*, Bulley demonstrates that the seeming 'impurity' that results from the impossibility of making a decision that would be fully ethical or just is not an impediment to politics but instead a true locus of the political.

Then, April Biccum introduces the interesting topic of pedagogy as a way of reflecting on Derrida's legacy. Opting for a post-colonial approach Biccum, using her diversity trainer's experience as a case study and a point of reference for her discussion explores the potential of disruption as a political praxis. Inspired by Bhaba and Spivak, themselves reliant on Derrida, Biccum proposes that the exploitation of ambivalences, regarding racist claims among other colonial narratives she inspects, offer a site for challenging those very narratives. She thus exposes a possible political strategy based upon post-colonial theory.

As all the chapters here underscore, and as Derrida insisted in a great number of his writings, European tradition, philosophy and political thought already contain a promise of open politics, a promise of the kind of politics that allows for the future, for dissymmetry and for a formulation of the political along less totalising and exclusionary lines.[23] And the chapters in this section demonstrate, in Derrida's spirit, that it is precisely in the places of greatest tension and impossibility, in the aporias and paradoxes that announce themselves that this possibility is exposed. The possibility of politics, in other words lies there where the problem of delimiting clean and coherent notion of the political announces itself. As Dan Bulley's argument tellingly proposes: the aporias and paradoxes are not something we ought to get rid of in order to achieve pure politics, but rather the very 'impurity' manifested through the return of the aporetic is where politics takes place.[24]

The closing section of the volume, 'Following and Breaking', is reserved for discussion about Derrida in relation to other contemporary philosophers. As we have hinted before, breaking and critiquing can be more faithful and move away from a dogmatic appraisal of the texts. This section begins with Christina Howells's chapter in which, incited by the recent death of Derrida, she explores his relation to another of his late contemporaries, Jean Paul Sartre, addressing the issue of ambiguity in relation to

Sartre and the lack of serious engagement with the Sartrean notion of subject in Derrida's writings. Through the parallel reading of the two philosophers and engagement with the themes of subjectivity, decision and future she demonstrates the proximity in their thought, arguing that many of the themes visited by Derrida have been dealt with in a similar fashion by Sartre.

Next, Jenny Edkins visits the themes of responsibility, sacrifice, singularity and plurality through the reading of Derrida and Jean-Luc Nancy organised around the photographs of Salgado's children and photographs from Cambodia's S-21 prison. Against Derrida's notion of aporia that presupposes a singular being as an original starting point, Edkins puts forwards the claim that if we instead take Nancy's idea of being-with as the initial point, then this aporia that forces sacrifice of other singularities does not occur in the same way as '[t]here is no way in which we *cannot* respond: existence *is* responsibility'.

Daniel Watt's chapter focuses both on Derrida's text and on the legacy of influential thinkers of the twentieth century such as Heidegger, Levinas, Blanchot and Barthes in his work. His catalyst for such an operation is the fragment, a literary genre that was characteristic of Derrida, and symptomatic of his philosophical endeavours. Viewing it as a destabilising technique, as a possibility for interruption, Watt assesses what remains – and the remainders – of the fragments in Derrida's texts and builds up a case suggesting that 'the fragment and Derrida survive (on) each other'.

The closing chapter by Lasse Thomassen addresses the Derrida–Habermas debate, and specifically focuses on fending off the claims that there has been a recent rapprochement; a point also rehearsed by Richard Beardsworth in the opening chapter. While the imminent political engagement of the two has been very similar in recent years, Thomassen points out that this hardly qualifies as a philosophical rapprochement but rather as a strategic alliance. His analysis demonstrates that affinities in certain spheres cannot erase the fundamental differences that exist in the philosophical approaches of the two, especially in relation to language and the goal of critical philosophy.

As inheritance is not an upfront business, as it consists both of an act of recuperating from the past and projecting into the future, the very way of approaching it practically speaking cannot be straightforward: the oblique approach once again imposes itself. It is thus a spirit inspired by the work of Derrida, intimately related to deconstruction as a way of inheriting. Within this context, the best we can hope for is a negotiation. But this should not be read as a way of bypassing the need to decide and to close, because we cannot ignore the fact that, to a certain extent it brings some form of closure. However, what we have attempted to achieve is to demonstrate that there is no single Derrida despite the fact that we always must appropriate *a* Derrida in our singular acts of inheritance. Consequently, it is only through this multiplicity of perspectives, united around both the theme of legacy and in the absence of Derrida that we can formulate in so many ways a faithful response to the unmatchable demands of loss and death.

Notes

1. Anabell Guerrero Mendez, 'Jacques Derrida', *The Economist*, 21 October 2004, online version:
   www.economist.com/people/displayStory.cfm?story__id=3308320.
2. Jonathan Kandell, 'Jacques Derrida, Abstruse Theorist, Dies in Paris at 74', *New York Times*, 10 October 2004, online version: www.select.nytimes.com/gst/abstract.html?res=F10B11FB385F0C738DDDA90994DC404482.
3. Jacques Derrida, 'Like the Sound of the Sea Deep within a Shell: Paul de Man's War', in Jacques Derrida, *Memoires for Paul de Man*, New York: Columbia University Press, 1989.
4. Jacques Derrida, *The Work of Mourning*, Chicago, IL: University of Chicago Press, 2003, p. 6.
5. Jacques Derrida, *Résistances à la psychanalyse*, Paris: Galilée, 1996, p. 40.
6. Jacques Derrida and Elizabeth Roudinesco, *For What Tomorrow: a Dialogue*, Stanford, CA: Stanford University Press, 2004, p. 3.
7. Jacques Derrida, *Rogues: Two Essays on Reason*, trans. Pascale-Anne Brault and Michael Naas, Stanford, CA: Stanford University Press, 2005, p. 9.
8. Jacques Derrida and Elizabeth Roudinesco, *De quoi demain . . .*, Paris: Fayard/Galilée, 2001, p. 39.
9. Ibid. p. 18.
10. Jacques Derrida, 'Je suis en guerre contre moi-même', *Le Monde*, 18 August 2004, online version: www.lemonde.fr/web/article/0,1-0@2-3230,36-375883,0.html.
11. Jacques Derrida, *Specters of Marx*, London: Routledge, 1994, p. xviii.
12. Ibid. p. 37.
13. Ibid. p. xix.
14. Jacques Derrida, *Politics of Friendship*, London: Verso, 1997, p. 1.
15. Derrida, *Specters of Marx*, p. xviii.
16. Maurice Blanchot, Jacques Derrida, *The Instant of My Death/ Demeure: Fiction and Testimony*, Stanford, CA: Stanford University Press, 2000, p. 97.
17. Maurice Blanchot, *Friendship*, Stanford, CA: Stanford University Press, 1997, p. 218.
18. Maurice Blanchot, *The Unavowable Community*, Barrytown, NY: Station Hill Press, 1988, p. 9.

19. Derrida, *Specters of Marx*, p. 133.
20. Derrida, *Politics of Friendship*, p. 14.
21. Derrida, *Specters of Marx*, p. xix.
22. Alex Thomson, 'Derrida's *Rogues*: Islam and the futures of deconstruction', this volume, p. 117.
23. Jacques Derrida, *The Other Heading: reflections on today's Europe*, trans. Pascale-anne Brault and Michael Naas, Bloomington, IN: Indiana University Press, 1992, p. 17 and Derrida, *Politics of Friendship*, p. 185.
24. Dan Bulley, 'Ethical assassination? Negotiating the (ir)responsible decision', this volume, p. 228.

I

Future of Deconstruction

I

Analytic Philosophy in Another Key: Derrida on Language, Truth and Logic

Christopher Norris

INTRODUCTION

Jacques Derrida's death in 2004 was a loss felt all the more keenly by his friends, readers and commentators for the fact that he was still – after nearly five decades of intensely productive work – at the height of his intellectual and creative powers. The event was marked by some eloquent and moving tributes, as well as by some rather mealy-mouthed token acknowledgements and also (predictably) a number of ill-informed, dismissive or downright vituperative pieces that told us rather more about the psychopathology of academic life than about any putative shortcomings in their subject. To this extent the pattern of negative response was much like that which had become all too familiar over the years, driven largely (one suspects) by resentment at Derrida's extraordinary range, originality and depth of engagement with issues that most of his detractors found either alien or too close for comfort to their own, more narrowly defined concerns.

Still, having aired these preliminary grouses, I propose now to do something more constructive by looking at some aspects of Derrida's work that might be expected to engage the interest of philosophers in the 'other', that is, broadly analytic line of descent. Since that work has tended to divide commentators along fiercely partisan lines my main purpose here is to offer a non-prejudicial account of the various issues that have given rise to such a long-running and (as it might seem) irreconcilable difference of views. I shall therefore focus on those elements in Derrida's thinking that conflict with certain deep-laid analytic aims and priorities, while none the less suggesting some points of contact between his project and the sorts of concern that typically preoccupy analytic thinkers. By so doing it may yet be possible to move beyond the often strident and ill-informed polemics that have hitherto characterised much of this debate.[1] At the same time I shall examine both the sources of resistance to Derrida's work from within the analytic tradition and – more constructively – some possible ways in which a reading of that work attentive to its different, more text-focused but none the less rigorous modes of analysis might help to overcome such resistance. A further aim is to provide a *vade mecum* – however brief and selective – for readers in search of guidance through the great mass of Derrida's writings and the thickets (or minefields) of commentary that now surround them. Hence the unusually high ratio of endnotes and bibliographical data to text, a disproportion which may appear less absurd in light of the above remarks. I should perhaps also apologise in advance for the frequent references – in text and endnotes – to my own earlier work. That this is not (or not merely) a piece of brazen self-advertisement will I hope strike the reader who is willing to accept what follows as in part a reflective *compte rendu* of some thirty years' fairly sustained engagement with Derrida's work.

I

There are already signs that attitudes are changing and that some analytic philosophers are starting to approach Derrida's texts without the kinds of fixed (mostly hostile) preconception that have marked the history of Anglophone responses over the past three decades. This growing interest is reflected in the number of articles, books and conference papers that have lately been produced by philosophers with a background in various main-stream 'analytic' areas of thought such as epistemology and philosophy of language and logic.[2] Some of these more positive overtures have come from thinkers who perceive a striking resemblance between Derrida's decon-structive reading of Austinian speech-act theory and developments of a broadly 'post-analytic' character.[3] Among them is the minimalist-semantic approach – the idea that we can and should make do without elaborate theories of meaning, intention, or propositional content – suggested in a well-known essay by Donald Davidson.[4] Thus, according to Davidson, quite simply 'there is no such thing as a language' if by 'language' one means the sort of thing that linguists or philosophers have mostly taken as their putative object of study, that is, a well-defined system of meanings, intentions, implicatures, structural constraints, logico-semantic entail-ments, etc., that can in principle be subject to detailed and rigorous specification. Rather, '[w]hat two people need, if they are to understand one another through speech, is the ability to converge on passing theories from utterance to utterance'. In which case, '[t]heir starting points, however far back we want to take them, will usually be very different – as different as the ways they acquired their linguistic skills. So also, then, will the strategies and stratagems that bring about convergence differ'.[5] In which case 'prior theories' are of little use, whether those that speakers and hearers supposedly apply to each new situation by way of basic linguistic competence, or those that philosophers and linguists produce in order to explain that competence. For it is just in so far as such theories are taken to possess a generalised, trans-contextual, or non-situation-specific scope that they fail – necessarily so – to grasp what is involved in particular cases of achieved communicative uptake. Thus, they are subject to a curious inverse law of sharply diminishing returns whereby the kind of theory concerned 'is, in its formal structure, suited to be the theory for an entire language, even though its expected field of application is vanishingly small'.[6]

It is here that promoters of the Davidson/Derrida *entente* claim to find just such a point of convergence, that is, in the idea of a minimalist semantics that requires no more than rough agreement on 'passing theories' (Davidson) or a barely specified notion of speech-act 'iterability' (Derrida) in order to explain – so far as explanation is required – how people do manage to communicate for most everyday or practical purposes.[7] I have argued elsewhere that this claim underestimates both the problems with Davidson's ultra-pragmatist theory-to-end-all-theories and the extent of Derrida's critical engagement with just those issues that Davidson so brusquely or breezily sets aside.[8] Thus, it takes no account of his keen awareness that, despite the problems with Austin's appeal to utterer's meaning, sincerity-conditions, or authentic *versus* inauthentic speech-acts – for example, those of a fictive, poetic, on-stage, ironic, cited-out-of-context, or likewise 'parasitic' character – and despite the kindred problems with defining what should count as a proper or valid context, all the same it is prerequisite to any adequate (remotely plausible) theory that speech-acts should somehow be conceived as retaining certain recognisable traits from one such utterance and context to another. Hence what he terms their 'iterability', that is, their capacity to function, signify and bear the appropriate kind of performative force across a potentially limitless range of unpredictable and non-standard situations whose extent or (presumed) common features cannot possibly be specified in advance.

My point is that Derrida insists on thinking these problems through with the utmost tenacity and logical rigour, unlike those other, more confidently orthodox speech-act theorists – such as John Searle – who refuse to acknowledge them and thus fall back on a vaguely pragmatic line of least resistance according to which such standards of conceptual precision are simply out of place (and designed to make trouble) when applied in the context of everyday, communicative utterance.[9] Hence Derrida's scandalised response when Searle thought to call his bluff by claiming that his talk of conceptual 'rigour' in this context should be seen as just a curious – strategic or unwitting – throwback to the antiquated discourse of logical positivism. Thus:

> from the moment that Searle entrusts himself to an oppositional logic, to the 'distinction' of concepts by 'contrast' or 'opposition' (a legitimate demand that I share with him, even if I do not at all elicit the same consequences from it), I have difficulty seeing how he is nevertheless able to write [that] phrase . . . in which he credits me with the 'assumption', 'oddly enough derived from logical positivism', 'that unless a distinction can be made rigorous and precise, it is not really a distinction at all'.[10]

Although this must surely have struck Searle as yet another piece of perverse and mischievous point-scoring it is none the less an argument strictly in keeping with the norms of analytic (not only logical-positivist) thinking and, beyond that, with the standards of all reputable philosophic discourse, Derrida's included. Thus, '[w]hen a concept is to be treated as a concept', he insists:

> one has to accept the logic of all or nothing . . . at any rate, in a theoretical or philosophical discussion of concepts or of things concep-tualizable. Whenever one feels obliged to stop doing this (as happens to me when I speak of différance, of mark, of supplement, of iterability and of all they entail), it is better to make explicit in the most conceptual, rigorous, formalizing, and pedagogical manner possible the reasons one has for doing so, for thus changing the rules and the context of discourse.[11]

This places Derrida squarely at odds not only with Searle but also with proponents of a minimalist-semantic approach along late-Davidsonian lines. That approach no doubt bears a suggestive resemblance to the idea of speech-act iterability as the rock-bottom, least 'metaphysically' encum-bered means of explaining how communicative uptake occurs across large (otherwise maybe insuperable) differences of utterer's meaning or operative context. However, the resemblance does not go very far – *pace* its current promoters – since Derrida's hard-pressed analysis of Austin's text contrasts very sharply with Davidson's idea that such uptake requires nothing more than intuitive 'wit, luck and wisdom' plus a charitable willingness to maximise the good sense, relevance, or rationality of what people say by picking up various context-specific cues and clues while pretty much ignoring the gist of their utterance as given by any kind of 'prior theory'.

Indeed, it is just in virtue of his *not* adopting an approach along such minimal-semantic or pragmatist lines that Derrida can justifiably protest against Searle's dismissive rejoinder. Thus the charges come back like so many boomerangs since it is Searle, not Derrida, who has muddied the waters by exempting not only 'ordinary language' but also the discourse of speech-act theory from standards of conceptual clarity, rigour and precision that properly apply to any philosophical argument worthy of the name. Now, of course, it may be said – and not without reason – that calling Derrida to witness on his own behalf is completely beside the point since such protestations do nothing to show that he actually observes those standards in his writings on Plato, Rousseau, Husserl, or Austin. And, indeed, this precept (more pithily expressed: that the proof of the pudding is in the eating) might be thought to apply with particular force in the case of a thinker whose statements to that effect go along with an overt commitment to exploring the limits of classical (bivalent) logic and indeed 'reinscribing' concepts such as truth and reference in 'more powerful, larger, more stratified contexts'.[12] After all, that process of reinscription could be taken to involve something very like the principle of symmetry invoked by 'strong' sociologists of knowledge, that is, that truth-claims of whatever kind – in the physical sciences, mathematics, or logic – and whatever their standing (or lack of it) as a matter of probative warrant are likewise subject to explanatory treatment in cultural or socio-historical terms.[13] Thus, Derrida's professed adherence to the strictest protocols of logical reasoning or bivalent truth/falsehood would have to be seen as thoroughly undermined by his treatment of them as products of the 'differential' force-field comprising various residual, dominant, or emergent ideologies. In which case the above-cited passage would amount to no more than a pious protestation designed to head off the standard philosophical arguments against full-fledged cultural relativism and, more specifically, to spike the guns of opponents like Searle.

Nevertheless, I would claim – and have sought to demonstrate at length elsewhere – that Derrida's assertions in this justificatory vein are amply borne out by a close scrutiny of those various, intensely analytical readings where they are put to the test through a detailed engagement with issues in philosophy of language and logic.[14] What has so far prevented recognition of this fact except amongst a small number of analytically-trained philosophers is the combined influence of three main factors. First, there is the deep-laid philosophical assumption that textual close-reading of this sort is the province of literary criticism rather than conceptual analysis, the latter taken to involve quite different, more rigorous standards of validity or truth. Secondly, there is the skewed reception-history whereby Derrida's work has enjoyed its most widespread and enthusiastic response – at least until the past few years – among literary and cultural theorists who are keen to play down that aspect of Derrida's work and thus leave the field open for a takeover bid from their own side of the fence. Whence, thirdly, the deceptive ease with which that work has been recruited in the name of a 'post-analytic', even 'post-philosophical' discourse which pretty much accepts the idea of deconstruction as spelling an end to the kinds of debate that have characterised mainstream philosophy from Descartes to the recent past. Yet this notion altogether lacks credibility if one considers, say, Derrida's reading of Foucault – in 'Cogito and the history of madness' – where he shows with the utmost logical force why reason cannot be relativised to this or that phase of cultural-historical development without such arguments (whether by Foucault or, one might add, by the 'strong' sociologists of knowledge) running into all kinds of disabling aporia or performative contradiction.[15]

One might also instance his early essay, 'The supplement of copula', which takes the linguist Emile Benveniste to task for maintaining that logicians from Aristotle down have been subject to the typical philosopher's delusion of supposing themselves to be reasoning 'in the absolute', that is, in accordance with certain *a priori* or universal laws of thought.[16] On the contrary, Benveniste argues: their thinking has always been constrained by the structural features of ancient Greek and various derivative or kindred languages, that is to say, those languages that happen to afford their particular, culture-specific range of concepts, categories, predicative judgement-forms, and so forth.[17] To which Derrida responds by pointing out – through a mode of transcendental (or condition-of-possibility) argument – that Benveniste's case depends at every stage on categorial distinctions such as those between language and thought or form and content which, however problematic their character, cannot be addressed except by way of the conceptual and logical resources provided by a strictly antecedent philosophical discourse. This is why, as Derrida remarks, there is something askew about Benveniste's reference to a certain 'small document' – Aristotle's *Categories* – which he (Benveniste) regards as nothing more than a product of that same universalist delusion. As a result of this curious blindness, '[w]hat is not examined at any time is the common category of the category, the categoriality in general on the basis of which the categories of language and the categories of thought may be dissociated'.[18] Thus, Benveniste takes it that the methodological priority of language over thought (or linguistics over philosophy) is conclusively borne out by the fact that the number and nature of the categories have been subject to so many revised estimates from within the mainstream Western philosophical tradition, let alone from the evidence of ethnolinguists who offer a yet more jolting reminder of their non-universal, language-based, or culture-relative status. Yet it is just Derrida's point – one that has been pressed to similar effect by analytic philosophers, the earlier Davidson among them – that such claims are demonstrably self-refuting since they presuppose what they purport to deny, that is, the possibility of comparing and contrasting such differences of cultural-linguistic framework on the basis of certain shared structures or attributes.[19]

Derrida puts this case in terms of the 'categoriality in general' (as distinct from the particular, no doubt to some extent language-specific range of categories) which Benveniste necessarily invokes when mounting his argument for the priority of language over that which philosophers deludedly ascribe to some supra-linguistic realm of *a priori* or 'absolute' truths. Thus he shows – convincingly, I think – that Benveniste avails himself of certain conceptual resources which cannot but enter into any such debate and structure the very terms of discussion whatever the position adopted by parties on one or the other side. That is to say:

> philosophy is not only *before* linguistics as one might find oneself facing a new science, a new way of seeing or a new object; it is also *before* linguistics, preceding linguistics by virtue of all the concepts philosophy still provides it, for better or worse; and it sometimes intervenes in the most critical, and occasionally in the most dogmatic, least scientific, operations of the linguist.[20]

It is here that his thinking comes closest to Davidson though not (to repeat) the later, 'minimalist-semantic' Davidson whose work has most often been taken as offering the best grounds for comparison.[21] Rather, it falls very much into line with those essays of Davidson's first period where he argued against a whole raft of cultural-linguistic relativist doctrines on the grounds that truth – or the attitude of holding-true – must be taken as basic to all languages whatever the otherwise large differences of worldview or (so-called) 'conceptual scheme' between them.[22] That is to say, they must share sufficient in the way of logical structure – a common apparatus of connectives, quantifiers, devices for cross-reference, negation, conjunction and disjunction, etc. – to guarantee that such differences will not impose an ultimate block on inter-lingual understanding.

Thus, theorists tend to be over-impressed by the Quinean problem of 'radical' translation (or interpretation) chiefly because they place too much emphasis on cases of *semantic* divergence between languages, such as different ways of dividing up the colour spectrum or picking out culturally salient objects and events.[23] This leads them to ignore those other, inherently more 'sociable' aspects of linguistic-communicative grasp, that is, the various logical constants – along with their closely related syntactic or sentence-forming structures – which offer an adequate basis for assigning propositional contents and attitudes. Focusing on these would help to draw the sting of sceptical doctrines such as Quine's idea of 'ontological relativity', Kuhn's notion of successive scientific paradigms as strictly 'incommensurable' one with another, or Whorf's ethnolinguistic thesis that some languages, like Hopi Indian, may embody a range of (to us) deeply alien metaphysical presuppositions, such that they might – for all we can know – be wholly untranslatable into our own or any other language that that we could understand.[24] Hence Davidson's response in the form of a transcendental *tu quoque*: that these theorists, despite their sceptical qualms, make a pretty good job of describing the sundry differences of paradigm, worldview, ontology, framework, or conceptual scheme which, on their own submission, should render such comparisons downright impossible.

II

My point here is that Derrida's argument *contra* Benveniste in 'The supplement of copula' runs closely parallel to Davidson's case against the proponents of cultural-linguistic relativism, especially when he remarks apropos Whorf that the latter, 'wanting to demonstrate that Hopi incorporates a metaphysics so alien to ours that Hopi and English cannot, as he puts it, "be calibrated", uses English to convey the contents of sample Hopi sentences'.[25] He can do so for just the same reason that Kuhn can give a lively sense of how it must have felt, scientifically or conceptually speaking, for an astronomer to undergo the experience of paradigm-conversion from a Ptolemaic to a Copernican–Galilean worldview, or for a biologist to make the transition from a pre- to a post-Darwinian understanding of the origin and history of species. What would, if true, constitute an obstacle to such understanding is Quine's claim that ultimately no line can be drawn – in point of principle – between, on the one hand, the kind of change whereby we might elect to revise or abandon certain axioms of classical logic (like bivalence or excluded middle) in response to some recalcitrant empirical finding and, on the other hand, the kind of change 'whereby Kepler superseded Ptolemy, or Einstein Newton, or Darwin Aristotle'.[26] For if that claim were valid – in whatever sense of 'valid' survived this wholesale revisionist move – then it would undermine Davidson's entire case against conceptual-scheme talk (along with its cultural-relativist upshot) since there could be no appeal to those logical constants which he takes to provide the strongest grounds for rejecting such talk. I have argued elsewhere that Quine's radical empiricist position self-deconstructs through its lack of any adequate normative criteria by which to make sense of its own more confident statements, let alone those episodes in the history of science that he somewhat casually calls to witness.[27] What I wish to stress here is the close kinship that exists between Davidson and Derrida, especially with regard to their shared conviction – borne out to most striking effect by Derrida's critique of Benveniste – that the priority of logic over language (or philosophical thought over its varied forms of linguistic expression) cannot be subject to challenge except by way of an argument which necessarily borrows its every last conceptual resource from that same discourse that it seeks to supplant.

Likewise, in his essay 'White mythology', Derrida starts out in Nietzschean mode by showing how pervasive is philosophy's reliance on various metaphorical turns, swerves, displacements, substitutions, and so forth, but then makes the case – through a sequence of passages mostly unremarked by his commentators – that one cannot address the problematic topos of metaphor without taking adequate account of those terms and distinctions developed by philosophers (or philosophically-informed rhetoricians and literary theorists) from Aristotle to the present.[28] Thus, on the one hand, 'there is no properly philosophical category to qualify a certain number of tropes that have conditioned the so-called "fundamental", "structuring", "original" philosophical oppositions: they are so many "metaphors" that would constitute the rubrics of such a tropology, the words "turn" or "trope" or "metaphor" being no exception to the rule'.[29] And again, in order to make good the claim for philosophy's power to comprehend and control its own constitutive metaphors,

> one would have to posit that the sense aimed at through these figures is an essence rigorously independent of that which transports it, which is an already philosophical thesis, one might even say philosophy's unique thesis, the thesis which constitutes the concept of metaphor, the opposition of the proper and the improper, of essence and accident, of intuition and discourse, of thought and language, of the intelligible and the sensible.[30]

From which it follows, *at the first stage* of a deconstructive reading, that philosophy will always find itself played off the field by the sheer proliferation of tropes since 'this entire philosophical delimitation of metaphor already lends itself to being constructed and worked by "metaphors"'.[31] Yet it is equally the case, as Derrida is at pains to insist, that one cannot so much as broach the topic of metaphor – or not in a sufficiently informed and critical way – except on condition that one works through the range of philosophic treatments wherein it has received the most detailed, attentive and elaborate discussion. For, as Derrida remarks, 'there is also a concept of metaphor: it too has a history, yields knowledge, demands from the epistemologist construction, rectifications, critical rules of importation and exportation'.[32]

To be sure, this attempt to categorise the various kinds of metaphor according to their structure, provenance, field of application, cognitive function, epistemic yield and so forth will always encounter a certain limit where philosophy turns out to rest upon metaphors that go so deep – or whose effects are so ubiquitous – as finally to defeat its best efforts. Still there is no avoiding that lengthy detour since, in Derrida's pithy phrase, 'metaphor, along with all the predicates that permit its ordered extension and comprehension, is a philosopheme'.[33] That is to say, any simple, unqualified assertion (in the quasi-Nietzschean or Rortian manner) that 'all concepts are sublimated metaphors', 'all truth-claims rhetorical through and through', 'all philosophy just a "kind of writing"', and so on, is thereby condemned to repeat these seemingly radical but, in fact, platitudinous claims without in the least helping to elucidate the complex patterns of reciprocal dependence and shuttling exchanges of priority that have always marked philosophy's dealings with metaphor. What these facile accounts have to ignore is the point that Derrida drives home through his critique of Benveniste, that is, the strict, *a priori* impossibility that thinking might be carried on to some purpose – even that of questioning its own received concepts and categories – while breaking altogether with the precepts of classical (bivalent) logic or 'categoriality in general'. Also they ignore Derrida's insistence – amply borne out in his readings of Plato, Rousseau, Kant and Husserl – that deconstruction is not a matter of seizing on localised aporias or isolated moments of textual undecidability but rather of applying the classical precepts in a rigorous and logically accountable way right up to the point where they encounter strong resistance from the text in hand.[34] Only then – as the result of such sustained and intensive scrutiny – should they at length give way to an alternative, 'deviant' logic by which to register the presence and the pressure of just those anomalous features. Such readings could have no warrant – no means by which to justify or motivate the shift – were it not for their implicit acceptance of the case (as argued by early Davidson) for the priority of language in its logical or truth-functional aspect as compared with those other, that is, semantic or context-variable aspects that lend *prima facie* support to arguments for cultural-linguistic relativism.[35]

Thus, Derrida is at odds with 'strong' revisionists like Quine as regards what would count as an adequate reason for renouncing or changing the ground-rules of classical logic. Certainly he would have thought it a great mistake – a virtual abdication of reason – to suppose (like Quine) that such revision might be mandated by certain anomalies or discrepant findings turned up through empirical research.[36] In this connection one might cite another passage from his second-round rejoinder to Searle where Derrida protested against the very idea that any problems with making strict (bivalent) logical sense of Austin's various distinctions can best be got around by adopting a sensibly relaxed 'empiricist' line. 'To this oppositional logic', Derrida writes:

> which is necessarily, legitimately, a logic of 'all or nothing' and without which the distinction and the limits of a concept would have no chance, I oppose nothing, least of all a logic of approximation [*à peu près*], a simple empiricism of difference in degree; rather I add a supplementary complication that calls for other concepts . . . or rather another discourse, another 'logic' that accounts for the impossibility of concluding such a 'general theory'.[37]

Still less, I would argue, can Derrida be lumped with those advocates of a 'minimalist-semantic' (late-Davidsonian) line which takes it that communication is very largely a matter of informed guesswork or ad hoc contextual adjustment.[38] On this account, to repeat, 'passing theories' (or intuitive 'wit, luck and wisdom') are enough to make up for what 'prior theories' inevitably lack on account of their inherent generality and, hence, their failure to offer any useful guidance with interpreting particular speech-acts by particular speakers in particular, always to some extent novel or unprecedented contexts of utterance. To be sure, there are interesting parallels here with Derrida's reading of Austin and his notion of 'iterability' as the furthest one can get toward explaining how it is that speech-acts retain a certain identity of meaning, role or performative function despite all the problems that emerge in attempting to specify the relevant felicity-conditions in terms of utterer's intention or proper context. However, as Derrida's response to Searle makes clear, it is only through a reading maximally attentive to the logic (and thereby the logical anomalies) of Austin's text that he is able to elicit those problems not just – *pace* Searle – in order to make mischief but with a view to raising serious issues about the scope and limits of responsibility for various kinds of performative commitment.

So there is something awry about attempts on the part of analytic (or 'post-analytic') philosophers to enlist deconstruction in the cause of such a minimalist-semantic or broadly pragmatist approach. Richard Rorty pushes farthest in this direction with his notion of Derrida as a brilliantly gifted and inventive writer whose texts are best read for their literary qualities and, hence, as happily pointing the way beyond all those problems – or pseudo-problems – that have vexed philosophers from Plato to the present.[39] Rather, we should take Derrida's point, give up the whole idea of philosophy as a 'serious', specialised, problem-solving activity, and treat it as just another 'kind of writing' whose chief virtue is to play a useful role in the 'cultural conversation of mankind' by constantly inventing new modes of metaphoric or narrative self-description. In which case we should tactfully ignore those texts where Derrida purports to advance substantive (albeit negative) philosophical claims with regard to such topics as 'logocentrism' or the Western 'metaphysics of presence'. This view is opposed by others who firmly reject the idea that we have now entered a post-analytic (let alone, as Rorty thinks, a 'post-philosophical') culture, and who are thus more concerned to stress the relevance of Derrida's work to various current and still very live issues in analytic philosophy, rather than its having pushed those issues right off the cultural agenda. These commentators often focus on his early engagement with Husserl's writings on philosophy of language, logic and mathematics, an engagement that is no less critical – and no less responsive to objections from the analytic (for example, Frege-influenced) quarter – for the fact of Husserl's formative influence at that stage in Derrida's thought.[40]

Others, including Graham Priest and myself, have examined the relationship between recent developments in philosophy of logic and Derrida's claims with regard to the deviant or non-classical logics (of *différance*, 'supplementarity', 'parergonality', 'iterability', and so on) which he finds everywhere at work in various philosophic texts.[41] Here again it needs saying – *contra* widespread report – that Derrida is a canny and exceptionally astute logician whose readings of Plato, Rousseau, Kant and Husserl are no less rigorous and pertinent to topics of present-day analytic interest (especially in the areas of modal, epistemic and tense-logic) for the fact that they adopt a heterodox stance on issues of interpretative meaning and truth.[42] Indeed, it is just this constant emphasis on the kinds of complication that typically arise in a reading attentive to the logical structure rather than the straightforward thematic content of some given (philosophical or literary) text which marks those readings out as belonging to philosophy of language as distinct from literary criticism. That is to say, such analyses have to do with 'a certain relationship, unperceived by the writer, between what he commands and what he does not command of the patterns of the language that he uses'.[43] And again: 'the writer writes *in* a language and *in* a logic whose proper system, laws, and life his discourse by definition cannot dominate absolutely', in so far as 'he uses them only by letting himself, after a fashion and up to a point, be governed by the system'.[44] Hence, as Derrida says of Rousseau, '[the] difference between implication, nominal presence, and thematic application' that emerges through a deconstructive reading alert to those moments in the text where expressive intent (the *vouloir-dire* of authorial meaning) is called into question by a 'supplementary' logic which contradicts that manifest purport. So likewise with the deviant, that is, non-classical but none the less rigorously-defined logics that mark Plato's treatment of writing, in the *Phaedrus*, as a *pharmakon* (= both 'poison' and 'cure') or Kant's attempt, in the *Critique of Judgement*, to distinguish those 'parergonal' (framing or extraneous) features of the artwork which should – yet which ultimately cannot – be shown to play no role in our aesthetic appreciation.[45]

What these readings have in common, together with his exegeses of Husserl on the movement of *différance* (differing/deferral) which compli-cates the phenomenological appeal to self-present meaning or time-con-sciousness, is Derrida's keenly analytic sense of the counter-logic that in each case runs athwart the express, overt, or intended meaning of the text. Nothing could be further from Rorty's idea that these are just the sorts of old-style, tedious 'philosophical' concern that we ought to have left well behind with the benefit of Derrida's various debunking treatments of philosophy as just another 'kind of writing'. Thus, the above brief account of how his thought relates to issues in philosophy of logic and language would no doubt strike Rorty as a vain attempt to reclaim Derrida for a mode of discourse – a 'serious', 'constructive', purportedly problem-solving mode – which maybe latches onto certain retrograde elements in his work but which thereby ignores its most liberating aspects. Above all it fails to grasp the pragmatist point: that logic-talk, like truth-talk, can simply drop out once we have come to see both as just that, that is, as optional and nowadays superannuated *façons de parler*. Most analytic – even 'post-analytic' – philosophers are understandably apt to cast a cold eye on this strong-descriptivist version of the claim that language in some sense goes 'all the way down', or that any criteria for values such as truth, goodness and justice can make sense only in relation to some given language-game or cultural life-form.[46] All the same it is a notion that Rorty can portray – not without a fair show of argument – as waiting at the end of various roads that analytic philosophy has been travelling for the past century and that have otherwise, failing this belated recognition, turned out to be sheer dead-ends.[47]

III

This raises the wider question of just how Derrida's project relates to the 'linguistic turn' which has been such a notable feature of philosophy in both traditions during the past near-century.[48] By now the phrase has become little more than a handy portmanteau, covering developments as diverse (indeed downright incompatible) as the Frege–Russell mode of logic-based linguistic analysis on the one hand and, on the other, Wittgensteinian or Austinian appeals to 'ordinary language' as the last, best source of philosophical guidance in such matters. Undoubtedly there is room for some sharply contrasting views of how Derrida's work stands in relation to these different ideas of the scope and limits of conceptual analysis as applied to natural language or to the norms of received, linguistically acculturated meaning and belief. It seems to me that his thought resists assimilation to either side of this continuing dispute within the (broadly) 'analytic' camp, while none the less engaging directly with the question as to just how far logic can take us in matters of natural-language interpretation. Thus he is closely attentive – no philosopher more so – to those nuances or complications of textual meaning that go beyond anything straightforwardly accountable in terms of a strictly regimented, that is, classical first-order propositional and predicate calculus. On the other hand, they emerge through a reading which exhibits its own, quite distinctive but none the less rigorous mode of logical engagement, one whose subtleties can best be brought out with the aid of alternative, more adequate resources from recent developments in modal, epistemic and tense-logic.[49] Beyond that, it remains to convince analytic philosophers – those who have yet to be convinced – that Derrida is a highly original and challenging thinker whose address to such topics itself fully merits the title 'analytic' in any but a narrowly parochial or honorific sense of that term.

In short, I would claim that his work gives every reason to question the typecast 'analytic' *versus* 'continental' view, especially with respect to that (supposed) parting-of-the-ways that ensued upon Frege's criticisms of Husserlian phenomenology and was further reinforced by Gilbert Ryle's much publicised change of mind about Husserl.[50] Over the past two decades I have approached these issues from both sides, so to speak, and have sought in particular to rectify some of the false (often second-hand) impressions of Derrida's thought that have gained currency amongst many analytic philosophers.[51] My aim in much of this work has been to bring out the close relationship – but also the productive tensions – between Derrida's thinking and analytic philosophy of language and logic. One area where this relationship stands especially in need of clarification is the debate between realism and anti-realism, whether conceived in traditional (that is, epistemological) terms or in the jointly metaphysical and logico-semantic terms that have recently come to define that issue as a result of Michael Dummett's decisive intervention.[52] Here I have argued against the widespread claim – by detractors but also some admirers – that deconstruction is a form of out-and-out 'textualist' idealism, or at any rate entails an anti-realist approach to questions of meaning, reference and truth.[53] That this claim is not lacking for plausible support from some of his texts – or from certain, much publicised passages within those texts – is further reason to specify exactly what Derrida means when he says that he has 'never put such concepts as truth, reference and the stability of interpretative contexts radically into question', at least if 'putting radically into question' means 'contesting that there are and that there should be truth, reference and stable contexts of interpretation'.[54] After all, that would seem to be just what he is doing not only in the deconstructive reading of Austin to which Searle so forcefully took exception, but also in those other early texts (such as the extended treatment of Rousseau in *Of Grammatology*) where concepts of reference and truth – at least on a classical construal – are clearly subject to a good deal of complex re-thinking.[55] Thus, any treatment of deconstruction that aims to locate it *vis-à-vis* the interests of current analytic philosophy will have to take adequate account of anti-realism, both as a prominent strain of thought within that tradition and also as offering what some might consider the closest analogue to Derrida's project with regard to its epistemological bearings.

Modern anti-realism takes a lead from Dummett's claim that it cannot make sense to think of any statement as possessing a definite truth-value – as objectively either true or false – unless we have some means of finding it out, that is, some method of empirical verification (in the case of the physical sciences), or documentary evidence (in historical research), or adequate proof procedure (in logic, mathematics and the other formal disciplines).[56] From which it follows that the entire 'disputed class' of meaningful and well-formed but unverifiable (or unfalsifiable) conjectures, hypotheses, theorems, etc., must be counted strictly neither true nor false, or as falling outside the scope of classical (bivalent) logic. This would apply to a vast range of statements in every field of thought, from mathematics (as with Goldbach's formally unproven conjecture that every even number greater than two is the sum of two primes), to astronomy (as with hypotheses concerning the existence or non-existence of celestial objects in regions of the expanding universe beyond the farthest reach of radio-telescopic observation), and historical hypotheses which make some perfectly intelligible claim with regard to the occurrence or non-occurrence of some specified past event but for which we lack any evidence either way. In such cases the realist considers it absurd to suppose that truth or falsehood could be 'epistemically constrained', that is, be somehow dependent on our given state of knowledge concerning them, while the anti-realist finds it just as absurd – indeed quite unthinkable – that truth should be conceived as surpassing or eluding our best powers of ascertainment.[57]

Most commentators, 'for' or 'against', take it as read that Derrida belongs to the anti-realist camp, if not in the *echt*-Dummettian ('technical' or logico-semantic) sense then at least in so far as he thinks – like Dummett – that language constitutes the limit or horizon of intelligibility, so that any statement whose truth-value exceeds the bounds of our linguistically manifestable cognitive grasp is one that *ipso facto* cannot make sense in classical (bivalent) terms. On the contrary, it is clear from Derrida's meticulously argued studies of Husserl, especially those having to do with topics in philosophy of logic and mathematics, that he is far from endorsing a wholesale anti-realist position even though he is keenly aware of the problems with an objectivist approach to the formal sciences that would seem to place truth inherently beyond reach of human knowledge.[58] Indeed, those writings are among the most acute and (again) the most *analytically* resourceful treatments of this issue to be found anywhere in the recent literature. What gives them an additional interest and value in the present context is that they come at it from a standpoint informed by Derrida's critical engagement with Husserlian phenomenology, an engagement none the less sustained and profound for his finding certain un-resolvable dilemmas at the very heart of that project. That is to say, anti-realists tend to stop short at the stage of concluding (rather hopelessly) that in philosophy of mathematics one can *either* have truth, objectively conceived, *or* knowledge within the bounds of formal provability, but surely not both unless at the price of manifest self-contradiction.[59] Derrida, on the other hand, approaches this dilemma through a deconstructive reading of Husserl – principally his late essay on 'The Origin of Geometry' and his writings on philosophy of logic and language – which takes it as the starting-point for a detailed and conceptually rigorous enquiry into the nature, origins and historical development of knowledge in mathematics and the formal sciences.[60]

IV

The same can be said of his claims with respect to those non-classical or 'deviant' logics (of supplementarity, parergonality, *différance*, and so forth) which Derrida advanced only as the upshot of a close, intensely analytical reading of specific texts. That is, they emerge by way of the encounter with moments of aporia or strictly unresolvable contradiction within those texts rather than (as with Quine) in consequence of adopting a radically empiricist, hence revisionist view of logic *vis-à-vis* the methods of the physical sciences or (as with Dummett) in keeping with certain foregone metaphysical commitments.[61] All this needs a great deal more in the way of argumentative support with particular reference to Derrida's writings on Plato, Rousseau, Husserl, Austin and others. Having offered such evidence and arguments elsewhere I must here rest content with the general point: that analytic philosophers (or most of them) have got Derrida wrong on a good many matters, especially as regards his supposed indifference to basic standards of logic, validity and truth.[62] All the same, as I have said, others of a broadly analytic persuasion are starting to show not only an interest in possible points of contact between his work and theirs but also a sense that the latter might have something to gain by considering what Derrida has to say about philosophers such as Husserl and Austin. Thus, their attention is now turning to just those elements in Derrida's work that relate most strongly to current analytical concerns and just those aspects of analytic thought that most pointedly invite or provoke such a reading.[63] It seems to me that this development holds the promise of clearing away those various sources of prejudice and misunderstanding that have so far acted as a block to more productive exchange across and between the so-called 'two traditions'.

Such is the belief that has motivated much of my writing over the past twenty years: namely, that all philosophical thought which merits that title is 'analytic' in the best (non-proprietary) sense of the term, and that this applies most certainly to Derrida's work whatever its departures from certain locally prevailing stylistic and generic norms. Moreover, when he does break with those norms it is in order to make some specific philosophical point, as, for instance, with regard to the problems involved in maintaining Austin's constative/performative distinction, or laying down firm (conceptually adequate) criteria for the 'use'/'mention' dichotomy, or again – a topic more frequently discussed by literary critics than philosophers – telling the difference (one that may be crucial for interpretative purposes) between various kinds of direct, reported, oblique, or 'free-indirect' discourse.[64] In each case Derrida argues his way through a mode of writing that enacts, rehearses, or self-consciously 'performs' the issue to which that writing is addressed, whether by means of a reflexive commentary on its own ambiguous ('undecidable') status with respect to certain orthodox generic conventions or through a subtle and keenly perceptive play with the modalities of speech-act utterance that is none the less cogent for raising questions as regards what counts as a 'serious', good-faith instance of the kind.[65] Clearly any treatment of Derrida's work that would bypass this performative dimension so as to stress its 'purely' analytic virtues must do that work a major disservice by ignoring some of its most distinctive (even if, to opponents like Searle, its most baffling and philosophically disreputable) aspects. All the same one can take those aspects into account whilst by no means endorsing Rorty's claim that his writings are of value chiefly (or solely) for their sheer stylistic inventiveness and their downright refusal to have any truck with such outworn conceptions of philosophic truth and method.

This would also offer a rejoinder to those, notably Jürgen Habermas, who maintain that Derrida's supposed blurring of the genre-distinction between philosophy and literature (as likewise of that between reason and rhetoric) signals his regression to a pre-Enlightenment stage of thought and hence a betrayal of the 'unfinished project of modernity'.[66] Such charges can most effectively be countered by a detailed analytical reading of his texts that would show, among other things, the depth and extent of Derrida's engagement with that project and the distance that separates his thinking from the strain of wholesale postmodernist scepticism with regard to values of truth, reason and critique which is really (and properly) the target of Habermas's attack.[67] Thus, despite the problems that he brings to light in the discourse of Kantian epistemology, ethics and aesthetics there can be no doubting his continued commitment to those same Enlightenment values, both as a matter of overt declaration (*contra* their various present-day detractors) and – more importantly – as a matter of demonstrative warrant borne out through the critical acuity of Derrida's texts. Such a reading would have the additional merit of helping to distinguish those various, often sharply opposed, strains of thought that are often lumped together by opponents under the monolithic heading of 'continental' philosophy. We might then hope to see a better, more informed and receptive (no matter how critical) response to Derrida's work amongst those in the broad analytic community who have so far been overly swayed by reports from the polemical front-line.

NOTES

1. See especially Jacques Derrida, 'Afterword: toward an ethic of conversation', in Gerald Graff (ed.), *Limited Inc*, Evanston, IL: Northwestern University Press, 1989, pp. 111–54; also Christopher Norris, 'Of an apoplectic Tone recently adopted in philosophy', in *Reclaiming Truth: Contribution to a Critique of Cultural Relativism*, London: Lawrence & Wishart, 1996, pp. 222–53.

2. See, e.g., Simon Glendinning (ed.), *Arguing with Derrida*, Oxford: Blackwell, 2001; also Reed Way Dasenbrock (ed.), *Re-Drawing the Lines: Analytic Philosophy, Deconstruction, and Literary Theory*, Minneapolis, MN: University of Minnesota Press, 1989; Newton Garver and Seung-Chong Lee, *Derrida and Wittgenstein*, Philadelphia, PA: Temple University Press, 1994; Christopher Norris and David Roden (eds), *Jacques Derrida, 4 vols*, London: Sage, 2003; Norris, 'Derrida on Rousseau: deconstruction as philosophy of logic', in Norris and Roden (eds), *Jacques Derrida*, Vol. 2, pp. 70–124; Graham Priest (1994), 'Derrida and self-reference', *Australasian Journal of Philosophy*, 72: 103–11; Samuel C. Wheeler, *Deconstruction as Analytic Philosophy*, Stanford, CA: Stanford University Press, 2000.

3. See Jacques Derrida, 'Signature event context', *Glyph*, Vol. 1, Baltimore, MD: Johns Hopkins University Press, 1975, pp. 172–97; 'Limited Inc abc', *Glyph*, Vol. 2, Baltimore, MD: Johns Hopkins University Press, 1977, pp. 75–176; 'Afterword: toward an ethic of conversation'.

4. See Derrida, 'Signature event context', and Donald Davidson, 'A nice derangement of epitaphs', in R. Grandy and R. Warner (eds), *Philosophical Grounds of Rationality: Intentions, Categories, Ends*, Oxford: Oxford University Press, 1986, pp. 157–74; also W. J. T. Mitchell (ed.), *Against Theory: Literary Theory and the New Pragmatism*, Chicago, IL: University of Chicago Press, 1985; Norris, *Resources of Realism: Prospects for 'Post-Analytic' Philosophy*, London: Macmillan, 1997; S. Pradhan (1986), 'Minimalist Semantics: Davidson and Derrida on meaning, use, and convention', Diacritics, 16: (Spring), pp. 66–77; Wheeler, *Deconstruction as Analytic Philosophy*.

5. Davidson, 'A nice derangement of epitaphs', p. 173.

6. Ibid., p. 170.

7. See note 4, above.

8. Norris, *Resources of Realism: Prospects for 'Post-Analytic' Philosophy*, and *New Idols of the Cave: On the Limits of Anti-realism*, Manchester: Manchester University Press, 1997.

9. See John R. Searle, 'Reiterating the differences: a reply to Derrida', *Glyph*, Vol. 1 (1975), pp. 198–208; also *Speech Acts: An Essay in the Philosophy of Language*, Cambridge: Cambridge University Press, 1969.

10. Derrida, 'Afterword: toward an ethic of conversation', p. 123.

11. Ibid., p. 117,

12. Ibid., p. 146.

13. See, e.g., Barry Barnes, *About Science*, Oxford: Blackwell, 1985; David Bloor, *Knowledge and Social Imagery*, London: Routledge & Kegan Paul, 1976; Steve Woolgar, *Science: The Very Idea*, London: Tavistock, 1988.

14. See notes 4 and 8, above; also Norris, *Derrida*, London: Fontana, 1987; *Against Relativism: Deconstruction, Critical Theory, and Philosophy of Science*, Oxford: Blackwell, 1987; *Deconstruction and the Unfinished Project of Modernity*, London: Athlone, 2000; *Minding the Gap: Epistemology and Philosophy of Science in the Two Traditions*, Amherst, MA: University of Massachusetts Press, 2000.

15. Derrida, 'Cogito and the History of Madness', in *Writing and Difference*, trans. Alan Bass, London: Routledge & Kegan Paul, 1978, pp. 31–63; Michel Foucault, *Madness and Civilization: A History of Insanity in the Age of Reason*, trans. Richard Howard, New York: Pantheon, 1965.

16. Derrida, 'The Supplement of Copula', in *Margins of Philosophy*, trans. Alan Bass, Chicago, IL: University of Chicago Press, 1982, pp. 175–205.

17. See Emile Benveniste, *Problems in General Linguistics*, trans. Mary E. Meeks, Coral Gables, FL: University of Miami Press, 1971.

18. Derrida, 'The Supplement of Copula', p. 182.

19. See especially Donald Davidson, 'On the very idea of a conceptual scheme', in *Inquiries into Truth and Interpretation*, Oxford: Oxford University Press, 1984, pp. 183–98.

20. Derrida, 'The Supplement of Copula', p. 188.

21. See note 4, above.

22. See Davidson, *Inquiries into Truth and Interpretation*.

23. See W. V. Quine, 'Two dogmas of empiricism', in *From a Logical Point of View*, 2nd edn, Cambridge, MA: Harvard University Press, 1961, pp. 20–46; also *Ontological Relativity and Other Essays*, New York: Columbia University Press, 1969.

24. Quine, 'Two dogmas of empiricism'; Thomas S. Kuhn, *The Structure of Scientific Revolutions*, 2nd edn, Chicago, IL: University of Chicago Press, 1970; Benjamin Lee Whorf, *Language, Thought and Reality: Selected Writings*, J. B. Carroll (ed.), Cambridge, MA: MIT Press, 1956.

25. Davidson, 'On the Very Idea of a Conceptual Scheme', p. 184.

26. Quine, 'Two dogmas of epiricism', p. 43.

27. See Norris, *Against Relativism* and *Minding the Gap* (note 14, above).

28. Derrida, 'White mythology: metaphor in the text of philosophy', in *Margins of Philosophy*, pp. 207–71.

29. Derrida, 'White mythology', p. 229.

30. Ibid., p. 229.

31. Ibid., p. 252.

32. Ibid., p. 264.

33. Ibid., p. 228.

34. See especially Derrida, *Margins of Philosophy*; also *Of Grammatology*, trans. Gavyatri C. Spivak, Baltimore, MD: Johns Hopkins University Press, 1976; *Dissemination*, trans. Barbara Johnson, London: Athlone Press, 1981; and *The Truth in Painting*, trans. Geoff Bennington and Ian McLeod, Chicago, IL: University of Chicago Press, 1987.

35. Davidson, *Inquiries into Truth and Interpretation*.

36. For further discussion, see Peter Gibbins, *Particles and Paradoxes: The Limits of Quantum Logic*, Cambridge: Cambridge University Press, 1987; Susan Haack, *Deviant Logic: Some Philosophical Issues*, Cambridge: Cambridge University Press, 1974; Hilary Putnam, *Mathematics, Matter and Method*, Cambridge: Cambridge University Press, 1979.

37. Derrida, 'Limited Inc', p. 117.
38. See note 4, above.
39. Richard Rorty, 'Philosophy as a kind of writing: an essay on Jacques Derrida', in *Consequences of Pragmatism*, Brighton: Harvester Press, 1982, pp. 89–109 and 'Is Derrida a transcendental philosopher?', in *Essays on Heidegger and Others*, Cambridge: Cambridge University Press, 1991, pp. 119–28; also Christopher Norris, 'Philosophy as *not* just a "kind of writing": Derrida and the claim of reason', in Dasenbrock (ed.), *Re-Drawing the Lines: analytic philosophy, deconstruction, and literary theory*, pp. 189–203 and Rorty, 'Two versions of "logocentrism": a reply to Norris', ibid., pp. 204–16.
40. See especially Derrida, *Edmund Husserl's 'The Origin of Geometry': An Introduction*, trans. John P. Leavey, Pittsburgh, PA: Duquesne University Press, 1973 and *'Speech and Phenomena' and Other Essays on Husserl's Theory of Signs*, trans. David B. Allison, Evanston, IL: Northwestern University Press, 1973; also entries under note 2, above, and Marian Hobson, *Jacques Derrida: Opening Lines*, London: Routledge, 1998.
41. Norris, 'Derrida on Rousseau' and Priest, 'Derrida and self-reference' (note 2, above); also Derrida, *Of Grammatology*; *Writing and Difference*, trans. Alan Bass, London: Routledge & Kegan Paul, 1978; *Dissemination*.
42. See note 2, above; also Priest, *Beyond the Limits of Thought*, Cambridge: Cambridge University Press, 1995.
43. Derrida, *Of Grammatology*, p. 158.
44. Ibid., p. 158.
45. Derrida, 'Parergon', in *The Truth in Painting*, pp. 15–147 and 'Plato's Pharmacy', in *Dissemination*, pp. 63–171.
46. See for instance Alan R. Malachowski (ed.), *Reading Rorty: Critical Responses to Philosophy and the Mirror of Nature, and Beyond*, Oxford: Blackwell, 1990 and Malachowski (ed.), *Richard Rorty, 3 vols*, London: Sage, 2002.
47. See note 39, above; also Rorty, *Consequences of Pragmatism*, Brighton: Harvester, 1982 and *Contingency, Irony, and Solidarity*, Cambridge: Cambridge University Press, 1991.
48. See Richard Rorty (ed.), *The Linguistic Turn*, Chicago, IL: University of Chicago Press, 1967, for a representative selection of essays.
49. See Norris, 'Derrida on Rousseau'.
50. For some astute historico-philosophical commentary, see Michael Friedman, *A Parting of the Ways: Carnap, Cassirer and Heidegger*, Chicago, IL: Open Court, 2000 and *Reconsidering Logical Positivism*, Cambridge: Cambridge University Press, 1999; also Gottlob Frege (1972), 'Review of Edmund Husserl's *Philosophie der Arithmetik*', trans. E.-H. W. Kluge, *Mind*, 81: 321–37; Gilbert Ryle, ' "Phenomenology" and "Phenomenology versus The Concept of Mind" ', in Ryle, *Collected Papers, Vol. 1*, London: Hutchinson, 1971, pp. 167–78 and 179–96.
51. See note 14, above.
52. Michael Dummett, *Truth and Other Enigmas*, London: Duckworth, 1978 and *The Logical Basis of Metaphysics*, Duckworth, 1991.

53. Norris, *Resources of Realism: Prospects for 'Post-analytic' Philosophy* and *New Idols of the Cave on the Limits of Anti-Realism*; also *Language, Logic and Epistemology: A Modal-Realist Approach*, London: Macmillan, 2004.

54. Derrida, 'Afterword: toward an ethic of conversation', p. 145.

55. Derrida, *Of Grammatology*.

56. See note 52, above; also Michael Luntley, *Language, Logic and Experience: the Case for Anti-Realism*, London: Duckworth, 1988; Christopher Norris, *Truth Matters: Realism, Anti-Realism and Response-Dependence*, Edinburgh: Edinburgh University Press, 2002; Neil Tennant, *Anti-Realism and Logic*, Oxford: Clarendon Press, 1987 and *The Taming of the True*, Oxford: Clarendon Press, 2002.

57. Crispin Wright, *Realism, Meaning and Truth*, Oxford: Blackwell, 1987 and *Truth and Objectivity*, Cambridge, MA: Harvard University Press, 1992.

58. See note 40, above; also Derrida, *La problème de la genèse dans la philosophie de Husserl*, Paris: Presses Universitaires de France, 1990.

59. See especially Paul Benacerraf, 'What numbers could not be', in Benacerraf and Hilary Putnam (eds), *The Philosophy of Mathematics: Selected Essays*, 2nd edn, Cambridge: Cambridge University Press, 1983, pp. 274–93.

60. Derrida, *Edmund Husserl's 'The Origin of Geometry': an Introduction*.

61. Dummett, *Truth and Other Enigmas*; also W. V. Quine, 'Two dogmas of empiricism', in *From a Logical Point of View*, 2nd edn, Cambridge, MA: Harvard University Press, 1961, pp. 20–46.

62. See Searle, 'Reiterating the Differences'.

63. See note 2, above.

64. See Derrida, 'Signature Event Context' and 'Limited Inc abc', op. cit.; also 'Of an apocalyptic tone newly adopted in philosophy', in Harold Coward and Toby Foshay (eds), *Derrida and Negative Theology*, Albany, NY: State University of New York Press, 1992, pp. 24–71.

65. For some striking examples, see Derrida, *Dissemination*, op. cit.; also *The Post Card: from Socrates to Freud and Beyond*, trans. Alan Bass, Chicago, IL: University of Chicago Press, 1987; 'Before the Law', in *Derrida: Acts of Literature*, Derek Attridge (ed.), London: Routledge, 1992, pp. 181–220; 'The Law of Genre', ibid., pp. 221–52.

66. Jürgen Habermas, *The Philosophical Discourse of Modernity: Twelve Lectures*, trans. Frederick Lawrence, Cambridge: Polity Press, 1987.

67. For further argument to this effect, see Norris, *What's Wrong with Postmodernism: Critical Theory and the Ends of Philosophy*, Hemel Hempstead: Harvester-Wheatsheaf, 1990 and *The Truth About Postmodernism*, Oxford: Blackwell, 1994.

2

The Future of Critical Philosophy and World Politics[1]

Richard Beardsworth

INTRODUCTION

The legacy of Jacques Derrida's thought is large, diverse and open. This chapter explores that legacy through the relation between critical philosophy and world politics. Its focus, which is on Derrida's work where it prolongs the tradition of 'critical philosophy', produces an ambivalence: respect for the manner in which he prolongs Enlightenment thinking, but distance towards the way in which he ultimately relates philosophy to current objects of society. I suggest that Derrida's legacy in the tradition of critical philosophy requires rethinking. Before outlining my argument, let me define my general terms.

Critical philosophy is characterised by four major traits.

1. It promotes reflective thought, thought that presupposes no determining instance except that which confronts it historically as its object (what Hegel called 'actuality').
2. This reflective dimension ensues from the modern negotiation between the transcendental and the empirical consequent upon Kant's ethical deduction of religion. As a result of this deduction, the tension between the transcendental and the empirical is rehearsed immanently by critical philosophy within the finite.
3. Such thinking is therefore concerned with society (however it circumscribes society).
4. This concern is engaged: moving within the tension between the transcendental and the empirical, the practice of critical philosophy is ethically disposed and, in some way or other, it is related to politics.

Critical philosophising means, in brief, reflecting upon actuality in such a way that helps, directly and/or indirectly, the betterment of humanity.

I understand world politics in two senses: first, the challenge of the political is to shape the world *as* a world, that is, as an organised but differentiated space that diminishes economic, military and political disequilibria through a praxis of the world; and secondly, that more local formations should be articulated within this overall shaping since world governance is necessary for sub-global differentiation in an integrated global economy to be possible in the first place.

However we conceive world polity (from a federation of states to a dense network of inter-regional relations; from institutions of world governance to a world state), this article's interest in Derrida's legacy lies in the articulation between critical thought, on the one hand, and the institution of the world, on the other. My question is therefore the following: what is the legacy of the critical thought of Jacques Derrida concerning this articulation?

My response is made in five stages: first, I examine the two basic gestures of recent critical thought and their apparent reconciliation in the late rapprochement between Derrida and Habermas concerning world politics; secondly, taking a historical step back from these recent political and philosophical events, I then consider our general historical actuality and the way in which its challenges undermine the basic gestures of 'post-modern' culture; thirdly, I examine the specificity of Derrida's thinking with regard to this culture, and within this specificity, the way in which deconstruction responds to our present challenges; fourthly, I focus on a hesitation in this response, specific to Derrida's overall adventure of thinking and invention; and finally, I sketch out what I consider our critical philosophical priorities regarding the world to be. My conclusion summarises the argument and underlines, in the context of Derrida's legacy, a distinction between two lines of critical philosophising regarding the world.

CONTEMPORARY CRITICAL PHILOSOPHY AND THE RECENT RAPPROCHEMENT BETWEEN HABERMAS AND DERRIDA

The critical philosophy of the last four decades can be divided into two basic gestures: one supposedly 'German', the other 'French'. These two gestures are usually exemplified by Jürgen Habermas, on the one hand, and Jacques Derrida, on the other. Within the problematic of critical philosophy defined above, these two gestures are the following.

German thought has been concerned to pursue the post-Kantian tradition of critique and to posit a normative horizon to thought and action within an intersubjective, speculative or phenomenological understanding of theoretical and practical reason. Habermas is the most imposing German thinker here, re-articulating philosophical modernity, after the eighteenth-century retreat of religion from the social sphere, in terms of a post-subjective philosophy of communicative rationality and action. The end of critical philosophy is accordingly to reinvent, after the twentieth-century political failure of the philosophy of the subject, the Enlightenment project of truth, reason and freedom.

French thought has radicalised the phenomenology of Martin Heidegger and Edmund Husserl in distinction to this post-Kantian critical tradition. It inscribes this tradition within a general metaphysics of temporalisation ('presence'), and it thinks determination and calculation within this temporal inscription. Unable to oppose to the metaphysics of reason another form of rationality, it interrupts this general circumscription with the problematic of difference and aporia, of singularity and event. Jacques Derrida is the most imposing French thinker here, re-articulating the teleological horizon of community and universality within an a-rational economy of reason and radical alterity. The end of critical philosophy is, for him, the deployment of the non-dialectisable oscillation between the common and the singular in order to negotiate the violent limits of any project of truth, reason or freedom.

The last twenty-five years of critical thought has been fuelled by this difference of approach to the 'critical' nature of critique. The difference is clear, for example, in Habermas's polemical *The Philosophical Discourse of Modernity*, in which Derrida is portrayed as a post-Nietzschean aesthete, and in Derrida's uncompromising *The Other Heading*, in which any formation of a common will always already constitutes fear of the stranger.[2]

The stridency of this difference, together with other work in French thought that considers the universalising processes of reason as destructive of difference, has helped to engender the philosophico-cultural distinction between the 'modern' and the 'post-modern'. This distinction follows the translation of French thought into English and its adoption by American academia from the 1970s. While Derrida's negotiations with reason and the event eschew the more Habermasian/Lyotardian/Rortyesque distinctions between the modern and the post-modern, the above difference in critical approach helps to define the major traits of recent French theory. These traits include the following: a radical critique of our understanding of the real; a deconstruction of the philosophy of the subject and its attendant epistemological, ethical and political attributes; attention to the excess of form and the excess of reason *qua* the excess of temporalisation (the unpresentable, the monstrous, the nomadic, the pre-ethical, radical alterity); strong engagement with literature as a field of singularity and non-representation; and, in the context of totalitarianism, the Shoah, and twentieth-century elisions among science, technology and politics, separation of the ethical from the political, and focus on the event, on the ethics of radical passivity and the aesthetics of successful failure.

Given the differences between recent French and German thought, in the context of our concern with the manner in which we assume the world, how should we understand the late rapprochement between Derrida and Habermas?

There are four important moments to this rapprochement: first, Derrida's acceptance of the Adorno prize in 2001;[3] secondly, their separate interviews with Giovanni Borradori in the jointly produced *Philosophy in a Time of Terror*;[4] thirdly, Derrida's co-signing of Habermas's letter – published simultaneously in *Frankfurter Allgemeine Zeitung* and *Libération* – which criticises the invasion of Iraq;[5] and fourthly, more indirectly, the earlier work, published in 2002, *Voyous. Deux essais sur la raison*, where Derrida reorganises the post-Heideggerian distinction between thinking and reason into a double-sided figure of two forms of reason (those of conditionality and of unconditionality) and argues for a contemporary deconstructive rationalism.[6] In the jointly signed letter, Habermas argues against the flouting of international law by the US and British governments and for the promotion of a common European will that affirms a 'domestic' world politics based on law. In a note added to the co-signed letter Derrida remarks that 'beyond the differends that may have separated [us] in the past', he and Habermas believe it important to join voices given the urgency of the situation, concluding: 'I share *in essence* the premises and perspectives of this letter'.[7]

In the context of the above two gestures of critical thought, Derrida puts aside here irreducible philosophical differences – concerning the commonality of the will, the philosophical exemplarity of Europe, and the use of reason – in the name of political pragmatics.[8] He argues that his own and Habermas's reflections on Europe, its future political role in the world, the establishment of the rule of international law and their thinking on religious fundamentalism intersect – notwithstanding their philosophical differences 'in the past'. Derrida emphasises hereby the reflective rationalism of deconstruction and a paradigm of European thinking and practice (whatever the complications).

Now, since Derrida's thought emerges from out of a specific negotiation with the empirico-transcendental difference that requires the deconstruction of any exemplary horizon of reason or will, the rapprochement seems a little quick. Rather than 'reconciling' two different gestures of thought, Derrida seems to demonstrate awareness of the importance of rational argument, and recasts his own development of an *a-rational* economy between reason and its other as a reflective rationalism. Being pragmatic, this recasting sits a little unhappily with prior philosophical moves in which the interest of reason and rational will were interrogated. The rapprochement suggests that Derrida senses that the practices of deconstruction could be caught out by the movement of history (and the challenges of recent world events), and that something else is going on, within history, beyond the terms of the deconstruction of metaphysics.

To understand the complexity of what is indeed taking place here, where deconstruction lies within this complexity in comparison with the overall gesture of French theory, as well as what challenges await critical thinking in general, I want to take an historical step back and appraise, behind September 11 and the third Iraq war, our actuality. The following historical account is not original, but it allows me to frame my concerns.

Our Historical Actuality, its Challenge, and the End of the Post-modern

One of the defining terms of our period is 'globalisation'. A materialist perspective on this process seems today to be generally accepted, whether this perspective is thought through philosophically or not, whereby globalisation is considered the ongoing effect of a capitalisation of economic and social relations that began in Europe in the fourteenth century. Following Marx, I understand 'capitalisation' as an economic dynamic whereby increasing parts of inanimate and animate nature are subordinated to the rule of value: exchangeability and valorisation (the process by which value is added to an object). During the Renaissance, Reformation and Counter-Reformation, capitalisation spread to large areas of western and central Europe and made inroads through colonisation into American and Asian societies. From the eighteenth to the end of the nineteenth century, industrialised and further divided at the level of production, distribution and finance, capitalisation was increasingly contained within the dual process of nation-state territorialisation and its attendant 'liberties', on the one hand, and imperialism and its attendant 'civilising processes', on the other hand. From within the historical process of capitalism the modern epoch came to be defined as an age of rapid economic, technological and social change, political liberalisation and national sovereignty.

Political responses to this epoch are fundamentally of two kinds. Within the parameters of nation-state territoriality, the state is conceived and shaped increasingly in the name of autonomy: its power is legitimated through the legal self-determination of its people; and it defines itself in difference to other states and other peoples' self-determination. This autonomy is simultaneously undercut, however, by the increasing exposition of relations of power between governing and governed and between the state and other peoples. The modern epoch is also constituted, therefore, by a second form of political invention which attempts to transcend the formalism of liberal polity and give content to the social relation. From Marx to the end of socialist internationalism in the 1930s this attempt was widely celebrated as 'communism' or 'radical social democracy'. The attempt constituted in theory a participatory, rather than representative, self-organisation of socio-economic life that extricated both objective and subjective worlds from the law of value. Before and after the First World War, historical attempts at its institutionalisation became limited again to the frontiers of the nation-state. Radical social democracy then disintegrated as an idea in the inefficient and unjust command economies of state socialism in the following decades. The frontiers of the nation-state were only undone by an alliance of capital and political power in the last quarter of the twentieth century with the emergence of economic and political neo-liberalism. Whereas in the eighteenth century capitalisation was restricted to a small part of the world, while in the twentieth century large parts of the world still refused the market system, but increasingly worked within its processes of capital accumulation, today, after the failure of the radical social democratic alternative to liberal democracy, we stand again in a process of capitalisation that is ever-expanding but is still structured by the legacies of its early historical and geographical formation.

This historical epoch, delimited by processes of capitalisation and thought in terms of liberal or social democracy within or beyond the nation-state, is at the same time understood in the reflective terms of 'modernity'. From Rousseau to Kant, Hegel to Marx, Nietzsche to Weber and Simmel and Freud, the liberal, republican or social democratic responses to capitalisation are conceived in terms of philosophical modernity.[9] Its particular traits are:

1. the domination of the socio-economic over society as a whole and the increasing withdrawal of religion from the public sphere;
2. with increasing capitalisation, on the one hand, and the marginalisation of religion, on the other hand, the progressive individualisation of society – the emergence of the individual as an autonomous social, cultural and legal person – and the increasing differentiation of society through monetarisation and the division of labour;
3. the attempt to rearticulate what is left unarticulated between individuals *qua* society (as the remainder of religion) in terms of ethical and political law;
4. the attempt, then,
   (a) to think the unarticulated relation between individual adventure

and collective spirit in terms of new ethical and political laws and new kinds of institution, and

(b) the consequent foregrounding of reflective political solutions to the injustices of capital social relations.

The historical epoch of the modern can be understood through capitalisation and the emergence of the nation-state. The philosophical problematic of modernity with regard to this history can be understood as a reflective response – at the level of ethics, politics and institutionality in general – to this historical process. The reflection is made in terms of the unarticulated relation between individual adventure and collective spirit that follows the marginalisation of religion. This problematic and response come in two waves, the second a response itself to the first. The first wave of modernity, the Scottish and European Enlightenment, is made in terms of the legal nation-state (parliamentary democracy and/or republicanism and/or constitutional monarchy); the second wave, the continental post-Enlightenment, is made in terms that go beyond the nation-state, but whose empirical concretisation, when attempted, fails in the twentieth century.

How does the above account of modern history, together with the reflective response to it, define historical and philosophical actuality? And what purpose does this definition serve with regard to my previous description of French and German thought in the context of the legacy of Derrida and world politics? I wish to make six broad points.

First, just as the thinkers of the Enlightenment stood from the middle of the eighteenth century to the middle of the nineteenth century in a material actuality that required the invention of the *polis* at a level and in terms that could politically embed or transform the social consequences of capitalisation, so we today have to re-invent the political at a level and in terms that will appropriate the planetarisation of these same relations. There is, in other words, an analogy between the political projects of the eighteenth and nineteenth century and the challenge of twenty-first-century political invention *given the background of capitalisation*.

Secondly, with the failures of the twentieth century to reorganise the capitalisation of the life world, all human beings, wherever they live on the planet, will become articulated in an increasingly particular form of socio-economic life that will require political shape in order for them to remain socially individuated. The project of the Enlightenment as a project of universalisation through which plurality and difference can be expressed is, in this sense, to be continued. *Contra* the undifferentiating logic of untamed capital markets, political institutions are required to give possibility and shape to the social relation between human beings and between human beings and their environments. To foreground this necessity demands, intellectually, a re-consideration of universality as a process of cognition that promotes difference. Following Hegel, I wish to call this universality 'concrete'.[10]

Thirdly, such a history and such an analogy reveal our challenge – to construct institutions of the universal that regulate and organise global capitalism in such a way that individual adventure and collective spirit are harnessed without reducing either the collective to the individual or the individual to the collective. This challenge is perhaps impossible, but inevitable. Contemporary religious instrumentalisation of politics constitutes the disavowal of this challenge.

Fourthly, we remain, therefore, not only within the history of the modern epoch, delimited by the capitalisation of social relations, but we remain also within the philosophical problematic of modernity: the attempt, following the social consequences of capitalism, to articulate the relation between individual adventure and collective spirit. After the failure of twentieth-century articulations of this relation, the attempt situates itself now in world terms. Habermas's general understanding of philosophical modernity is, indeed, 'in essence' correct as long as we keep in mind the relation between the economic, the political and the reflective. Habermas's own move into a pragmatic transcendentalism of language to articulate substantive rationality anew loses this focus, however, and remains vulnerable to deconstruction.

Fifthly, the late-twentieth-century theoretical distinction between the modern and the post-modern has been overstated. There are certainly excellent reasons for this distinction concerning the diversification of subjective identity and citizenship within and beyond the nation-state. However, when the distinction marginalises the philosophical problematic of modernity, it ignores historical movement. For example, the recent return of religion or intensification of religious identity does not invalidate the modern thesis of secularisation particular to philosophical modernity as much post-modern theory has argued (often interestingly).[11] Rather, the contemporary return of religion and new forms of irrationalism emerge, broadly, out of the failure of the second response of modernity to the inequalities of the nation-state and colonisation. This failure happens both in the north (with state socialism) and in the south (with post-colonial independence, nationalisation and socialism). The return of religion constitutes a symptom, therefore, not of the end of modernity, but of the continuing process of historical modernity and the endurance of its philosophical problematic. To overcome irrational responses to contemporary economic, social and political life, contemporary forms of capitalisation need to be appropriated. This appropriation requires the mobilisation of our rational powers and the practice of concrete universality (the relation between unity and plurality).

Sixthly, post-modern thought has been inspired by the traits of the overall gesture of French theory defined above. Radicalising this inspiration in more cultural than philosophical terms, it has therefore spoken of the 'end' of the modern. In the context of the above history, the post-modern has thought in abstraction from material, historical processes. In the context of the twentieth-century fates of modernity, its mourning of historical materialism has, therefore, been poor when radical phenomenology and ontology have diverted it from thinking the movement of the real. When, furthermore, post-modern thought has undercut the modern primacy of the political and the differentiating effects of universality, it has largely been responding to the second response within modernity (the fate of radical social democracy *qua* totalitarianism and totality-thinking), but not to the historical and philosophical problematic of modernity as such: the constant re-articulation of the relation between individual and collective. Prioritising the ethical, the nomadic and the unilaterally deconstructive over construction, law and institution, it has short-circuited history and underestimated the creative powers of reason and institution.

The American translation of the French heritage of phenomenology and structuralism, together with the recent focus of critical thought on the relation between philosophy and literature, have contributed to this side-lining of critical thought from the movement of history and its constellations of force. When, today, the modern responses to capitalisation are so historically inadequate, we should rethink our ideational framework and reinvent, from within historical and philosophical modernity, the *polis* beyond its modern inventions. This paradox – we are beyond the modern within modernity – is outstanding.

At the moment when the weak aspects of post-modernism come to an end, what happens to the thought of Jacques Derrida within the overall legacy of critical philosophising? Does the thought of Jacques Derrida resist the above material history and its terms, and does it allow us to think reflectively our political future? Derrida's co-signing with Habermas of the Iraq letter of 2003 and his recasting of deconstruction in *Voyous* do constitute displaced recognitions of a problem within deconstruction concerning the relations between reason, history and matter. Yet Derrida's thought can be assumed to a large extent to be within the above account of modernity. I now wish to consider Derrida's specificity within French thought and its post-modern derivatives as well as the singularity of his own response to our challenge: the political architecture of world space.

DECONSTRUCTION, POST-KANTIAN MODERNITY AND DERRIDA'S RESPONSE TO WORLD POLITICS

As the two essays in *Voyous* emphasise (especially 'The "World" of the Enlightenment to come'), Derrida's thinking with regard to Enlightenment thought and its inventions can and should be placed within the legacy of his thinking on metaphysics. His deconstruction of reason in terms of an a-rational economy between rationality and alterity leads to a form of thought and invention that is neither pro-Enlightenment nor anti-Enlightenment. With regard to the above history and problematic, one can therefore argue that Derrida has:

1. clear critical purchase on historical and philosophical modernity in terms of his own reading of the future of Enlightenment reason;
2. a particular 'theory' of invention, one critical to understanding how to respond to and invent world democracy beyond the nation-state reinvention of the democratic *polis*; and
3. a philosophy of democracy that affirms, above all other political regimes, the rule of the people, but shows how, within the self-delimitation of democracy, critical philosophy will remain in oscillation between institution and alterity, law and singularity in the very name of people.

A Derridean might argue, therefore, that, unlike post-modern thought, and despite the overall traits of French thought in their particular exportation to the USA, deconstruction is very much alive given, precisely, its aporetic understanding of reason and institution. It is, therefore, formative regarding the challenge of the political appropriation of world capitalisation. Given the necessary violence of all form, critical philosophy cannot not take distance from any act of political appropriation, all the while also affirming those political acts that are more respectful of their own violence.[12] This argument underpins Derrida's recent response to world democracy.

For Derrida, there is no such thing as democracy.[13] In the tension between liberty and equality, more of one means less of the other, and, in the tension between legislative sovereignty and executive sovereignty, democracy must limit itself. The first aporia is well rehearsed by political liberalism, so I will concentrate on the second aporia, between law and force. If law is to be law, then it must be enforced. Without coercive force, law is not law. With the enforcement of law, however, law is necessarily made particular to the interests of executive sovereignty. The early Enlightenment distinction between the legislative and the executive can do nothing, as Rousseau and the young Hegel analysed, but defer this necessary appropriation of the law by executive sovereignty. Regularly held elections constitute one important way of limiting this corruption as much as possible.

For Derrida, the tension between the modern sovereignty of a self-determining people and the moment of executive sovereignty in enforcing the law over any other intra-state power requires that real sovereignty lies with the monopoly of violence and with the indivisible moment of decision proper to the executive instance. This sovereignty comes into its own in democracy when, as in Algeria in 1992, democracy is suspended, and a state of exception is declared for the sake of democracy. The aporia between democratic legislative autonomy and sovereign force, necessary to the definition of democratic law, means that there can be no such thing as democracy (at any level). Derrida thus agrees with Kant's 'Perpetual Peace' essay which states that a world cosmopolitan order is impossible as such.[14] But he does so for reasons that go beyond Kant's empirical fear that, given the spatial geography of the world, a world republic would be despotic. For Derrida, the specific enforcement of universal cosmopolitan law, through the executive sovereign, undercuts the very universality it is enforcing as it enforces it. As soon as there is a legislative will, sovereignty, there is enforcement. As soon as there is enforcement, there is executive sovereignty. As soon as there is executive sovereignty, there is in principle abuse of power. Following these aporias, Derrida concludes in *Voyous*, 'Executive sovereignty will always betray world democracy'.[15]

Given this aporia between law and force within the rule of the power of people, any invention of world democracy must attempt to transcend the terms of nation-state sovereignty and its monopoly of violence. If international law is to be upheld over the sovereignty and interests of nation-states, international law must have legitimacy and must be enforced. Both the legitimacy of the justice of the law and the monopoly of violence particular to the enforcement of its rule remain problematic. Any democratic appropriation of the logic of market forces and of the neo-liberal alliance between economic and political power cannot not force these aporias back onto the table. To be effective, international law must be both legitimate and sovereign. If not, a world order of international law will be imperial law. By being effective, however, international law will become at the same time particular. This aporia is irreducible.

Derrida notes in *Philosophy in the Age of Terror*:

> I cannot hide away from the apparently utopian character of what I am
> suggesting, that of an international institution of law or an international
> institution of justice, etc. that has its own force at its disposal. Although I
> do not take law to be the last word in ethics, in politics, in anything,
> although this unity of force and law (demanded by the very concept of
> law) is not only utopian, but aporetic . . . one is reconstituting a new
> figure, not necessarily in the form of the state, of universal sovereignty,
> of absolute law, that has at its disposal the autonomy of force it needs,
> and I persist in thinking that it is faith in the possibility of this impossible
> thing . . . that must command all our decisions.[16]

This aporia of law within democracy reveals three things. First, the unity of
justice, law and force (pure democracy) is a radical impossibility: it is utopian
and aporetic. Secondly, being aporetic, this impossibility, as Derrida has
argued since the 1980s essay 'Psyché: Invention of the Other', becomes the
condition of good invention.[17] Aware that the equation between justice,
law and force is radically impossible, as one institutionalises justice as law,
one can invent democracy in world terms in an interesting manner by
giving more chance to the other than less. Thirdly, given the radical
impossibility of their unity, the good statesperson will work for world
democracy in the simultaneous understanding of the necessary dissociation
between democracy and autonomy, law and justice, sovereignty and
unconditionality. The unity of justice, law and force commands his or
her decision, but such a decision works, always, to allow for the reinvention
of the law. Since unity and dissociation cannot be held together in the
decision, the decision is possible in the first place. Impossibility and aporia
are therefore *creative* not negative. The aporia of law and force within the
rule of the power of the people (demos-kratos) will insist at all levels of
democracy: from the city-state to the nation-state, from the nation-state
to regional alliance, from a world order/federation of law to a 'city' of
humanity. How, therefore, would deconstruction conceive the specific
invention of world democracy within the process of capitalisation that I
have foregrounded here? In his last works Derrida makes at least three
moves in this regard.

First, he pushes for the rule of international law: both for the increasing
legitimacy of international law and for its force. He thereby encourages
continued reform of the UN General Assembly and radical reform of the
Security Council in the name of the democratic legitimacy and force of law.
Here we understand why Derrida, despite what he wrote in *The Other*

Heading regarding the non-exemplary exemplarity of Europe, can co-sign Habermas's Iraq letter of May 2003. The letter argues for the construction of universal institutions of law, for the continuation of the European project of Enlightenment world-wide, and for a common European will underpinning this project. Both Derrida and Habermas conceive of world politics in terms of law and institution. Universal legality is what the Enlightenment gave the world, consequent upon the socio-political marginalisation of religion. The difference between Derrida and Habermas lies in Derrida's critical focus on the *remainder* of this law and institution, proper to the limitation or auto-immunity of democracy. It also lies in the fact that Derrida thinks this remainder through religion (the messianic, the promise, radical faith) not through history (see section 'Our historical actuality, its challenge, and the end of the post-modern', pp. 49–54).

Secondly, breaking with what international relations theory calls the 'domestic analogy' between the national and the international, Derrida argues for the invention of new forms of supra-national sovereignty distinct from nation-state sovereignty. In this respect he alludes in *Voyous* to the possible sharing of sovereignty across different instances of local, metro-politan, national, regional and global governance. Towards the end of the first essay he also points to the idea of sovereignty without sovereignty, of a law without force. Like the unity of justice, law and force, the idea constitutes another impossible condition of invention. Hence Derrida's further re-reading, at the end of the first essay of *Voyous*, of Heidegger's pronouncement in the *Spiegel* interview: 'Only a god can (still) save us'.[18]

Thirdly, Derrida reiterates the point of the indivisibility of sovereignty for the rule of law to be possible through enforcement. He argues for the necessity of executive sovereignty and for the consequent self-limitation of world democracy. The notion of sovereignty without sovereignty remains a quasi-concept, something 'always to come'. For Derrida, again: 'Executive sovereignty will always betray world democracy'.[19]

These three steps cannot be transformed into a coherent strategy. Each step in its non-synthesisable relation to the others forms part of an aporetic negotiation with the aporias of world democracy that spring from the irreducible incompatibility between force and law within democratic gov-ernance. Consequently, the quasi-concept of 'democracy to come' has profound purchase upon world politics. It allows world politics to be thought and practiced critically within its non-horizontal horizon because it deploys both the relation and the dissociation between justice, law and force. This negotiation of aporia is, in essence, the 'reasonable' practice of reason Derrida recasts in *Voyous*:[20] hence the hyper-rationalism of decon-struction.

DERRIDA'S HESITATION AND THE DEVELOPMENT OF SOVEREIGNTY

The problem of this argument as a response to our historical actuality emerges with these three aporetic steps which work within the quasi-concept of 'democracy to come'. The tension between the invention of sovereignty without sovereignty and the impossibility of such sovereignty in the very definition of sovereignty speaks less of the validity of creative aporetic than of an intellectual hesitation. This hesitation resides in the tension between the aspiration to a new concept of sovereignty, the reflection on the divisibility of sovereignty at a world level, and the simultaneous argument that all forms of sovereignty will be the same given the irreducible indivisibility of executive sovereignty in the coercion of law. Derrida cannot, rightly, imagine an institution of sovereignty without sovereignty, of law without force. Yet he is aware that, historically, it is towards this conception of law without force that critical thought must move in order to invent forms of world democracy. The quasi-concept of 'democracy to come' covers over the critical need to flesh out this *new* relation between law and force. This does not require the disentangling of this relation from metaphysically loaded moral and political thought (for example, the moral idealism inherent to liberal internationalism). It requires the *developing* of new relations between law and force from out of the socio-economic and political history of an increasingly integrated and hierarch-ised human world. The quasi-concept of 'democracy to come' with its aporias stands at a distance from the material real and from its re-determination. This distance implies that Derrida is *also* caught out by the present development of history given his post-Heideggerian focus on the indeterminate and incalculable in the relation between the incalculable and calculation. The reconciliation between Derrida and Habermas, Derrida's appendix to the Iraq letter of May 2003, the shift from 'thought' to 'reason' in *Voyous*, the stress on the rationalism of deconstruction in distinction to the concerns of the 1996 essay 'Faith and Knowledge' – all translate this theoretical hesitation and distance from the real that informs it. And so, despite Derrida's singularity in comparison with the 'post-modern', his thinking also refuses to countenance the rational development of alterity, not in terms of the excess of time, but in terms of the material dynamic of history. We would need to look here in detail at Derrida's understanding of reason and determination, and his 1980s consideration of the 'post-Leibnizian modern' of rational calculation and programmaticity to get a purchase on his understanding of determination.[21]

Briefly, for Derrida the only invention possible is that of the real *as* the other: otherwise invention becomes a programme of the possible. Since all invention programmes the other, invention is therefore impossible. This impossibility constitutes the creative condition of invention. In this logic the other as other lies beyond determination, and modern reason is unilaterally determined *as* calculation, be it determinant or reflective in the Kantian sense, reflective or speculative in the Hegelian sense. *Qua* horizonal, reason always already anticipates the event. This is a phenomenologically inspired reading of reason. While giving access to singularity and difference, reason cannot not close down difference. Since for Derrida reason does not give rise to difference, critical thought must work between the incalculable and calculation, between the unconditional and conditionality. It is therefore unwilling to consider reason as a force of thought that promotes the possibility of the singular in the first place.

If these points are correct, the manner in which deconstruction thinks leads to a heavy irony, an irony to which the political history of the American post-modern in part testifies. The endeavour of deconstruction is to promote alterity and difference. In refusing to determine alterity, however, *contra* the less reflective determinations of other forces, deconstruction risks closing down alterity. By not determining the real in the name of alterity, *contra* other determinations that reduce it to the same, deconstruction risks giving less chance to alterity rather than more chance. Conversely, by determining the real, one risks opening up the possibility of chance as much as one may close it down; by determining the other, one does not simply subsume or master it, one equally gives it its chance. Thus, by refusing mastery, deconstruction risks mastering the real because it disengages from the real at the very moment that one needs to determine it against other forces of determination. I sense this disengagement in the aporia of world democracy. Derrida leaves the sovereignty of the world too much to chance by signalling the critical disposition necessary to invent its possible forms solely in terms of aporia and by implicitly justifying the suspension of the work of reflective thought through the quasi-concept of democracy to come. This suspension takes place at the precise moment when sovereignty is being over-determined by economic, military and political hegemony. The engagement and disengagement of democracy to come is thus, in the historical context adumbrated throughout this paper, a form of mastery over life and less the invention of it.

The above argument only has purchase if one sees the power or faculty of reason within the continuum of history as one force counteracting others, if one sees reason, differentially and non-ontologically, as a process of distinction, determination and universalisation that emerges immanently within history in distinction to other determinations of history. Derrida's reading of reason through Heidegger's destruction of metaphysics in terms of presence, on the one hand, and Emmanuel Lévinas' first ethics, on the other hand – whatever the deconstructive complications – blocks this historical, material path. Thinkers such as Deleuze and Foucault who have this genealogical perspective also refuse however, *contra* Hegel, a determining relation between universality and alterity. It is where French thought, above and beyond its Anglo-American translations, remains skewed with regard to our actuality. Concrete universal institutions need to be invented in order to release the difference of the world from under the determinations of capital and the nefarious political alliances and compromises with it. Without determining the real through such institutions, the world risks subordination to oligarchy. The powers of reason should be focused on the invention of institution and law for new forms of sovereignty to emerge.

Considered from this perspective the aporias of democracy and sovereignty do not constitute creative conditions of invention. Rather, these aporias should be left to one side as one builds institutions that allow for the difference of the world in the first place. It will be for the following generations to work with the necessary exclusions that come with any determination of the real. That is the logic of history. It is not, however, the logic of invention – unless one formalises history to the point that one risks disengaging from it. Deconstruction runs this risk.

PRIORITIES AND PROJECTS

How and where, then, should critical philosophy proceed in its engagement with world politics? The following brief comments propose an ideational framework and orientation for critical thought at this moment of radical historical change.

Philosophically

First, we should focus on universal law and institution in the context of our histories, whatever the level (local, national, regional, global) at which we work for this law and institution. The power of reason is thereby to be affirmed as providing, through determination of the relations between universality and difference, a set of as yet unarticulated strategies for differentiation. If French thought has led reflection to avoid the construction of concrete universality, it underestimates significantly how much ideas can help change history and how much reason can release difference. During the Cold War, and in the context of the failure of communism, this philosophical disposition was understandable, although it underestimated from the outset the necessary relation between universality and difference. In an increasingly integrated global economy, under the law of competition, difference and singularity only have their chance through universal mechanisms of law and institution in co-ordination with sub-global assembly.

Politically

Secondly, that we should focus on new forms of concrete universality in the context of our histories requires an embracing of the necessary relation between democracy and institution. The basic disposition of French critical thought, and post-modern culture more loosely, have encouraged people to shy away from the institution of the political. Yet both the movement of history and the present undermining of international institutionality require invention of a form of politics that includes clear promotion of potential world bodies. This defence means promotion of the democratic reform of the UN (particularly its deliberative assembly and executive council) and of its associated agencies (the Bretton Woods institutions) in co-ordination with state and non-state actors according to the principles of reciprocity, universality and subsidiarity. It means, second, a new institutional approach to world economic and social governance that redefines, after neo-liberalism, world macro-economic policy.[22] Initial steps to world governance along the legal and political lines of subsidiarity could then converge with co-ordination between global, regional, national and local economic policy-making bodies. It is only *as a result of this approach* that new modalities of sovereignty will emerge. The process will be very slow, full of compromise and set-backs. This democratic expansion nevertheless constitutes the major challenge for sub-national, national and regional democracies in the next hundred years.[23]

Disciplinarily

Thirdly, we need to rehearse rigorous, hard-headed formulations of world governance in the long-term perspective of institutional forms of world democracy. Intellectuals need to place to the foreground of the international and political stage, therefore, a clear, policy-oriented framework for a world ethical community of law, endowed with political mechanisms of implementation in the context of a regulated planetary economy. Research projects concerned with the principles of economic globalisation, together with forms of political institutionality to concretise them, are on the increase. To be co-ordinated and realisable, yet set within the horizon of a world polity, such projects must be trans-disciplinary, require careful teamwork between, at least, economics (particularly international political economy), politics and critical philosophy, and they must be as publicly mediated as possible. We must promote emerging paradigms of thought that are reflective and concretely universal, that open up new spaces between social science and the humanities. In the context of my negotiation with Jacques Derrida's legacy, I would suggest, therefore, that we intensify the reflective power of critical philosophy within empirical and normative social science and open up a set of constructive, informed dialogues between ethics, political institution and critical articulation of regional and global economy. To do so will help foster a forward-looking *political* mindset that can respond concretely to the challenges of our age.

CONCLUSION

This chapter constitutes a call to a series of re-engagements between critical philosophy and social science within a negotiation with the legacy of the critical thought of Jacques Derrida. Analysing first how Derrida returns to a form of deconstructive rationalism (and to a rather rapid rapprochement with the critical gesture of Jürgen Habermas), I have claimed that the basic gesture of both French thought in general and of deconstruction in particular is caught out by the post-1989 movement of history. I then analysed the deeper reasons for this with an account of modernity that prioritised the relations between religion, economy and politics and the problematic relation between the individual and society that emerged from the diremption of these relations under capitalism. I argued that we are still in modernity but beyond the modern solutions to its diremptions. I next showed that Derrida's thought is complex with regard to this history (unlike much post-modern culture and poor post-modern readings of Derrida). While continuing to work within the discursive strategies of European Enlightenment thought, deconstruction shows at the same time the necessary limits to these formations. This means that Derrida's late work focuses on aporias between justice, law and force that will always already undermine the practice of world democracy. Derrida can thereby both criticise all unilateral attempts to scupper the move to world democracy and question the very possibility of it. I then argued that while this engagement with law and institution is singular among French thought, the manner in which it is carried out underestimates the affirmative relation between the determining powers of reason and history. As a result, any thought of new forms of polity on Derrida's part remains within a formal logic of the incalculable and calculation, one that does not open up the interdisciplinary places where work needs to be done for these new forms of polity to emerge.

That said, I understand the power of Derrida's aporetic thinking for critical studies of social and political determination. I believe, today, however, that critical thought needs to do more, that it is a question of apprehending our actuality in such a way as to determine it for the greater good of humanity. This demands a re-engagement with reason understood as a process of thought that works towards the articulation of concrete universality (a notion of reason underestimated by French thought in general). In Marxian vein, I assume that history has its own dynamic, that this dynamic is material and, in large part, economic, and that present economic structures are causing immense political and cultural strain. I have argued that a response to this strain requires that world democracy and world sovereignty constitute part of our actuality, even if their empirical forms disappear for many in a hazy, distant, if not, precisely, impossible future. In this sense they constitute the major challenge of critical thought and practice, whatever the difficulty of assuming this challenge. I ended with a short reflection on some of the disciplinary implications of such a challenge that would encourage a public, political culture of world democracy to emerge.

What is to become of the legacy of Jacques Derrida within the articulation between critical philosophy and world politics? What is the basic distinction between the kind of rationalism Derrida argued for at the end of his life in the immediate context of political, economic and religious irrationality, and the kind of rationalism I am arguing for in the context of the continuing problematic of modernity within which these irrationalities are understood? I conclude with two possible responses.

Minimally, there are important questions which any Derridean legacy must address, after post-modern culture, concerning the relation between reason, history and transformation. These questions do not qualify, however, the critical gesture with which Derrida and those inspired by him are concerned: delimitation of the violent limits of any finite form, reflection upon the political from out of this delimitation.

Maximally, there is a clear difference in the understanding of the powers of reason: one understanding places focus on the differentiating powers of reason within the context of historical force and looks to construct a more encompassing universality beyond given forms of it; the other understanding, while promoting these forms, looks to deconstruct them in order to give witness to the differences that they exclude. In the former understanding of critical reason there is a political engagement with the world and with its articulations that the latter understanding of critical reason cannot countenance. From its perspective, such engagement is either dangerous or naive. I would argue rather that it signals an engagement with the real from which a phenomenologically inspired account of post-Kantian modernity remains distant. I have argued that the critical philosophical gesture of the future should move to where the real is being determined and give it critical shape from out of the evolving historical continuum of reason, institution, economy and force. From within the present diremptions between religion, polity and economy, I am making an argument for a trans-disciplinary apprehension of present and future lines of force that could help foster a strong, responsible sense of world polity that is increasingly transparent, accountable and politically and culturally ambitious. The difference between these two conceptions of reason is philosophically and disciplinarily decisive.

NOTES

1. A longer version of this article first appeared in *Millennium: Journal of International Studies* (2005) 34: 1 and is reproduced with the permission of the publisher.
2. See J. Habermas, *The Philosophical Discourse of Modernity*, trans. Frederick Lawrence, Cambridge, MA: MIT Press, 1987; J. Derrida, *The Other Heading: Reflections on Today's Europe*, trans. Pascale-Anne Brault and Michael Naas, Bloomington, IN: Indiana University Press, 1992.
3. J. Derrida, *Fichus*, Paris: Galilée, 2002, p. 50.
4. J. Derrida and J. Habermas with Giovanna Borradori, *Philosophy in a Time of Terror*, Chicago, IL: Chicago University Press, 2003.
5. J. Derrida and J. Habermas, *Frankfurter Allgemeine Zeitung* and *Libération*, 1 May 2003.
6. J. Derrida, *Voyous*, Paris: Galilée, 2002, p. 208. Partly trans. Pascale-Anne Brault and Michael Naas as 'The "World" of the Enlightenment to Come (Exception, Calculation, Sovereignty),' *Research in Phenomenology* 33:9–52 at 45.
7. Ibid., my emphasis.
8. Compare, precisely, Derrida, *The Other Heading*, pp. 48–56.
9. I owe the phrase to Habermas. See *The Philosophical Discourse of Modernity*, pp. 31–43.
10. See G. W. F. Hegel, 'Preface', *Philosophy of Right*, pp. 1–13.
11. See Peter Berger, *The Desecularization of the World: Resurgent Religion and World Politics*, Grand Rapids, MI: Eerdmans, 1999 and John Esposito and Ali Tamimi, *Islam and Secularism in the Middle East*, New York: New York University Press, 2000. For a strong version of post-modern reflection on religion, culture and politics, see M. A. Vasquez and M. F. Marquardt, *Globalizing the Sacred: Religion across the Americas*, Chapel Hill, NC: Rutgers University Press, 2003.
12. This was the basic thesis of my *Derrida and the Political*, London: Routledge, 1996.

13. For this, and the following arguments, see Derrida, *Voyous*, pp. 115–51; and Derrida and Habermas with Borradori, *Philosophy in a Time of Terror*, pp. 170–81 (French version, my translation).

14. Immanuel Kant, 'Perpetual peace: a philosophical sketch', in Hans Reiss (ed.), *Kant: Political Writings*, trans. H. B. Nisbet, Cambridge: Cambridge University Press, 1996, p. 105.

15. Derrida, *Voyous*, pp. 146–7.

16. Derrida and Habermas with Borradori, *Philosophy in a Time of Terror*, pp. 170–1 (French version, my translation).

17. See J. Derrida, 'Psyche: the invention of the other,' in Lindsey Waters and Wlad Godzich (eds), *Reading de Man Reading*, Minnesota, MN: University of Minnesota Press, 1989.

18. Derrida, *Voyous*, pp. 153–61.

19. See note 16.

20. For the choice of terms, see Derrida, *Voyous*, pp. 208 and 217.

21. See J. Derrida, 'Psyche: the Invention of the other', a seminal essay for Derrida's delimitation of the relation between invention and reason.

22. See Sam Daws and Frances Stewart, 'An Economic and Social Security Council at the United Nations,' 2000, at www.christianaid.org.ok/indpeth/0006unec/unecon2.htm.

23. My argument is indebted to the work of David Held and other radical liberals who emphasise that social democracy is now only possible through global and regional institution. See, particularly, David Held, Anthony McGrew, David Goldblatt and Jonathan Perration, *Global Transformations: Politics, Economics and Culture*, Cambridge: Polity Press, 1999 and D. Held's argument for a legal cosmopolitanism, *Global Covenant: The Social Democratic Alternative to the Washington Consensus*, Cambridge: Polity Press, 2004.

3

Derrida's Rogues: Islam and the Futures of Deconstruction

Alex Thomson

What I am going to say is inspired . . . by a painful love for Algeria, an Algeria where I was born and that I left only for the first time, literally, at age nineteen before the war of independence, an Algeria to which I have often returned and that deep down I know I have never really left and that I still carry in what is most profound in me: a love for Algeria which, though it is not the love of a citizen, precisely, and thus the patriotic attachment to a nation-state, is nonetheless what makes indissociable for me heart, thought, and the political taking of sides – and thus dictates all that I will say in a few words.[1]

The final years of Derrida's work are dominated by a set of questions which connect politics and religion. Reading and responding, we may be tempted either to ask what his views on politics or religion are or to see deconstruction as a methodology which we could simply apply to theology or political science. But either of these approaches will abolish and neutralise in advance the full force of the demands which deconstruction places upon us. For Derrida, as I have argued at length in *Deconstruction and Democracy*, deconstruction *is* a political practice, a form of negotiation between the contextual inscription of every utterance.[2] Derrida's work needs to be read as an exemplary performance of the kind of critical political strategies which might allow for a just response to the world. Faced with an apparent gap between the prescription and moral practice of an authority figure we might accuse them of telling us 'to do as I say, not as I do'. In Derrida's case we have to understand that he means us to do not as he says, but as he does.

This suggests that in responding to his written texts, as to his interviews or his public political statements and gestures, our attention should be directed first and foremost to the form, rather than the content of his actions. To take one example, in May 2003 Derrida was a co-signatory, with

Jürgen Habermas, of an open letter, published in both France and Germany, which appears to back down from his earlier furious critique of Eurocentrism in *The Other Heading*. The letter urges Europe to face up to its unique responsibility as the fortunate site of a specific political mutation, a democratic system in which everything may be put into question. 'The party system that emerged from the French Revolution has often been copied', write Habermas and Derrida: 'but only in Europe does this system also serve an ideological competition that subjects the socio-pathological results of capitalist modernization to an ongoing political evaluation'.[3] This might be taken as the sign of a political and philosophical rapprochement with Habermas: indeed, in his chapter, 'The Future of Critical Philosophy and World Politics', Richard Beardsworth treats it as one amongst a number of symptoms of such a shift in Derrida's position. But Derrida would be the first to distinguish between the point at which one must take a specific and pragmatic political stance, which will always be the product of a calculation between finite possible alternatives, and the ultimate horizon of deconstruction, which is an opening to the infinite, to the unpredictable and the incalculable.

In fact, there is a strong underlying continuity between *The Other Heading* and the May 2003 letter: it is the political emphasis which diverges, perhaps in acknowledgement of what the letter refers to as a change of 'mentality' since 1989–90 and the end of the Cold War.[4] In *The Other Heading*, first delivered as a paper in 1990, Derrida addresses the notion of European reunion, following the fall of the wall which since 1961 had come to symbolise the post-war division of Germany, in order to warn Europe against a celebration of its own spiritual exemplarity: 'Europe has . . . confused its image, its face, its figure and its very place, its taking-place, with that of an advanced point, the point of a phallus if you will, and thus, once again, with a heading for world civilization or human culture in general'.[5] In 2003, Derrida and Habermas stress that 'taking a leading role does not mean excluding. The avant-gardist core of Europe must not wall itself off into a new Small Europe'.[6] In neither case does Derrida seek to simply celebrate or denigrate the idea of Europe. In both he affirms the existence of something like a European identity as an opportunity for an advance which might open up the concept of identity itself ('*what is proper to a culture is to not be identical with itself*'[7]), but equally as the risk of a terrifying retreat into insularity and enclosure. The deployment of the idea of 'Europe' in both texts is like every political position: in seeking to interrupt a state of affairs, it may allow for the possibility of more justice, but it is also necessarily closes down other possibilities. Every political event is in this sense violent. Our responsibility is to locate ourselves in this economy of violence.

So the fact that Derrida might at first appear to have changed his mind (a warning against Europe becomes a plea for Europe) should be less important than our attempt to grasp the general economy of political violence which deconstruction seeks to expose and our acknowledgement that, since writing always takes sides in that economy, we can neither justify nor avoid being committed to such violence ourselves. It is in this light that I want to turn to Derrida's book *Rogues*. What I wish to emphasise is the continuity of *Rogues* with the kind of political negotiation evident in *The Other Heading* and the May 2003 letter, despite the fact that it may at first appear more abstract or schematic. Like most of Derrida's more reflective and less occasional texts, the political position taken in the text is complex and ambivalent. Its arguments cannot be equated with the more direct political statements given in Derrida's interviews, just as such commitments cannot be reduced to the outcome of some deconstructive political programme, but must be treated as contingent political calculations.

In particular I am interested in the way that 'Islam' figures in the text. In the context of Derrida's association of deconstruction with democracy (through the complex conceptual topography of what he calls 'democracy to come'), and of a certain thinking of democracy with a particular European heritage, it seems striking that Derrida should weave into *Rogues* the image of an opposition between democracy and Islam. Elsewhere Derrida rejects this opposition, so why flirt with it in *Rogues*? Not only does deconstruction give us good reason to be suspicious of it – as of any such opposition – in general but Derrida's deliberate flaunting of it in *Rogues* serves to challenge us directly. The difficulty, as so often in Derrida's work, is that his exhibition of a particular point of political dissensus, which must be approached from one side or another in order to avoid claiming a spurious neutrality, can be mistaken for the reinscription of the divide he wishes to place into question. Accordingly I will argue, *contra* Beardsworth, that Derrida's strategy is consistent with that of his earlier work. Moreover, while this argument may certainly be read as *qualified* support for that philosophical project of Enlightenment which he expressly identifies as European in the May 2003 letter, it must also undermine the confidence with which we oppose philosophical democracy to religious anti-democracy, and unsettle the kind of critical programme proposed by Beardsworth.

Monstrous Democracy

The context for *Rogues* is the same horizon which rings most of Derrida's work of the last ten years: an ill-starred constellation of globalisation, advanced communications technologies and religious fundamentalism.

The question posed is always that of the future of democracy, or of how we might think democracy in such a situation so as to allow for an opening to the future. As we have already observed, in much of Derrida's work 'democracy to come' has been identified as both the product of a specific philosophical and geo-political history and as the only political regime which is itself open to a certain idea of historical possibility. This position seems to be sustained in the first essay in *Rogues*, 'The reason of the strongest (are there rogue states)'. On the one hand, democracy belongs to 'what is called the European tradition (at the same time the Greco-Christian and globalatinizing) that dominates the worldwide concept of the political'; on the other hand, it is 'the only name of a regime, or quasi-regime, open to its own historical transformation, to taking up its intrinsic plasticity and its interminable self-criticizability, one might even say its interminable analysis'.[8] Particularly because of its link with secularisation, also highlighted in the May 2003 letter, 'European' democracy seems to offer the only future for democracy. But for Derrida this does not mean a particular political and institutional model which could be directly implemented elsewhere so much as an idea of politics as not merely open to internal self-criticism but characteristically exposed by virtue of its electoral or constitutional structures to a change of government, or even of regime. Something like a democratic vulnerability is a precondition for the possibility of democratic justice.

This image of democratic exposure must be troubling if it is not to degenerate into the piety of tolerance, a concept about which Derrida has stated his concerns. The guiding idea of tolerance is that of a guarded hospitality, a suspicious and hostile stance which makes allowance for, or reserves space for, another's views or beliefs. But tolerance allows no chance of what Derrida describes in a long series of his writings as the unconditional horizon of hospitality: that situation in which the guest is offered not merely temporary shelter but residence, not a place at the table but the head of the table, not the use of one's home but possession of it. I take this to mean that the possibility of genuine hospitality is only at stake when offering it appears as crisis, when the gesture of welcome is made in the shadow of a threatened dispossession. In *Of Grammatology*, Derrida remarks that 'the future can only be anticipated in the form of an absolute danger. It is that which breaks absolutely with constituted normality and can only be proclaimed, *presented*, as a sort of monstrosity'.[9] If our understanding of 'democracy to come' (*démocratie à venir*) is to realise a genuine sense of the future (*avenir*), we need to recover a sense of its monstrosity. This is, I believe, a central plank of Derrida's intention in *Rogues*: if we read and are reassured, we are not reading hard enough. So although we may recognise his treatment of democracy in this book as continuous with his arguments elsewhere, we should also emphasise the ambivalence with which it is treated.

As the product of the European tradition, democracy is also, Derrida suggests, bound up with the economic globalisation whose affinity with linguistic and cultural factors is underlined by Derrida's neologism globa-latinisation. For 'democracy to come' to fulfil its promise of democratic openness this must become not the domination of the world by one idea of democracy, or of international law, but the establishment of a democratic community or a new international law, which no longer perpetuates the economic and political dominance of certain States, but allows for the full participation of others. This is the burden of Derrida's analysis in *Specters of Marx*,[10] and is not directly rescinded in the May 2003 letter, since the call for a European foreign policy is directed towards the Kantian vision of world government, understood not as the domination of one idea of law, but of an institutional framework in which the very idea or tradition from which such a framework emerged should be open to self-transformation. Yet the situation Derrida describes in *Rogues* feels more like that of a cultural and conceptual imperialism: which is, of course, the exact risk run by the kind of foreign policy objectives he and Habermas underwrite in their letter. It is at this point that the figure of Islam emerges in *Rogues*, as the only point of resistance to the hegemony of the European (and thus Greek and Judeo-Christian) idea of democracy:

> Islam, or a certain Islam, would thus be the only religious or theocratic culture that can still, in fact or in principle, inspire and declare any resistance to democracy. If it does not actually resist what might be called a real or actual democratization, one whose reality may be more or less contested, it can at least resist the democratic principle, claim, or allegation, the legacy and old name of 'democracy'.[11]

The phrase 'old name' should give us pause for thought. It is axiomatic in Derrida's work on politics that the old names are not enough, but that we cannot simply invent new names. In *Politics of Friendship* Derrida considers the possibility that because of its conceptual entanglement with the rhetoric of masculine virility, politics as we know it might never be able to adequately address both the equality and difference of women. This leaves two options. First, 'to admit that the political is in fact this phallogocentrism in act. . . . This structure can be combated only by carrying oneself beyond the political, beyond the name "politics"'. 'Or else', secondly, to 'keep the "old name", and analyze the logic and the topic of the concept differently'.[12] Characteristically, Derrida insists that there can be no choice: we could never justify choosing the incalculable while neglecting the actual, but nor should we allow our entanglement in the here and now to obstruct the movement *beyond*: 'deciding without excluding, in the invention of other names and other concepts, in moving out *beyond this* politics without ceasing to intervene therein to transform it'.[13] In *Rogues*, as in *Politics of Friendship*, 'democracy to come' entails putting the 'old name' of democracy under pressure which it might not survive: 'this name, democracy . . . will last as long as it has to, but not much longer'.[14] Derrida's audacity in *Rogues* is to juxtapose the 'old name' of democracy to that of Islam.

If Islam is the signal point of opposition to the 'old name' of democracy, could it also, and despite appearances, be the site from which something new might emerge? We have to take this possibility seriously to understand the full force of Derrida's argument that the confrontation between Islam and democracy is:

> perhaps, in the end, the greatest, if not the only, political issue of the future, the most urgent question of what remains to come for what is still called the political. The political, which is to say, in the free play and extension, in the determined indetermination, of its meaning, in the opening up of its meaning, the democratic.[15]

If the question of the future of democracy involves Islam, deconstruction must also be directly implicated, for in *Politics of Friendship* Derrida directly associates the two concepts: 'no deconstruction without democracy, no democracy without deconstruction'.[16] The futures of deconstruction would be inseparable from the future of democracy, itself entwined with the future of Islam. This is a potentially enormous and abyssal problem, and one that it seems to me Derrida's followers have been slow to acknowledge. My modest aim here is to offer some suggestions as to how the political dimensions of such an investigation might work out. To do so we need to turn to a deeply problematic example, introduced by Derrida immediately following the introduction of these geopolitical concerns in *Rogues*, and which illustrates all the ambiguity of trying to read 'democracy to come' (that is, deconstruction) at work within the democratic process. The example is all the more striking for being drawn from Algeria, Derrida's place of birth, and as both the comments cited in the epigraph to this essay, and the lengthier exploration in *Monolingualism of the Other*,[17] suggest, close to the heart of deconstruction.

ALGERIAN DECONSTRUCTION

On 11 January 1992 President Chadli Benjedid resigned his post as President of Algeria.[18] Into his place slipped a shadow committee of national security which suspended the elections due five days later, and in doing so effectively stalled the fragile democratisation process which Chadli had initiated in 1988 in the face of massive civil unrest. This open intervention by the military rescinded the formal separation of military and executive authority marked by the resignation of army officers from Chadli's reforming government in March 1989. From 14 January, power rested with a governing committee which used emergency powers to deploy troops to quell unrest among fundamentalist supporters of the Front Islamique Salut (FIS) angry that their anticipated victory at the polls had been denied them. In swift succession came further dismantling of the short-lived democratic infrastructure, with the arrest of a number of journalists in the last weeks of January and the subsequent banning of the FIS on 9 February. Within two months of the first multi-party elections to the National Assembly in Algerian history all the main innovations contained in the 1989 Constitution, whose popularity had been confirmed by referendum at the time, had been erased: freedom of the press; freedom to organise in political parties; and the breaking of the authoritarian grip of the post-independence elite consisting of the army and the Front de Libération Nationale (FLN) party. What had been proclaimed as measures necessary for the restoration of stability and the preservation of democracy instead plunged Algeria into a sickening cycle of political violence in the face of widespread insurgency matched by the ruthless and criminal activities of the state. As French historian Benjamin Stora puts it: 'State violence also occurred on a vast scale: the use of torture, . . . detention without trial in camps in the south, special jurisdictions that pronounced death sentences, sweep operations, and summary executions. In the face of armed groups that were striking with terrible cruelty, law enforcement conducted an indiscriminate campaign of repression that extended far beyond Islamist ranks'.[19] Despite a dramatic fall in levels of violence and the initiation of a reconciliation process in recent years, NGOs such as Amnesty International and Human Rights Watch still report widespread torture, abduction and general suppression of political and civil liberties.

It may be tempting to see the intervention of the military as a direct attack on democracy, and on the legitimate election of a popular party. In December 1991 the FIS had won 188 out of 231 available seats in the first round of elections, taking 47.54 per cent of a 59 per cent turnout. However, as Derrida points out in *Rogues*, any interpretation of the events of January

1992 must recognise that 'the electoral process . . . risked giving power, in accordance with perfectly legal means, to a likely majority that presented itself as essentially Islamic and Islamist and to which one attributed the intention, no doubt with good reason, of wanting to change the constitution and abolish the normal function of democracy'.[20] Although not explicitly committed to the dismantling of democracy, the FIS were, in the words of Esposito and Voll, at the very least guilty of 'equivocation about democracy and equal rights for women', which 'left them vulnerable to criticism and scepticism regarding the true nature of their ultimate agenda'.[21] But if Derrida himself sounds somewhat equivocal about the threat to democracy posed by the FIS and, therefore, the legitimacy of the actions of the military, this may be for good reasons. The unexpectedly high turnout for the FIS can be interpreted in a number of ways, for example, as a convenient protest vote against the long rule of the FLN, which suggest, that it might have been impolitic, or at least difficult, for the FIS to implement extreme or anti-democratic measures. Equally, it is by no means clear that the FIS can be realistically seen as a uniform or even a coherent body, consisting as it did of a number of competing factions whose alliance might have dissolved rapidly on the outcome of a successful election.

Derrida has scrupulously refused to take sides on this issue in the past. In a 1993 interview he acknowledges the point of view of 'some of my Algerian friends' that the military response was the 'only possible reply to a well-prepared, long-standing strategy of takeover, which was hostile to democracy itself'.[22] While urging understanding, Derrida deliberately sits on the fence: the threat to democracy, the crime against politics, comes from both sides. I take this strategy to be in part a response to another structural and political double bind. Since independence the state of Algeria has been officially Islamic. A key element of the confrontation between the FLN and the FIS in the run-up to January 1992 rested on the claim to be the legitimate party of Islam, with the FLN cast as a degenerate and westernised influence on the country. Because of this one needs to take extreme care in portraying the conflict as one between Islam and democracy, the Arab world and the European, or between East and West. Just as the military government's assumed legitimacy stemmed from its claim to be the defender of democracy against an Islamist threat, so the actions of the FIS could be presented as the only road to a truly Islamic form of government. The more polarised and violent the rhetoric, the more entrenched the divisions appear, and the greater the political capital gained on both sides.

Whether this problem is in Derrida's mind or not, it is clear that one effect of the kind of depoliticisation for which he calls in his 1994 text

'Taking sides for Algeria' might be progress in defusing the stand-off. In his 1993 interview Derrida is explicit:

> The unity of Algeria is certainly in danger of dislocation, but the forces that are tearing it apart do not, as is often said, oppose East and West, or, as with two homogeneous blocks, Islam and democracy. They oppose different models of democracy, representation, or citizenship – and, above all, different interpretations of Islam. One of our responsibilities is to be attentive to this multiplicity and to demand constantly that not everything be confused.[21]

This refusal to directly oppose Islam and democracy is characteristic of Derrida's work, which is what makes his apparent flaunting of that opposition in *Rogues* so unusual. However, Derrida qualifies his use of that opposition: it is only 'a certain Islam' which is directly opposed to democracy, and we should certainly lend our support to those within Islam who

> fight not only for the secularization of the political . . . for the emergence of a laic subjectivity, but also for an interpretation of the Koranic heritage that privileges, from the inside as it were, the democratic virtualities that are probably not any more apparent and readable at first glance, and readable under this name, than they were in the Old and New Testaments.[24]

Derrida takes the events of January 1992 as an example of a suicidal possibility always inherent within democracy – I have explored this account elsewhere, as another figure of what Derrida calls auto-immunity, not a catastrophic perversion of democracy but a necessary possibility of any democratic regime, in which the very openness which constitutes the democratic space must always expose the polity to the risk of its own abolition.[25] We can draw a direct parallel with the necessary confrontation of democracy with its apparent limits in certain forms of Islam: in both cases Derrida wishes to emphasise that deconstruction must think democracy to the limit, '*there where I do not know* . . . what a democracy worthy of this name might presently be or what it might mean properly speaking'.[26]

This does not mean a capitulation to theocracy. Derrida insists in both *Rogues* and the earlier writings on the Algerian situation on the secularisation also identified in the May 2003 letter. This European idea would need to be fully carried through in Europe, in order to allow for a democracy which might be hospitable to other religions. However, it would also be a precondition for democracy in Algeria. So it is clear that Derrida's attitude to Islam is differentiated: and by no means that exaggerated gesture of respect which would simply affirm Islamic difference as in itself a source of value. In practical terms this must mean, as Derrida argues in his interview following September 11, that 'we must help what is called Islam and what is called "Arab" to free themselves from such violent dogmatism'.[27] To insist on the necessity of dialogue with Islam as well as of the dialogue within Islam is to attack the illusion of a fundamental cultural chasm between Occident and Orient.

ISLAM AND THE FUTURE

'Deconstruction' is how Frédéric Volpi describes the events of January 1992: 'as the Algerian population slowly began to realise that the democratic transition was seriously endangered, the deconstruction of the democratic institutional framework continued to unfold'.[28] Volpi does not mean to use the term in anything like Derrida's sense. Yet if deconstruction needs to be understood as meaning 'what happens, what is happening today in what they call society, politics, diplomacy, economic and historical reality', as Derrida has claimed, it should be possible to see these events as deconstruction in operation.[29] Certainly, to the extent that there are both democratic and anti-democratic tendencies on both sides, and that any detailed examination of the events unsettles the possibility of a clear opposition between 'Islam' and 'democracy', this seems to be the case. Moreover, the harder it becomes to draw a limit to the event, as broader factors including the legacy of colonialism and Algeria's economic poverty are taken into consideration, the more 'we are all concerned and accountable'.[30] The practical recognition that supposedly homogeneous identities are never what they appear or claim to be partners the theoretical attempt to displace the notion of the unity of sovereignty: Derrida's work combines both gestures, joining genealogical analysis of concepts to something very like a philosophy of history, although one in which both terms would themselves be under suspicion. Derrida's use of the notion of auto-immunity seems to generalise the enigmatic statement in the introduction to *Politics of Friendship*, '*At the centre of the principle, always, the One does violence to itself, and guards itself against the other*', into something like a historical principle.[31]

Yet in his chapter, 'The Future of Critical Philosophy and World Politics', Richard Beardsworth suggests that we need to undertake what Derrida does not, by pursuing deconstruction further into 'actuality'. For Beardsworth, *Rogues* must be understood as indicating a late acknowledgement that this project must be both secular and rational: philosophical. Where earlier writing such as 'Faith and Knowledge' had offered us 'a radical Faith', *Rogues* argues for 'a deconstructive rationalism'. But this fails to account for Derrida's continuous insistence that he gestures towards a principle of messianicity without messianism which subtends both faith and reason, rendering the distinction Beardsworth draws moot. Indeed, Derrida concludes the longest essay in *Rogues* with a reiteration of Heidegger's notorious appeal, in his interview with *Der Spiegel*, to a God to come, yet is unstinting in his commitment to a secularised political sphere. What distinguishes deconstruction from critical philosophy is not a lack of attention to the here and now, but the construction of a double strategy which recognises that the urgency of the here and now may always obscure the vital question of the future.[32]

Heidegger comments: 'A decisive question for me today is: how can a political system accommodate itself to the technological age, and which political system would this be? I have no answer to this question. I am not convinced that it is democracy'.[33] As I have suggested, it is essential to the trajectory of what Derrida calls 'democracy to come' that the possibility be posed that what is to come will no longer be recognisable as democracy. From this stem both the ambivalence of the figure of Islam in *Rogues* and its absolute centrality to the question of a future for deconstruction, and of a future for democracy. Despite his political and theoretical distance from Derrida, this is also a point recognised by Slavoj Žižek:

> Instead of . . . bemoaning the fact that, of all the great religions, Islam is the most resistant to modernization, one should, rather, conceive of this resistance as an open chance, as 'undecidable': this resistance does not necessarily lead to 'Islamo-fascism', it can also be articulated into a socialist project. Precisely because Islam harbours the 'worst' potentials of the Fascist answer to our present predicament, it can also turn out to be the site for the 'best'. In other words, yes, Islam is indeed not a religion like the others, it does involve a stronger social link, it does resist integration into the capitalist global order – and the task is work out how to use this ambiguous fact politically.[34]

To negotiate with Derrida's legacy must mean facing up to this ambivalence. The distinction Beardsworth draws between the finite calculation which would characterise the invention of new forms of sovereignty and the infinite melancholia of deconstruction in Derrida's hands is a false one. Derrida means us to undertake both, and suggests that to make such a distinction would be the very mistake he is arguing most vigorously against. To believe yourself to have definitively escaped the sovereignty of the theological, to have reached the security of a critical philosophy which can now tackle 'actuality' is to have foreclosed on the future. Derrida's return to Heidegger indicates the impossibility of a definitive secularisation of thought, even while he insists on the unique and virtuous institution of a secularised political sphere. To calculate with Islam must mean a rejection of theocracy, as it would for Christianity or Judaism; but this should not become a blindness to what Islam promises of democracy, or of something which might no longer answer to the name democracy.

In 1925 a French magazine invited Paul Valéry to comment on the relationship between Europe and the Orient. On a number of occasions in Derrida's work – for example, in *The Other Heading* and *Of Spirit* – Valéry has served as an exemplary model of the difficulty of disentangling philosophy and the spiritual identification of Europe: 'the philosophemes [in Valéry's work] come under the same program and the same combinatory as those of Hegel, Husserl, and Heidegger'.[33] So there is some justification to take Valéry as exemplary once again. He comments:

> From the cultural point of view, I do not think that we have much to fear *now* from the Oriental influence. It is not unknown to us. We owe to the Orient all the beginnings of our arts and of a great deal of our knowledge. We can very well welcome what now comes out of the Orient, if something new is coming out of there – which I very much doubt. This doubt is precisely our guarantee and our European weapon.[36]

Valéry answers the question which, eighty years later, Derrida's late writings seek to keep open. For the thrust of deconstruction is always towards an unpredictable and unprogrammed future; and in *Rogues*, awkwardly and hesitantly, the question of the future emerges in terms of democracy and Islam. Derrida's account structures the question into two parallel strands. If Islam appears opposed to democracy, is this because there is no future for democracy there? Or if (as a European tradition, a Greek name, a feature of the globalatinisation of the world) democracy appears opposed to Islam, is that because there is no future for – the 'old name' – democracy? Against Valéry, Derrida specifically requires us to take seriously the prospect that the future of 'the West' might come from 'the East'.

Derrida outlines two conflicting duties: to resist the attack on democracy present in some forms of Islam, just as we resist the crimes against democracy which are necessarily constitutive of every democratic state; but also to allow for the possibility that the future of democracy might itself come from Islam, once we understand Islam to be not the opposite of democracy, or of Europe, or of the West, and above all *not any one thing*, but

– just as much as the purportedly 'democratic' tradition – the site from which the future might emerge. This entails at the very least some hesitation before the kind of militantly critical philosophy urged upon us by Richard Beardsworth. But it also goes further than the argument of a reformist Muslim and democrat such as Khaled Abou el Fadl that 'the best thing the West can do is to observe its own ideals when dealing with the Muslim world and to let the struggle for Islamic democracy run its evolutionary course'.[37] Non-intervention might mean an armed silence, a limited hospitality; yet we are only open to the future when we risk everything. 'Democracy to come' requires auto-immunity, that is the possibility of suppressing our own immune reactions in order to allow contact with the outside: a constant negotiation with what seems to threaten our security, but may in fact be our only chance of a future. For deconstruction, as for democracy, that may mean not only religion in general, but Islam in particular.

NOTES

1. Jacques Derrida, 'Taking sides for Algeria', trans. Elizabeth Rottenberg, *Negotiations*, Stanford, CA: Stanford University Press, 2002, pp. 117–24 at 119.
2. Alex Thomson, *Deconstruction and Democracy: Derrida's Politics of Friendship*, London: Continuum, 2005.
3. Jacques Derrida and Jürgen Habermas (2003), 'February 15, or what binds Europeans together: a plea for a common foreign policy, beginning in the core of Europe', trans. Max Pensky, *Constellations*, Vol. 10, no. 3, pp. 291–7 at 295. Reprinted from *Frankfurter Allgemeine Zeitung*, 31 May 2003.
4. Ibid. p. 295.
5. Jacques Derrida, *The Other Heading*, trans. Pascale-Anne Brault and Michael Naas, Bloomington, IN: Indiana University Press, 1992, p. 24.
6. Derrida and Habermas, 'February 15', p. 292.
7. Derrida, *The Other Heading*, p. 14 [emphasis in original].
8. Jacques Derrida, *Rogues: Two Essays on Reason*, trans. Pascale-Anne Brault and Michael Naas, Stanford, CA: Stanford University Press, 2005, pp. 28 and 25.
9. Jacques Derrida, *Of Grammatology*, trans. Gayatri Spivak, Baltimore, MD: Johns Hopkins University Press, 1976, p. 5.
10. Jacques Derrida, *Specters of Marx*, London: Routledge, 1994.
11. Derrida, *Rogues*, p. 29.
12. Jacques Derrida, *Politics of Friendship*, trans. George Collins, London: Verso, 1997, pp. 158–9 [emphasis in original].
13. Ibid. p. 159.
14. Ibid. p. 105.

15. Derrida, *Rogues*, p. 29
16. Derrida, *Politics of Friendship*, p. 105.
17. Jacques Derrida, trans. Patrick Mensah, *Monolingualism of the Other*, Stanford, CA: Stanford University Press, 1998.
18. For the details of these events I have drawn on the following sources: John L. Esposito and John O. Voll, 'Algeria: democracy suppressed', chapter 4, in, *Islam and Democracy*, Oxford: Oxford University Press, 1996; Hugh Roberts, *The Battlefield: Algeria 1988-2002*, London: Verso, 2003; Benjamin Stora, *Algeria 1830-2000: A Short History*, trans. Jane Marie Todd, Ithaca, NY: Cornell University Press, 2001; Frédéric Volpi, *Islam and Democracy: the Failure of Dialogue in Algeria*, London: Pluto, 2003.
19. Stora, *Algeria 1830-2000*, p. 216.
20. Derrida, *Rogues*, p. 31.
21. Esposito and Voll, 'Algeria: democracy suppressed', p. 165.
22. Jacques Derrida, 'The deconstruction of actuality', in Elizabeth Rottenberg (ed. and trans.), *Negotiations*, Stanford, CA: University of Stanford Press, 2002, pp. 85–116 at 114
23. Ibid. p. 116.
24. Derrida, *Rogues*, pp. 32 and 33.
25. Alex Thomson, 'What's to become of "democracy to come"?', *Postmodern Culture*, Vol. 15, no. 3 (2005).
26. Derrida, *Rogues*, p. 8.
27. 'Auto-immunity: real and symbolic suicides', trans. Giovanni Boradorri, *Philosophy in a Time of Terror: Dialogues With Jürgen Habermas and Jacques Derrida*, Chicago, IL: University of Chicago Press, 2003, pp. 85–136 at 113.
28. Volpi, *Islam and Democracy*, p. 55.
29. Jacques Derrida, 'Some statements and truisms about neologisms, newisms, postisms, parasitisms, and other small seisms', trans. Anne Tomiche, in David Carroll (ed.), *The States of Theory*, New York: Columbia University Press, 1990, pp. 63–94 at 85.
30. Derrida, 'The deconstruction of actuality', p. 114.
31. Derrida, *Politics of Friendship*, p.ix.
32. See Geoffrey Bennington's comments on Beardsworth's *Derrida and the Political*, (London: Routledge, 1996) in *Interrupting Derrida*, London: Routledge, 2000, pp. 172–9.
33. Martin Heidegger, 'Only a god can save us', trans. Maria P. Alter and John D. Caputo, in Richard Wolin (ed.), *The Heidegger Controversy: A Critical Reader*, Cambridge, MA: MIT Press, 1993, pp. 91–116 at 104.
34. Slavoj Žižek, *Iraq: The Borrowed Kettle*, London: Verso, 2004, pp. 48–9.
35. Jacques Derrida, *Of Spirit*, trans. Geoffrey Bennington, Chicago, IL: University of Chicago Press, 1989, p. 123.
36. Cited in Edward Said, *Orientalism*, Harmondsworth: Penguin, 1995, p. 250.
37. Khaled Abou El Fadl et al., *Islam and the Challenge of Democracy*, Princeton, NJ: Princeton University Press, 2004, p. 52.

4

Force [of] Transformation

Michael Dillon[1]

I. Force Transformation

Transformation should be thought of as a process, not an end state. Hence there is no foreseeable point in the future when the Secretary of Defense will be able to declare that the transformation of the Department has been completed. Instead, the transformation process will continue indefinitely. Those responsible for defense transformation must anticipate the future and wherever possible help create it.

Elements of Defense Transformation, Office of Force Transformation,
US Department of Defense, October 2004

II. Force of Transformation

This vulnerable force, this force without power, opens up unconditionally to what or who comes and comes to affect it.

Jacques Derrida, *Rogues: Two Essays on Reason*, p. xiv

THE MESSIANIC

Recalling Derrida's celebrated essay 'Force of Law' in which he engages Benjamin's 'Critique of Violence', this chapter seeks to champion the non-negotiability of Derrida's legacy in terms of how it finds expression in a messianic 'Force of Transformation.'[2] What is non-negotiable in Derrida is the aporia of justice. He expresses and explores how the aporia of justice impacts on us by using a powerful figure of political speech; that of the messianic. Derrida is not alone, however, in being powerfully committed to the force of transformation. The epigraphs that head this chapter indicate an equal if quite different commitment to force transformation operating, for example, throughout the United States' techno-scientific military strategic complex. Messianic talk is the talk of the age. Note, however, the difference. On the one hand, the commitment to the force of transformation. On the other hand, a commitment to force transformation. An equal but opposite expression of, and commitment to, transformation is none the less at work here. For Derrida and the Pentagon alike, transformation is 'to come', on the way towards which we are continuously heading but at which we never arrive. But that is the limit of their agreement.

The US Office of Force Transformation is committed to the infinite realisation of the promise of techno-scientific revolution in the cause of maintaining the global liberal hegemony championed by the United States. Its messianism is founded in the aspiration to a power of force so great that its 'shock and awe' might prevail with the minimum application of force, or even without it ever having to be deployed. This is the dream of the lesser violence of that politically strategic deployment of necessary killing upon which the very promise of modern politics – of peace and progress – has been founded since Machiavelli.

Derrida's messianic talk fundamentally contests that of the age. It challenges the reason, the force and the very promise of that talk. The messianic in Derrida derives instead from the (im)possibility of justice. It is impossible to become just. Justice is a responsibility that continuously devolves upon us because it is always 'to come'. If justice had already arrived, we would have to attend to no more appeals for justice. That there will never be justice is the condition of possibility for us continuously to attend to the incessant call of justice. It is, therefore, always possible to be open to the appeal for justice. Derrida describes this as an aporia; a difficulty from which there is no escape; a problem for which there is no resolution. His work continuously interrogates what is required of us – of our reasoning and of our force – if our living is to be done in respect of this condition. For that reason his philosophy is politically charged even when it is not explicitly expressed politically. As a matter of fact, Derrida almost always expresses it in explicitly political terms. The terms he uses are the very same as those that comprise our traditional political lexicon: sovereignty, power, spirit, community, language, friendship, hospitality, force, witness, testimony, futures, archives, secrets and so on. There is one crucial difference. Derrida's political lexicon is governed by a different 'grammar'; that of *différance* or deconstruction. His political lexicon, therefore, operates differently. It does not simply mean different things, or point to different things. It entails different things. Living according to it would change our individual and collective experience. Derrida devoted his work to interrogating how that entailment arises aporetically, and what that aporia demands of us.

An aporetic condition is not an abstract condition. Aporias take place. They do not exist except in that they materialise historically, and differently. Among other means an aporia materialises through powerful figures of political speech which respond to the incitement posed by the aporia as it is experienced in a particular time and in a particular place.[3] Amongst the most powerful figures of political speech which Derrida deploys in response to the aporia of justice is that of the messianic. Indeed, I think it possible to reinterpret almost all of Derrida's work as changing our political lexicon into terms – described in *Rogues* as forms of 'weak force'[4] – which champion the non-negotiability of the aporia of justice at this time and in this place.

Much depends here, of course, on what one means by politics as distinct, for example, from government, governance or rule. For brevity, and risking untold hostages to fortune, I would say that politics is what takes place when a site of antagonism forms around a specific clash of the calculable and the incalculable. It is redundant to say historically. When something takes place, that is history.

Some discount this talk of the messianic as a turn to religion and a theologisation of the political and of the ethical in Derrida. It is said that this vitiates his earlier work, or compounds the mystification for which it has long been criticised.[5] I dismiss the charge that the messianic is further evidence of Derridaean mystification, but I do not contest the charge that there has been a turn to religion and a certain re-engagement of theology. Manifestly, Derrida became preoccupied not only with the question of religion in his later work but also with the question of God.[6] I do not, however, think this disqualifies that work politically. On the contrary, I would propose that the turn to religion can be construed as a politically important manoeuvre, one of a number through which Derrida figures the aporia of justice in politically compelling ways.

The moment one introduces God into the political mix one is speaking directly about the clash of the calculable and the incalculable. It is hardly necessary to observe that the question of God could not be more politically charged today, but then it never lacked political charge. And there was never a time when it was not a site of antagonism and, therefore, also a powerful political incitement. Removing God from politics does not eliminate the incitement of the incalculable and the invaluable. It channels 'the God question' into different courses, where it finds its expression in different forces, removed from the critique of theological interrogation and left to a political theory evacuated of its capacity to think sensibly about incalculability. A theological interrogation of the messianism obtaining in the current Office of Force Transformation in the US Department of Defense, for example, would yield critical military-strategic as well as political purchase on the prevailing significance of that (in)calculable investment in global force transformation.

Despite the price paid for the active inclusion of God and theology in politics – a price regularly paid in violence – something vital may also be violently excluded when policing politics from God and the theological.[7] The reason is simple: the incalculable and the invaluable cannot be eliminated from the grid of political calculation and intelligibility because the calculable and the valuable are always contoured by the incalculable and the invaluable, however calculated or valued. The incalculable has always been integral to grids of political calculation and political intelligibility – not least in a political modernity that claims to be governed exclusively by the purely immanent calculus of reason. In military strategic terms consider only Clausewitz's philosophy of war, and in particular the undecidable (in)calculability of the moment of combat and the clash of forces.[8] Immanence in short never shakes off transcendence; often violently aligning itself against its 'enslavement' to that which none the less conditions it.

Talk of the messianic has, therefore, always been political talk. There is nothing about it that necessarily disqualifies it from being political. Indeed, contrary to its secular pretensions, messianic transformation is precisely what distinguishes modern political talk as 'modern'; 'new time', renewing time, a time of continuous renewal, modernisation. One wonders if we have ever been secular.[9] Messianic talk may be dangerous political talk. After all it speaks of transformation (to come); over whose legitimate expression modern economic as well as political authorities seek a monopoly. A certain kind of violence may also be a necessary entailment of – immanent to – the messianic; and Derrida in his engagement of Levinas as well as in his reflections on 'the binding' of Abraham and on sacrifice was well aware of this.[10] But all political talk is dangerous talk in its own way, and every politics entails its own violence. The violence that the messianic may threaten does not exclude it from political calculation or from being political talk. Rather it poses a greater incentive to interrogate – politically, philosophically and theologically as well as culturally and socially – the enormous political valences and political entailments of such talk; to interrogate the very charge that it carries.

Derrida does precisely this in a novel political as well as philosophical register; that of the claim of an insatiable justice exterior to both law and politics. It is hardly the exteriority of justice to law and politics, however, which is novel in Derrida. It is the way in which he figures how that exteriority will never materialise as such, but is instead always already at work on the inside, so to speak, continuously contesting and unsettling the good conscience to which all law, rule and calculation is given, and the very promissory economies upon which they themselves rely. However much impelled by the logic of his philosophical reflections from their very inception, it is perhaps no surprise that Derrida should talk of the messianic. These days, once also his days, are days saturated in a different 'to come' than that which Derrida espoused. Modernity is founded in the very inter-articulation of the violent and violating promissory economies of techno-scientific development, military strategic dominance, consumer capitalism and political emancipation, while claiming to be exclusively instrumentalist, materialist and realist. The messianic in Derrida may, therefore, be figured as one way of speaking about the very resource of ethical and political renewal against the moralising rage of political renewal that goes by the name of modernisation and globalisation (or what he calls *mondialisation*). Derrida's messianic – affirmatory promise – fundamentally contests, for example, the 'to come' of global liberal capitalism; it also opens-up, even if it does not very much pursue, the fundamental difficulty that Islam has with the political economy and cultural entailments of the modern promise.

In his messianic political talk Derrida was evidently not expert on political institutions; witness his crude analysis of the United Nations in *Rogues*. But that does not diminish the political significance of his messianic talk. Institution talk can be as messianic as any talk, not least in those political institutions which sport 'United' in their names. The universality figured in the unification such names invoke is a promise bloodily imposed when contested by other particularisms and universalities; the war between the states of the United States, otherwise known as the American Civil War, is not the least of such examples. However important institutions are to rule, politics has never been confined to institutions. Moreover, those with experience of political institutions know how fragile they appear from the inside when dealing precisely with the intersection of the calculable and the incalculable; which they encounter all the time and at every mundane level of institutional activity however calculated and routinised it may appear from the outside.

One has therefore to ask: what is being presumed about both religion and politics, in order for this turn to religion in Derrida to be questioned or discounted politically? For to discount the messianic move in Derrida courts making certain questionable assumptions about both religion and politics, together with their shared history, as well as more broadly about what Claude Lefort called 'the permanence of the theologico-political'.[11] In presuming the sovereignty and authority of reason, for example – itself a faith – it may presume that something foreign in the form of theology is being re-introduced into politics and thinking politically.

However, Western politics was thoroughly theologised from its inception and not simply in the way that Carl Schmitt contended.[12] It claims to have outgrown this birth in the theologico-political, but it may be more pertinent to ask into what kind of monster has it subsequently matured. In the process it may also be more pertinent to assume that the theologico-political is not a passing but a permanent issue, precisely because it concerns the inescapable interface of the calculable and the incalculable which is so vital to any politics. Finally, it may also be more pertinent to ask if our capacity to respond to intersections of the calculable and the incalculable, by continuously interrogating the intersection of theology and political theory, has itself been vitiated by the decline of the theological and the rupturing of its relation to thinking politically. I want to hazard the thought in this chapter that this line of questioning may offer a more fruitful way of responding to Derrida's religious turn, at this time and in this place.

I want, therefore, to broach a different thought to those of his critics: the thought instead that this so-called turn to religion in Derrida may be interpreted less as a turn to religion, or a theologisation of the political, rather as a materialisation of the aporia of justice. I want to propose that the 'weak force' of the messianic which he talks about in *Rogues*, for example, is the very locus of the force of transformation to which Derrida's political lexicon continuously appeals and in reference to which his 'politics' might best be understood. Talk of the messianic is one way in which the aporia of justice finds political and ethical voice in Derrida. I want to emphasise, in addition, that Derrida is not exceptional in this respect. Transformation is a political trope deeply installed in the very term modern itself; one indeed that defines the modern as modern. Moreover, that trope is most widely expressed and most fervently deployed at the very centre of modern technicity; specifically the techno-scientific military strategic discourse upon which its economies and its politics are so pervasively and so corrosively dependent.

My proposal that the messianic turn may be of profound and positive political significance is prompted in addition by the following allied thoughts: that religion and politics are indissolubly related; that our understanding of both religion and politics is obscured more than it is clarified by what these terms have come to mean today, and by the concordat currently obtaining between failed institutional religion and failed institutional politics; that when we talk of any politics we are always addressing a specific religio-political nexus; *a fortiori*, that when we are talking about a self-confessed secular politics we are addressing a particular religio-political nexus founded upon certain expression of faith that denies itself as faith in order to institute itself as the particular religio-political nexus that it is; that political modernity did not dissolve, or resolve, but re-tied religion and politics; that its very own conviction of the power of reason demands the re-interrogation of that nexus; that Derrida was true, more remorselessly true than many, to this very conviction of the power of reason, while continuously reminding himself and us of the limits within which it operates, the necessity of continuously operating at those limits and the violent price to be paid for refusing them.[13]

I do not have the space to develop these arguments more fully here, but I do want to broach them by drawing attention also to Derrida's deployment of the messianic in his recent text, *Rogues*. *Rogues* was prompted by the charge of 'rogue state' that the Anglo-American alliance regularly issues against states that defy its geopolitics. Playing with '*voyous*', a French word for rogue, Derrida returns to many of his well established political, philosophical and ethical themes. He pushes these themes further in respect of both a trenchant attack on the rogue character of all states (not least the United States and the United Kingdom), and a pungent interrogation of both political 'sovereignty' and the sovereign 'unconditionality' of reason. In the process he pursues and plays these themes against a continuous re-affirmation of that 'act of messianic faith – irreligious and without messian-ism'[14] which came to characterise his later work and for which he has received much criticism. Here the messianic can be construed not only as inaugurating a host of problems in relation to Derrida's work, which it does, but also as inaugurating a literature of hope and protest against the cult of modern imperial power; a cult long associated with its own brand of political and economic, as well as military-technical, messianism to which I draw attention briefly here.

Political theology

For Plato, the problem of theology was most closely connected with political theory.

Jacob Taubes

One needs to proceed first, however, by restoring political theology to political discourse. The theologico-political has a history. That history is yet to be written. Carl Schmitt, for example, did not write it. He polemicised it as a form of advocacy on behalf of his own theologico-political subscrip-tions.[15] Cryptically sketching some of its most important features, however, Jacob Taubes tells a different story. Recalling the deep-seated relation that has long obtained between thinking politically and thinking theologically, neither category is fixed and their historically changing relation is not that of the mere etiological rise of secularism. In the process, he provokes us into thinking critically, and politically, about it once more.

Taubes wisely notes that:

> It is important to keep one's eye on the original position of theology in order to understand that its connection with political theory is not derivative, but touches the very centre of both fields. In fact, there is no theology that is irrelevant to the order of society.[16]

He went on: 'Just as there is no theology without political implications, so there is no political theory without theological preconditions either.' In a short, but astonishingly acute and compact, survey Taubes reviews the history of the relation between theology and political theory. He notes how the very problematic of theology is first posed by Plato in a dialogue between Adeimantus and Socrates – in which Adeimantus questions: 'But which are these forms of theology; *typoi peri theologieas*, that you mean?' The question is asked and answered at that point when the narrative myth of the divine in Greek culture was being made accountable to reason. It is posed, along with many other fundamental questions, in relation to Plato's political concern for the community: 'A society that accepts sophistic epistemological relativism is doomed according to Plato, to anarchy and tyranny, because political authority cannot be founded on the basis of relativism.'

Even a theology that claims to be entirely apolitical, conceiving of the divine as entirely foreign, the absolute Other of man and world, Taubes explains, 'can have political implications.' He then records the familiar story of how throughout the nineteenth century God is replaced by man and Providence is replaced by progress, a development culminating in Nietzsche's announcement of the death of God; although Taubes observes how Hegel had already quietly recorded His demise in the *Phenomenology of Spirit*. Sovereignty passed to 'the people'. With the passing of God also went the passing of a social and cosmic experience of hierarchy that was,

> not just a political term that expresses the ideology of a feudal society, not just a theological analogy that has been translated into the political order . . . [but was] so fundamental for man, cosmos and God that even the epistemological notion of an 'idea' was determined by the image of hierarchy.

Thus: 'An "idea" in the Platonic sense did not "mirror" things visible in the universe, but those things from the "lower", changeable order shared in the unchangeable realm of ideas and reflected in them.' The death of God was also 'the collapse of the hierarchical order in thinking, believing and acting.'

Hierarchy of unequal forces was subsequently replaced by the balance and counter-balance of equal ones. Although Taubes observes that the idea of balance has not received the attention it deserves as one of the key elements in the grammar of the motives of the modern era, students of Hobbes, pluralism, international relations and strategic studies, for example, will hardly need reminding of its significance. Taubes does, however, recall that the idea of balance, think Adam Smith's hidden hand as well, had a transcendent other worldly point of reference in deist vocabulary as the hand of Providence. 'This development from heteronymous theism to the autonomous atheism of the nineteenth and twentieth centuries,' says Taubes, 'contains the inner history of theological-political thinking in the modern period.' But matters did not stop there.

When the last traces of transcendence had been eliminated from the general consciousness and the principle of immanence took its place, 'then the principle of balance [lost] its transcendent point of reference: balance has [then] to result exclusively from the immanent relationship of the powers involved.' The autonomous reason on the basis of which the counter-balancing law of immanent forces relied for its authority – in pluralist liberal political thought and military strategic studies alike, for example – none the less also quickly loses this authority when once it, too, is re-construed as rationalisation (ideology critique), as concealing irrational motivations (the unconscious), or as itself ultimately conditioned by the unconditional (deconstruction, see especially Derrida's account of the 'sovereignty' of both reason and power in *Rogues*). By the nineteenth century the conjugation of the theologico-political had, therefore, arrived at the point where: 'if God exist[ed] then man must be his slave and, therefore, Bakunin arrives at the opposite conclusion to Voltaire: if God existed, man would have to kill him . . . The idea of progress crushes the myth of providence.' Dead or alive God none the less remained a pole of reference while the messianic message progressively became 'modernisation'.

Pursuing his review, and turning it into a powerful critical hermeneutic, Taubes observes how ideology, in particular, 'is only a first step towards a new, mythical existence.' Provocatively proposing Sorel's theory of violence as offering the key 'to any present day political theory', Taubes's conclusion is directly to the point and important to quote at length:

Only myth delivers a criterion for societal action and only myth can work as a driving force behind the historical process. It should be obvious that the rise of myth as a political force goes hand in hand with the demise of religion as a bourgeois platform . . . These mythical energies cannot be ignored without danger to society, but have to be formed into a *nomos*.

The uncreated consciousness of our time that pulsates through various mythologies would have to be coined through a new perception of reason. This is a task for philosophy, in the sense in which Plato and Hegel understand the term. Today's chaos of antagonistic mythologies can then lead to the realisation, if to nothing else, of the inseparable unity of theology and political theory. The secret interface between both domains is based on the notion of power. Only when the universal principle of power has been shattered will the unity of theology and political theory be abrogated. A critique of the theological element within political theory is ultimately founded on critique of the principle of power itself.[17]

Derrida's entire oeuvre is preoccupied with the continuous deconstruction of that new *nomos* of reason. Indeed, he engages and breaks open the very idea of *nomos*; of the conception and force of law that lies behind all law talk. Similarly also he contests 'the principle of power itself', whether in speaking, writing, thinking, welcoming, giving or acting as well as in the cult of contemporary global imperial power. To the degree that the politically modern, not least but not only in its cardinal principle of sovereign power, might be represented as 'the unity of theology and political theory', whose effect obscures the thought of the divine as much as it does thought of the political because of the ways in which it unites them in the thought of the modern state and the messianism of the politically modern, then Derrida does no more than offer grounds for repealing their conflation. His turn to religion might be nothing, one may then say, but a means of resourcing a renewed interrogation of 'the secret interface' between the thought of the divine and the thought of the political. In many respects nothing could be more politically urgent today.

An aporetic condition is one from which there is no escape. While it is a forceful provocation to figures of political speech, the aporia is itself, however, no speech-act. It takes place, but not of our volition 'The coming of this event exceeds the condition of mastery and the conventionally accepted authority of what is called the "performative". It thus also exceeds, without contesting its pertinence, the useful distinction between the "constative" and "performative".'[18] Its ramifications, therefore, also exceed the political economy of speaking. That is why other forms of speaking are important, including, for example, those of gesture and the poetic. Plato's hostility to the poetic of political talk and gesture only testified to its enduring force. Policing it politically in the cause of rule no doubt contributes to keeping it alive; indeed to its very liveliness.

The aporia is, however, that speaking cannot ultimately rule, and rule cannot ultimately command the force of speech. But speech does remain forceful, no more so than when it is messianic and, therefore, necessarily also dangerous. The civil enlightenment of seventeenth-century Europe, and the Atlantic republicanism of the eighteenth century, were not without their allied messianisms. From outwith that culture, the messianic promise in Derrida offers a resource for not only questioning what that modern messianism of political freedom consisted in, but also what has become of the contemporary cultic military, political and economic expression of it.

THE APORIA OF JUSTICE

The play on terms between 'Force of Law' and 'Force of Transformation' in my title is, therefore, deliberate, but it does not claim that they are the same thing. The 'Force of Law' is the force of the politically strategic 'necessary killing' for there to be law. 'Force of Transformation' derives from what Derrida calls the aporia or (im)possibility of justice. Its force is 'a weak force' or 'vulnerable force . . . without power' that 'opens up unconditionally to what or who *comes* and comes to affect it.'[19] Yet the two titles are also intimately related. Juxtaposing them is meant to prompt reflection on the relation between the two; to suggest in particular that since politics and law cannot elide the aporia of justice, and the claim it issues through them, they are always already also enmeshed in a force of transformation from which they themselves cannot escape. That, indeed, the promise of 'force transformation', to which politics and law regularly have recourse, is no secure escape from it either.

Between them, Benjamin and Derrida agree on the radical disjuncture between law and justice, the violence integral to law, and the fundamental inadequation of law to justice because of the radical exteriority of justice to law. One can stretch the point and speak, in addition, of a triangulation of politics, law and justice. Justice is as exterior to politics as it is to law. In other words, there is a fundamental inadequation also between politics and law and justice. This exteriority of justice to law and politics does not rupture the relation between politics and the other two. It ties politics, law and justice together in ways that exceed the teachings of our political and philosophical traditions. Specifically, it tells us that politics cannot be oriented toward the good since there is no metric to provide the mean that would serve this navigational purpose. It also tells us that politics does not derive solely from the brokering of interest, because without a meta-metric the brokering of interest is ultimately also incalculable. Political justice cannot similarly also be confined to re-distribution. However important they are, and they are, the distributive questions of who gets what, where, when and how do not exhaust what politics is about. The antagonisms issuing from the call of justice around which politics ultimately revolve, and which government seeks to domesticate, ultimately derive from the clash of the calculable and the incalculable, the valuable and the invaluable. It tells us also that reason alone cannot resolve these clashes since it is the very unconditional condition of the calculus of reason itself that is at issue within them. It tells us finally that the politically strategic logic of necessary killing required for the foundation and preservation of political order, which claims to limit killing by monopolising it in the hands of the state while thereby reserving it for political purposes alone, the *ultima ratio* of political modernity since Machiavelli, is a chimera. It is ultimately governed by a law – that more politically strategic killing is always necessary – which subverts its appeal to a calculus of force that secures lesser violence. It does not.

Despite their measure of agreement, Derrida none the less deconstructs the distinction that Benjamin makes between law-constituting and law-preserving violence. The relation between law-founding and law-preserving is not dialectical, in which the one succeeds and critiques the other. There is founding in every act of preservation and every act of foundation presupposes the iterable preservation of law. Politics is not two separate moves. It is a single double move. The relation between its elements is not a sequential one. The very relationality of the political – (in)calculability – is a deconstructive not a dialectical one. A material effect of this relationality is that every act of law and politics is always already a response to the non-negotiable claim of justice. Another material effect is that however much the claim of justice requires re-calculation it none the less exceeds critique. It calls for transformation, not least a transformation of the imaginable, as well. A third material effect is the urgency upon which Derrida insists in relation to justice. The an-economic relation we have with the call of justice – an-economic because it does not follow the logic of economy but that of the gift – is urgent because it arises in each instance, in every time.[20] However promissory the call of justice may be – the promise of the very affirmation of existence announced in every act and with every enunciation – it is not to be deferred. The claim is always issued here and now.

While politics and law are transactions of the possible, the calculable and the valuable, justice is intractable, incalculable and invaluable. For us mortals, the claim of justice is thus an aporetic condition. The claim of justice is not brokered as a bargain or a deal. Its demand is non-negotiable. The (im)possible aporia of justice to which politics and law perforce must speak is not, however, an impasse. Neither does it suppress valuation, calculation or the possible; so long as 'possibility' is understood within the wider sense of undecidability that Derrida derives from the Nietzschean 'the dangerous perhaps'.[21] It is itself a locus of transformation.

Aporias do not disarm. They empower. They do not negate. They provoke. They do not close down our capacity to respond. They open it up. The aporia of justice is the condition of the possibility of justice. But it is not only a condition of possibility. It is also a condition of operability inflecting how justice, issuing from the very affirmation of existence that attends each act and utterance, invokes an infinitely welcoming disposition towards its claim. The aporia of justice is thus also a beginning not an end. It does not silence. It incites. An aporia is lived out and through figures of political speech. And figures of political speech may be – have been – transformative of the very metrics obtaining in politics and law. Derrida's writing is thus a political lexicon that continuously explores how one can speak, performatively, to this challenging condition even if we are not performatively responsible for its advent and are incapable, therefore, of exercise sovereign power over it. Performativity is a species of the force of transformation required to contest the security (salvation) induced force transformation with which we are globally threatened.

Notes

1. I would like to express my thanks to Richard Beardsworth, Arthur Bradley and Paul Fletcher for conversations that have fuelled this piece.
2. Walter Benjamin, 'Critique of violence', in Marcus Bullock and Michael W. Jennings, (eds), *Walter Benjamin. Selected Writings. Volume 1 1913–1926*, Cambridge, MA: The Belknap Press, 2004). Jacques Derrida, 'Force of law. The mystical foundation of authority', in Drucilla Cornell, et al., (eds), *Deconstruction and the Possibility of Justice*, New York: Routledge, 1992.
3. Points forcefully made by Bernard Stiegler, *Technics and Time 1. The Fault of Epimetheus*, Stanford, CA: Stanford University Press, 1998, and by Richard Beardsworth, *Derrida and the Political*, London: Routledge, 1996.
4. Jacques Derrida, *Rogues: Two Essays on Reason*, Stanford, CA: Stanford University Press, 2005.
5. The most carefully laid, and therefore serious, of these charges are made by Stiegler and Beardsworth. In an equally careful and challenging way, Arthur Bradley reviews them in detail and develops them further in, 'Derrida's God: a genealogy of the theological turn', *Paragraph*, 30:3, November 2006. This chapter is provoked in particular by Beardsworth and Bradley. I take a very different tack here but I am very much indebted to my conversations with them on these and related questions.
6. Jacques Derrida, 'Faith and knowledge: the two sources of religion within the limits of reason alone', in Jacques Derrida and Gianni Vattimo (eds), *Religion*, London: Polity Press, 1998. See also Hent de Vries, *Religion and Violence.*

Philosophical Perspectives from Kant to Derrida, Baltimore, MD: Johns Hopkins University Press, 2002; Yvonne Sherwood and Kevin Hart (eds), *Derrida and Religion: Other Testaments*, New York: Routledge, 2004; and John Caputo, *The Prayers and Tears of Jacques Derrida. Religion without Religion*, Bloomington, IN: Indiana University Press, 1997.

7. The political means by which that 'exclusion' was pursued in the early modern civil enlightenment, only for God to re-enter the political domain philosophically via Kant, are detailed in Ian Hunter, *Rival Enlightenments. Civil and Metaphysical Philosophy in Early Modern Germany*, Cambridge: Cambridge University Press, 2001.

8. Carl von Clausewitz, *On War*, Michael Howard and Peter Paret (eds/trans.), Princeton, NJ: Princeton University Press, 1984; see also Azar Gat, *The Origins of Military Thought. From The Enlightenment to Clausewitz*, Oxford: Clarendon Press, 1989.

9. See, Talal Asad, *Formations of the Secular. Christianity, Islam, Modernity*, Stanford, CA: Stanford University Press, 2003.

10. See, Derrida's, 'Violence and metaphysics: an essay on the thought of Emmanuel Levinas', in Derrida, *Writing and Difference*, London: Routledge and Kegan Paul, 1981; and Derrida, *The Gift of Death*, Chicago, IL: Chicago University Press, 1995.

11. See, Claude Lefort, 'The permanence of the theologico-political', *Democracy and Political Theory*, Oxford: Polity Press, 1988.

12. In Carl Schmitt, *Political Theology. Four Concepts on the Concept of Sovereignty*, Cambridge, MA: MIT Press, 1988.

13. It should go without saying that Derrida's reflections re-cast the question of religion and the divine as much as they do that of the political.

14. Derrida, *Rogues*, p. xiv.

15. For a critical engagement of Schmitt's political theology see, Heinrich Meier, *The Lesson of Carl Schmitt, Four Chapters on the Distinction Between Political Theology and Political Philosophy*, Chicago, IL: Chicago University Press, 1998.

16. Jacob Taubes, 'Theology and political theory', trans. Paul Fletcher, *The Journal of Religion*. I am indebted to my colleague Paul Fletcher for introducing me to Taubes, for the translation of Taubes's essay that I draw on extensively here, and for many conversations about the modern co-relation of politics, religion and political theology.

17. Taubes, 'Theology and Political Theory'.

18. Derrida, *Rogues*, p. xiv

19. Derrida, *Rogues*, p. xiv.

20. Jacques Derrida, *Given Time: 1 Counterfeit Money*, Chicago, IL: Chicago University Press, 1992; Derrida, *The Gift of Death*.

21. For an excellent discussion that compares and contrasts Derrida with Agamben see Adam Thurschwell (2003), 'Specters of Nietzsche: potential futures for the concept of the Political in Agamben and Derrida', *Cardozo Law Review*, 24:8–9.

II

Interrupting the Same

5

Derrida's Memory, War and the Politics of Ethics

Maja Zehfuss

The Second World War and its memory are frequently invoked by the Bush administration in relation to the 'war on terror'.[1] Today Americans have to fight for civilisation and freedom as they did then; another 'great generation' is needed. This chapter explores these invocations of memory in the context of Jacques Derrida's thought, especially his reflections on temporality and memory, and shows that they rely on an impossible temporality around which they necessarily unravel.[2]

THE 'WAR ON TERROR' AND SECOND WORLD WAR MEMORIES

In what one might describe as something of a time warp, the reactions to the events of September 11 started with memory. Jenny Edkins observes that at 9.31am, not even half an hour after the second plane had hit the World Trade Center, President George W. Bush asked his audience at a press conference in Florida, to 'join him in a moment's silence'. Meanwhile, in New York '[f]rantic callers trapped in the upper floors of the World Trade Center Towers were ringing the emergency services. People were plunging to their deaths from the burning buildings. Fire fighters were speeding to the scene.'[3] Both towers of the World Trade Center were yet to collapse, the third plane was yet to crash into the Pentagon and the fourth into a field in Pennsylvania.[4] In other words, most of the 'victims' upon whom Bush wished God's blessing were still alive, many of them desperately fighting not to become what they were already being commemorated as. The first commemoration thus not only came with great haste, immediately after the second plane had hit the towers, but preceded much of what we now refer to as 'September 11'. Edkins discusses this 'premature rush to commemoration' or 'unseemly rush to memory' and particularly the implications of the 'reversal in the assumed temporal order'.[5] Edkins's focus is on how those who died or were 'disappeared' were commemorated by the state but also by other groups and individuals who disrupted the government's representation and in particular its instrumentalisation of the 'victims' to justify 'Bush's heroic global strategy against America's enemies'.[6]

In this chapter, I examine not the problematic commemoration of the 'victims' but the way in which memory quickly became part of speaking about the events in a different sense. Bush did not merely note time and again his determination to 'remember the dead and what we owe them'[7] and to 'always honor their memory.'[8] He also invoked memories of another event that was presented as similar: the Second World War. In a general sense, Bush observed that, '[a]s Americans did 60 years ago, we have entered a struggle of uncertain duration'.[9] Yet there was more to relating Second World War memories to the events of September 11 and the United States' reaction to them. Bush repeatedly likened the 'terrorists' to the Nazis. For example, only days after September 11, Bush asserted:

> We are not deceived by their pretenses to piety. We have seen their kind before. They are the heirs of all the murderous ideologies of the 20th century. By sacrificing human life to serve their radical visions – by abandoning every value except the will to power – they follow in the path of fascism, and Nazism, and totalitarianism.[10]

In October 2001, Bush referred to the 'Nazi terror in Europe',[11] suggesting again some link to the current 'terror'. On Pearl Harbor Day 2001, clearly warming to the theme, Bush declared:

> We've seen their kind before. The terrorists are the heirs to fascism . . . Like all fascists, the terrorists cannot be appeased: they must be defeated. This struggle will not end in a truce or treaty. It will end in victory for the United States, our friends and the cause of freedom.[12]

Thus, the observation that today's terrorists are like yesterday's fascists implies the necessity of war. Indeed, in one speech Bush moved directly from this comparison to responding to a question he claimed Americans were asking: 'How will we fight and win this war?' Whilst he noted other tools, such as diplomacy and law enforcement, he affirmed that 'every necessary weapon of war' would be used.[13] Thus, the alleged similarity of fascists and terrorists suggests that the situation faced by the United States is one in which war is the only option.

Indeed, given that today's enemies are like the fascists of the past, this new war has much in common, in this reasoning, with the Second World War. Americans have to fight for freedom and civilisation now as they did then, something that Bush dwells on especially whenever he addresses the armed forces. In his remarks on the USS *Enterprise* on Pearl Harbor Day 2001, he claimed not only that 'just as we were 60 years ago, in a time of war, this nation will be patient, we'll be determined, and we will be relentless in the pursuit of freedom'.[14] He also compared directly those who fought in the Second World War and those in the United States armed forces today: 'Many of you in today's Navy are the children and grandchildren of the generation that fought and won the Second World War. Now your calling has come. Each of you is commissioned today to face freedom's enemies.'[15] Similarly, at the Air Force Academy graduation in June 2004, Bush quoted General Eisenhower telling troops before the invasion of Normandy in 1944 that the 'hopes and prayers of liberty-loving people everywhere' marched with them and then remarked that '[e]ach of you receiving a commission today in the United States military will also carry the hopes of free people everywhere.'[16] In sum, like the 'great generation' of the Second World War, the current generation is called upon to defend liberty on behalf not merely of their compatriots but 'free people everywhere'.

Although Bush concedes that in some ways 'this struggle we're in is unique', he stresses that in 'other ways, it resembles the great clashes of the last century – between those who put their trust in tyrants and those who put their trust in liberty'.[17] This leads on to what is perhaps the most surprising attempt at analogy: he asserts that '[l]ike the Second World War, our present conflict began with a ruthless, surprise attack on the United States'.[18] The rather puzzling and indeed outrageous idea that the Second World War started with an attack on the United States highlights the failure of the analogy; for, as *The Guardian* dryly noted, this was surely 'news to the Poles'.[19] It would be easy to note how the attack on Pearl Harbor was unlike the events of September 11 and how, more broadly, the Second World War was unlike the 'war on terror'. In fact, the differences are obvious; clearly, historical accuracy is not the point. The attack on Pearl Harbor led the United States to enter the Second World War, or so the argument goes, which ended in victory for the United States and its Allies. The topos of this reference and those to the 'great generation' and their fight for freedom thus seems to be one of heroism, of 'being on the right side', of fighting for a good cause, of defending not only one's country but civilisation. In Bush's representation American troops today are not only 'commissioned by history to face freedom's enemies' but also fighting 'for the security of our people and the success of liberty'.[20]

POLITICS OF MEMORY: CRITICAL OBJECTIONS

Calling on memory and thereby likening the 'war on terror' to the Second World War took centre stage as the sixtieth anniversary of the Allied invasion of Normandy approached. Bush explained at the US Air Force Academy that he would

> go to France for the ceremonies marking the 60th anniversary of D-Day, at a place where the fate of millions turned on the courage of thousands. In these events we recall a time of peril, and national unity, and individual courage. We honor a generation of Americans who served this country and saved the liberty of the world.[21]

He linked that great generation and today's troops; the latter also 'carry the hopes of free people everywhere'. Although Bush acknowledged that in some ways today's conflict is different, 'unique', the 'goal of this generation', he said, was 'the same: We will secure our nation and defend the peace through the forward march of freedom'. Finally, he asserted that 'our will is strong. We know our duty. By keeping our word, and holding firm to our values, this generation will show the world the power of liberty once again'.[22] Again, a parallel between the Second World War and the 'war on terror' is produced, revolving around the supposed defence of freedom.

This parallel was challenged by critics of the 'war on terror' because – despite its obvious limitations – it was powerful. The French government – which was opposed to the Iraq war – was concerned that France's liberation would be instrumentalised by the US administration to legitimise the war. According to The Guardian, advisers 'close to Jacques Chirac' warned 'that any reference to Iraq during the 60th anniversary of the Allied invasion of France . . . would be ill-advised and unwelcome'.[23] Indeed, the speeches at the commemoration ceremony did not mention Iraq. However, Bush's claim that 'our alliance of freedom is still needed today' was an undisguised if implicit reference to the 'war on terror'. In his turn, Chirac criticised Bush by noting that 'our two countries, our two peoples have stood shoulder to shoulder in the brotherhood of blood spilled, in the defense of a certain ideal of mankind, of a certain vision of the world – the vision that lies at the heart of the United Nations Charter.'[24] Where Bush underlined similarities between the two wars, Chirac pursued the opposite strategy: he stressed differences and asserted that the Iraq war violates the principles defended by the Allies in the Second World War.

Crucially, Chirac's intervention disputed the comparability of the wars but left untouched another fundamental assumption, that the generation who fought in the Second World War 'saved the liberty of the world'.[25] Chirac did not question that the Second World War was as Bush invokes it: about the 'power of liberty',[26] the 'pursuit of freedom'[27] and 'the hopes of free people everywhere'.[28] Simon Schama, in contrast, has been sharply critical of the Second World War memorial dedicated in Washington in May 2004 precisely for promoting and reinforcing such an heroic memory at a particularly dangerous time. According to Schama, we should not 'embalm the memory in stone-faced reverence in the manner of the banal neo-classical monument just opened on the Mall in Washington DC, with its meaninglessly feeble euphemisms for sacrifice and slaughter.'[29] He added that 'the last thing we need, 60 years on, are platitudes in marble'.[30]

Schama uses letters from soldiers involved in D-Day to construct a counter-memory, to illustrate that the war was not simply a glorious fight for freedom. He describes the letters as 'a moving antidote to empty monumental platitudes';[31] memories of the war turn out to be diverse and painful. This is even more obvious when memories on what was then the other side are taken into account. Germans' memories are in many ways disconcerting. For example, the terror of bombing and in some cases incinerating cities, killing civilians in atrocious ways, raises the spectre of 'unethical' implications of the Allied Second World War. The notion of the glorious war blanks out not only soldiers' horrific experiences but also the implications for civilians. The bombing of German cities is not mentioned nor is the exposure of 'friendly' civilians to bombing. The memory of the Second World War invoked by both Bush and Chirac is sanitised.

It is precisely the idea of investing the 'war on terror' with some of the glory of the Second World War – that is, the aspect not challenged by Chirac – that makes the analogy so attractive to supporters of the war. In other words, this analogy is not merely about making sense of events; it is about justifying a particular course of action. Schama's critique addresses this. He challenges the memory of the Second World War as an heroic fight for freedom or, in his words, as 'the Good War', but also, importantly, locates the reason for the current monumentification of this war in the present. He observes: 'How the memory craves the reassurance of the Good War . . . while we're in the middle of a bad one.'[32] In Schama's representation, the problem is not only the questionable comparability of the two wars, but the sanitising of the memory of the Second World War. Moreover, Schama points out how the invocation of memory itself – designed to underline the moral validity of the 'war on terror' – ironically points up the moral uncertainty that it is to conceal. In other words, Schama argues that the turn to memory betrays ethical insecurity: we seek refuge in what we

think we know, in the moral certainties of what appears as a less complicated time. It is precisely because it is not certain that the 'war on terror' is
a glorious fight for freedom that the connection with an heroic memory of
the Second World War is so attractive. But, as Schama's counter-memory
shows, this move – calling on memory in order to obscure ethical uncertainty – always already carries the possibility of failure. In order to further
elucidate this it is useful to consider Derrida's reflections on memory.

DERRIDA'S MEMORY

Derrida's work might, at first sight, not appear to be 'about' memory.[33] Yet
Dissemination discusses at length the pharmakon of writing,[34] which poses a
problem to Plato because of its relationship with memory. *Specters of Marx*
revolves around mourning and haunting,[35] both closely linked to memory.
And many of Derrida's more overtly political texts use the term, although
what precisely 'memory' signifies on those occasions appears to be left
tantalisingly unexplained.[36] In a reading of Paul de Man's work, Derrida
suggests that one might reach the conclusion, which he does not immediately subscribe to, that 'memory work' is all that is needed for deconstruction to take place:

> One might then be inclined to reach this conclusion: deconstruction is
> not an operation that supervenes *afterwards*, from the outside, one fine
> day; it is always already at work in the work; one must just know how to
> identify the right or wrong element, the right or wrong stone – the right
> one, of course, always proves to be, precisely, the wrong one. Since the
> disruptive force of deconstruction is always already contained within the
> architecture of the work, all one would finally have to do to be able to
> deconstruct, given this *always already*, is to do memory work.[37]

Although Derrida defers judgement on this conclusion, the association of
memory work with deconstruction is intriguing. In order to explore this
further, I start from what is usually regarded to be at the heart of Derrida's
thought: his critique of the 'metaphysics of presence'.[38]

Derrida questions the way in which Western thinking is arguably based
on the possibility and value of presence; for, according to Derrida, pure
presence is impossible. He points out that the present is always marked by
traces of the past and the future. As Jonathan Culler explains, using the
flight of an arrow as an example, the 'presence of motion is conceivable . . .
only insofar as every instant is already marked with the traces of the past
and the future.'[39] It would be impossible to grasp the motion of the arrow if

the present was uncontaminated by the non-present, free of traces of the past or future; for at every moment – in the present – the arrow is only ever in one place and never in motion. Hence, '[i]f motion is to be present, presence must already be marked by difference and deferral . . . The notion of the present is derived: an effect of differences.'[40] Thus, Derrida challenges thinking that takes pure presence as possible and, indeed, as the starting point of any argument. What interests me here is the effect of this challenge on thinking time and, relatedly, memory. After all, in Derrida's words, the 'rhetoric of temporality' is the rhetoric of memory.[41]

Derrida observes that the 'present is that from which we believe we are able to think time, effacing the inverse necessity: to think the present from time as différance.'[42] In the thinking he criticises, the 'past is a former present, the future an anticipated present, but the present simply is: an autonomous given.'[43] Attention seems to have focused on how Derrida undermines the notion of presence and, as a consequence, strategies of argumentation that are fundamental to Western thought. Yet he challenges not merely presence or the present but the linear development of time from the past (which once was the present) through the present to the future (which will become the present). Derrida's thought is an assault on the linear conception of time. There is not only a problematic dominance of presence in our thinking but an impossible distinction between and ordering of past, present and future. Of course, this does not mean that linear time does not exist or is insignificant. To the contrary, Derrida stresses that the linear conception of time is crucial. He speaks of the linearity of 'the traditional concept of time' as 'an entire organization of the world and of language'.[44]

Memory occupies an intriguing position with respect to time. Although it occurs, as it were, in the present, it is somehow about the past. To remember does not, however, mean that the past is revived in the present. As Derrida notes, 'limitless memory would . . . be not memory but infinite self-presence'.[45] Moreover, although the operation of memory assumes that there is something that is in the past, its pastness is obscured by the act of remembering or invoking memory: 'the rhetoric of memory . . . recalls, recounts, forgets, recounts, and recalls forgetting, referring to the past only to efface what is essential to it: anteriority.'[46] The temporality of memory is complex, arguably more complex than the linear conception of time allows. Reflecting on de Man's work, Derrida observes:

> The memory we are considering here is not essentially oriented toward the past, toward a present deemed to have really and previously existed. Memory stays with traces, in order to 'preserve' them, but traces of a past

that has never been present, traces which themselves never occupy the form of presence and always remain, as it were, to come – come from the future, from the *to come*.[47]

At least two points are significant. First, and as we would by now expect, Derrida refers to a past 'that has never been present', in defiance of the idea that memory recalls a past that has previously been present. Second, he reads memory not merely within the intertwining of past and present, inasmuch as these exist at all, but also as related to what he calls the future.

Derrida observes that to speak of memory is 'also to speak of the future'.[48] Thus, Derrida's reflections on memory have to be read together with his conceptualisation of the future. He distinguishes two significations of 'the future'. On the one hand, the 'future is that which – tomorrow, later, next century – will be. There's a future which is predictable, programmed, scheduled, foreseeable.'[49] This is the future as it would be understood in a linear conception of time: though it has not yet arrived, we have some notion of how it will follow on from the present, allowing us to plan for it. There is, however, Derrida explains, another future:

> there is a future . . . to come which refers to someone who comes whose arrival is totally unexpected. For me, that is the real future. That which is totally unpredictable. The Other who comes without my being able to anticipate their arrival. So if there is a real future behind this other known future, it's l'avenir in that it's the coming of the Other. When I am completely unable to foresee their arrival.[50]

Thus, Derrida is interested in the future to come, that is, he wants to think the future in the sense in which it may not be anticipated and, therefore, offers possibilities we are not able to imagine. This means that the future may be seen as dangerous: before it arrives we do not know what it will be. This is underlined when Derrida describes his work as 'a way of thinking that is faithful and attentive to the ineluctable world of the future which proclaims itself at present, beyond the closure of knowledge', only to observe that the 'future can only be anticipated in the form of an absolute danger'.[51] Crucially, the danger entailed by the future is not one we should seek to overcome, as, according to Derrida, 'without risk, there is nothing'.[52] There is clearly no politics without risk. Put differently, without the risk of the future there could be no decision. Not least because of this memory is inextricably linked to the political.

MEMORY, WAR AND THE POLITICS OF ETHICS

Bush's references to the heroic fight for freedom rely, not least, on our understanding of the evilness of the enemy; today's terrorists are, in this story, the new Nazis. As the Nazis remain in our political imagination the personification of evil, this means not only that the Americans were then and are now on the side of the Good but that there is a clear divide between Good and Evil. This rhetoric thus obscures the contradictory imperatives to which we are exposed in deciding whether and how to lead a war. If the war against Iraq is like the liberation of Germany and Japan in the Second World War,[53] then the right course of action is a foregone conclusion: it is obviously right to fight for freedom.

One ethico-political problem related to war is whether it is permissible to kill and whom it is permissible to kill for which goals. As wars inevitably involve killing, this question cannot be excluded. In it we encounter an aporia: the 'right way' is not clear and therefore we agonise over the decision.[54] The decision, whatever it will be, will never be ethically satisfactory. Of course, in waging war there is no time or opportunity for moral uncertainty: as Bush infamously put it, 'you are either with us or against us'. The invocation of memory seems designed to indicate the 'right way' by noting that the Americans have been in a similar situation before, they did the right thing then and so whatever they did then is likely to be right today. Thus, a decision is no longer needed; the uncertainty of the aporia is replaced with the certainty of a 'lesson' from the past. The United States administration seems to deny or seek to escape from the experience of the aporia through references to heroic memories of the Second World War, which not only obscure enemy casualties but also render them insignificant by representing the enemy population not as human but as the personification of evil. Thus, the problem of whose life may be taken all but disappears.

The crucial move in this denial of the need for a decision is the assumption that the past reveals what to do in the present. Bush's invocations of memory suggest that the present is like the past and that therefore doing what was right then will also be right now. The obvious critique of this line of reasoning is to highlight the ways in which the present is unlike the past, and Chirac's insistence that it would be unacceptable for Bush to mention Iraq at the celebrations of France's liberation follows this pattern. The second approach is to query quite how 'right' what was done in the past really was, something that forms part of Schama's reasoning. Significantly, these critiques do not seem to have had any significant effect. Bush still argued in July 2005, after giving a list of achievements of defenders of the United States culminating in the Second World War, that '[t]oday, a new generation of Americans is defending our freedom against determined enemies'.[55]

It is important to note that both lines of critique seem to allow that a more differentiated version of memory might be appropriately used for a sophisticated comparison that would highlight differences as well as similarities and take account of the less heroic aspects of the past. Such a memory could then inform our political choices today. If only we remembered correctly, these critiques seem to say, there would be no problem: we could invoke our memories of the past in order to guide our actions in the present. In this they seem to agree with Bush. Thus, whilst Schama offers a counter-memory of the Second World War that takes into account the recollections of individual soldiers, he does not go as far as examining the assumptions of invoking memory in the rhetoric of the 'war on terror' in the first place. It is now useful to press further the idea of 'memory work' and in particular to examine the aspect of temporality.

The rhetoric of Bush and others suggests, first of all, that there was a set of events in the past, called the Second World War, which may now usefully be remembered in order to grasp the 'war on terror' and guide our conduct with respect to it. This story is firmly based on a linear imagination of time where the Second World War comes before our present and hence may serve as a source of knowledge about how to cope in such difficult times. The Second World War occurs first, bringing about the triumph of freedom in western Europe and parts of Asia, thus saving 'freedom-loving people' (not quite) everywhere. This story is firmly linear. At first sight, so is the invocation of memory. Now, in our present which comes after this past, we remember the Second World War: the memory is now, what it remembers was in the past. This, however, poses at least two challenges to linearity. First, identifying the Second World War as the defence of the free world already involves a reversal of time. Second, such a story fails to acknowledge that memory refers not just to the event in the past that it is meant to recall but to a boundless context including not least other attempts at recounting this past.

What is 'the Second World War' is not a question of what happened in some past that was one day the present. Rather 'the Second World War', 'Pearl Harbor' and 'September 11', as we understand them, are produced after the event and indeed continuously reproduced. Thus, the Second World War becomes synonymous with the liberation of western Europe, for example, not because of the military actions that make up what we now understand to be the Second World War but crucially because of the success of liberal democracy in this part of the continent since the end of military hostilities. It is what occurs – in a linear understanding of time – after the war that makes the Second World War what we now understand it to be. Time is reversed: the past, inasmuch as it exists, becomes what it 'is' because of the present, retrospectively. It is in this sense that memory stays with traces of a 'past that has never been present'.[56]

Moreover, recalling the past never involves merely this past; rather memory operates according to the logic of iterability. Every performance of memory is also a citation or rather iteration. Iterability, Derrida explains, 'supposes a minimal remainder . . . in order that the identity of the selfsame be repeatable and identifiable *in*, *through* and even *in view of* its alteration. For the structure of iteration . . . implies *both* identity *and* difference'.[57] Bush never says much about his precise understanding of the Second World War. In referring to 'the great generation' and the fight for freedom, he is able to invoke an already existing context of the memory of the Second World War as the Good War. Martin Kettle observes that the idea of 'another great generation', called into action by the acts of Osama bin Laden frequently appears in Bush's speeches after September 11, but also that the celebration of the 'heroic myth about the benevolence of American power' dates back at least to Bill Clinton's speech commemorating D-Day in 1994 and has since been reinforced by popular culture.[58] Films, such as Steven Spielberg's *Saving Private Ryan*, have played a role,[59] as have popular books, such as those by Stephen E. Ambrose. Ambrose writes about the Second World War generation that they were 'a special breed of men and women who did great things for America and the world.'[60]

Despite being critical of this '1944 myth' Kettle observes that Ambrose's – and presumably by extension Bush's – assertion that we owe our freedom to the men of D-Day is 'the truth, of course'.[61] In other words, Kettle suggests that the story of D-Day is so powerful because there is some truth to it, even if it has since been mythologised. Kettle's representation, like Bush's, which it seeks to critique, assumes that there is a truth of D-Day and the Second World War, which is presumably about what really happened at the time. Yet 'truth' is an unhelpful category here. Bush's invocations of the Second World War are not powerful because they are true, because his audience has independently verified that the courage of the men of the 'great generation' was instrumental in bringing about a freer world. Rather their power shows that his audience is predisposed to subscribe to such an interpretation because it relates to what they have been told all along; Bush cites previous invocations of the Good War and simultaneously alters them to read, for example, 'September 11' as recalling 'Pearl Harbor'.

CONCLUSION

Exploring the rhetoric of memory shows that what is significant is what we do not easily see and, therefore, find difficult to challenge, although the invocation of memory itself already does. Bush's rhetoric of memory requires and reinforces the story of linear time, a story that is crucial to the idea that the state saved its citizens from danger and brought freedom to the world. Telling this story as part of political rhetoric produces a significant closure. The past teaches us what to do in the present thereby ensuring a favourable future. Bush is credited with remarking that 'the future will be better tomorrow', most likely an urban myth. The point is that we have no way of knowing what the future will be. This uncertainty offers an opportunity. It is not through doing the 'right thing' as established by the past, but in facing the impossible decision and embracing the danger of the future that we may move towards the ethical. Responsibility only becomes possible beyond the apparent security of knowledge: 'it is always in a dilemma and a certain non-knowledge [non-savoir] as to what it would be best to do, it is at the moment when two contradictory imperatives are in competition, that a responsible freedom can be exercised as such.'[62] Knowledge is necessary for the responsible decision, but it is never enough.[63] Derrida associates the responsible decision with the 'real future' for which we may not plan; for the 'real future' is that 'which is totally unpredictable'.[64] This does not mean, however, that the responsible decision is postponed until another day, to what is more commonly called the future. Rather, the 'responsible decision must also and above all . . . be made *with the utmost urgency*.'[65]

Derrida claims that to speak of memory is also to speak of the future, that is, of that which is totally unexpected. One might suggest then that 'memory work' offers an opportunity to move towards grasping the challenge of ethico-political problems. Indeed, we saw that at the same time as apparently underlining the conception of linear time, invoking memory challenged its very possibility, thereby blocking the smooth path from the lesson of the past to the recipe for the future. Memory, therefore, has the potential to underline the aporia, the uncertainty with which we are confronted when we face ethico-political questions, and the failure of knowledge, especially because knowledge of 'the past' relies on an impossible conception of linear time.

Critiquing the 'war on terror' has proved astonishingly difficult. The widespread opposition to it seems to have made little headway politically. Christian Parenti notes that one of the problems is that given the 'shockingly blunt official arguments made by the Bush administration and elements of the pundit class *for* American domination of the globe' there 'hardly seems much room for critique'.[66] Perhaps, in focusing on what are construed as the central political claims, the critique has chosen the wrong target. Perhaps what is necessary is a consideration of the basic assumptions on which the arguments rest and of how they come apart. Edkins usefully discusses the reversal of time in the reaction to September 11 and how this has enabled the Bush administration to produce consent. In a similar vein, what I have sought to highlight is that invoking memory always already involves a reversal of time – producing a past in the present – thereby undermining the argument it is meant to perform which requires, above all, that the past occurred before the present. The retrospective character of memory makes Bush's invocation of the Second World War in support of the 'war on terror' possible; at the same time his arguments necessarily unravel around their ambiguous temporality.

NOTES

1. I would like to thank Jenny Edkins and the editors for their insightful comments.
2. The themes of this chapter are further developed in Maja Zehfuss, *Wounds of Memory: Politics of War in Germany*, Cambridge: Cambridge University Press, 2007.
3. Jenny Edkins (2003), 'The rush to memory and the rhetoric of war', *Journal of Political and Military Sociology*, 31:236.
4. Ibid. p. 236.
5. Ibid. pp. 231 and 235.
6. Ibid. p. 246. See also Maja Zehfuss (2003), 'Forget September 11', *Third World Quarterly*, 24:513–28.
7. George W. Bush, Remarks by the President at 'The World Will Always Remember September 11th' Ceremony, 11 December 2001, http://www.whitehouse.gov/news/releases/2001/12/200111211-1.html.
8. George W. Bush, Remarks by the President at the Department of Defense Service of Remembrance, 11 October 2001, http://www.whitehouse.gov/news/releases/2001/10/print/20011011.html.
9. Ibid.
10. George W. Bush, Address to a Joint Session of Congress and the American People, 20 September 2001, http://www.whitehouse.gov/news/releases/2001/09/print/20010920-8.html.
11. Bush, Remarks, 11 October 2001.
12. George W. Bush, 'We're Fighting to Win – And Win We Will', Remarks by the President on the USS *Enterprise* on Pearl Harbor Day, 7 December 2001, http://www.whitehouse.gov/news/releases/2001/12/print/20011207.html.
13. Bush, Address to Congress, 20 September 2001.
14. Bush, 'We're Fighting to Win', 7 December 2001.

15. Ibid.
16. George W. Bush, Remarks by the President at the United States Air Force Academy Graduation Ceremony, Falcon Stadium, 2 June 2004, http://www.whitehouse.gov/news/releases/2004/06/print/20040602.html.
17. Ibid.
18. Ibid.
19. 'Past and present', *The Guardian*, 4 June 2004, p. 25.
20. Bush, 'We're Fighting to Win', 7 December 2001.
21. Bush, Remarks, 2 June 2004.
22. Ibid.
23. Kim Willsher, 'Anniversary anxiety', *The Guardian*, 2 June 2004, p. 14.
24. Remarks by President Bush and President Chirac on Marking the 60th Anniversary of D-Day, The American Cemetery, Normandy, France, 6 June 2004, http://www.whitehouse.gov/news/releases/2004/06/print/20040606.html
25. Bush, Remarks, 2 June 2004.
26. Ibid.
27. Bush, Remarks, 7 December 2001.
28. Bush, Remarks, 2 June 2004.
29. Simon Schama, 'If you receive this, I'll be dead', *The Guardian G2*, 28 May 2004, p. 4.
30. Ibid.
31. Ibid.
32. Ibid, p. 3.
33. Though see David Farrell Krell, *Of Memory, Reminiscence and Writing: On the Verge*, Bloomington, IN: Indiana University Press, 1990.
34. Jacques Derrida, *Dissemination*, trans. Barbara Johnson, London: Athlone Press, 1981, especially pp. 95–117.
35. Jacques Derrida, *Specters of Marx: The State of Debt, the Work of Mourning, and the New International*, trans. Peggy Kamuf, New York: Routledge, 1994.
36. See, e.g., Jacques Derrida, *The Other Heading: Reflections on Today's Europe*, trans. Pascale-Anne Brault and Michael B. Naas, Bloomington, IN: Indiana University Press, 1992, p. 13; Jacques Derrida, *Deconstruction Engaged: The Sydney Seminars*, Paul Patton and Terry Smith (eds), Sydney: Power Publications, 2001, pp. 63, 79 and 102; and, with more elucidation of the concept, Jacques Derrida and Bernard Stiegler, *Echographies of Television: Filmed Interviews*, trans. Jennifer Bajorek, Cambridge: Polity Press, 2002, pp. 56–67.
37. Jacques Derrida, *Memoires for Paul de Man: The Wellek Library Lectures at the University of California, Irvine* (revised edn), trans. Cecile Lindsay, Jonathan Culler, Eduardo Cadava and Peggy Kamuf, New York: Columbia University Press, 1989, p. 73.
38. Jacques Derrida, *Of Grammatology*, trans. Gayatri Chakravorty Spivak (Corrected edn), Baltimore, MD: Johns Hopkins University Press, 1998, p. 49.
39. Jonathan Culler, *On Deconstruction: Theory and Criticism after Structuralism*, London: Routledge, 1983, p. 94.

40. Ibid. p. 95.
41. Derrida, *Memoires*, p. 57.
42. Derrida, *Of Grammatology*, p. 166.
43. Culler, *On Deconstruction*, p. 95.
44. Derrida, *Of Grammatology*, p. 85.
45. Derrida, *Dissemination*, p. 109.
46. Derrida, *Memoires*, p. 82.
47. Ibid. p. 58.
48. Ibid. p. 93; see also p. 3.
49. Derrida in Kirby Dick and Amy Ziering Kofman, *Derrida*, Jane Doe Films 2003, subtitles.
50. Ibid.
51. Derrida, *Of Grammatology*, pp. 4–5.
52. Jacques Derrida, *Negotiations: Interventions and Interviews 1971–2001*, ed. and trans. Elizabeth Rottenberg, Stanford, CA: Stanford University Press, 2002, p. 238.
53. James Dao, 'Experts debate meaning of regime change', *New York Times*, 22 September 2002.
54. Derrida, *Other Heading*, p. 41; see also Jacques Derrida, *Aporias*, trans. Thomas Dutoit, Stanford, CA: Stanford University Press, 1993, especially p. 8.
55. George W. Bush, President's Radio Address, 2 July 2005, http://www.whitehouse.gov/news/releases/2005/07/20050702.html.
56. Derrida, *Memoires*, p. 58.
57. Jacques Derrida, *Limited Inc*, trans. Alan Bass and Samuel Weber, Evanston, IL: Northwestern University Press, 1988, p. 53.
58. Martin Kettle, 'Bush's war has nothing to do with the spirit of D-day', *The Guardian*, 1 June 2005.
59. Trevor B. McCrisken and Andrew Pepper, *American History and Contemporary Hollywood Film*, New Brunswick: Rutgers University Press, 2005, ch. 4.
60. Stephen E. Ambrose, *Citizen Soldiers: The U.S. Army from the Normandy Beaches to the Bulge to the Surrender of Germany June 7, 1944–May 7, 1945*, New York: Simon & Schuster, 1997, p. 472.
61. Kettle, 'Bush's war'.
62. Derrida, *Negotiations*, pp. 210ff.
63. Jacques Derrida, *The Gift of Death*, trans. David Wills, Chicago, IL: University of Chicago Press, 1995, p. 24.
64. Derrida in *Derrida*, subtitles.
65. Derrida, *Negotiations*, p. 296.
66. Christian Parenti, *The Freedom: Shadows and Hallucinations in Occupied Iraq*, New York: The New Press, 2004, p. ix.

6

The (International) Politics of Friendship: Exemplar, Exemplarity, Exclusion

Josef Teboho Ansorge

At the centre of the principle, always, the One does violence to itself, and guards itself against the other.[1]

Jacques Derrida

INTRODUCTION

International Relations (IR), if there is such a thing, is an academic discipline which intends to describe, analyse and explain international relations.[2] It is taught at universities through a variety of courses consisting of various quantitative and qualitative approaches; history and theory modules. Theory modules offer different competing stories about international politics: some write that the world is a multi-civilisational system;[3] others claim that the world is an anarchic order;[4] whilst another group of scholars propose that the world is reaching an endpoint in its ideological evolution.[5] If there is any consensus in the IR academic community, it is that these theories represent separate methodologies and conclusions. A result of this assumption is that the intellectual exchange in IR is organised into and around various 'great debates': such as the liberalism–realism debate or the neo-neo debate. Instead of focusing on the differences of contending approaches to IR this essay endeavours to work out some commonalities of IR theories.

Through a close reading of Jacques Derrida's *Politics of Friendship* the main texts of three academics whose works have been contested and re-contested in IR, Samuel Huntington, Kenneth Waltz and Francis Fukuyama, are going to be studied through the lens of friendship. This paper tries to 'bring the political back'[6] into our discourses on friendship and politics by pointing to their intimate link. To enable this, the first section introduces Derrida's writings on friendship. The second section deploys Derrida's writings towards Samuel Huntington's seminal *Clash of Civilisations*, the third section applies the same model to Kenneth Waltz's influential *Theory* of *International Politics* and the fourth section extends Derrida's writing on friendship to a critique of Francis Fukuyama's famous *The End of History*.

The thesis of this paper is that all three of the IR theoreticians share the same model of friendship, a model which Derrida has uncovered as distinctly Ciceronian in character. This model of friendship is explicitly expressed in some texts, whilst it functions as a more implicit presupposition in others. The possibility that our conflicting theories of IR rely on one mutual foundation of a model of friendship is both important and alarming to the study of IR. Not only does this discovery point to the inherent limitation of the canonised discourses of IR, it could also problematise the very horizon in which we think the political. Furthermore, by uncovering a constructed model of friendship at work in our main IR theories one of the conditions for violent prevalent modes of exclusion might be identified. The next section presents Derrida's approach to the complications of friendship and introduces a number of crucial concepts for the later analysis of texts.

Jacques Derrida

Derrida employs various moves and concepts which make his political contribution very rewarding, yet at times difficult to comprehend. The following section gives one reading of his project entitled *The Politics of Friendship* and introduces two important terms for our analysis: teleiopoesis and exemplum. Once a reading of his politics of friendship is developed in this section it is only one strand out of a patchwork – restraint must be shown not to graffiti teleology[7] onto his oeuvre.

Sketching a theme of *The Politics of Friendship* it is helpful to tackle the Derridean term of teleiopoesis. The book begins with and works through various different iterations of 'Oh my friends, there is no friend', a quote attributed to Aristotle. In the second chapter, Derrida coins the neologism teleiopoesis to describe the logic and the genetics of another quote, this time by Nietzsche: 'Alas! If only you knew how soon, how very soon, things will be – different!'.[8] The sentence speaks of an action to come which it then fulfills. The special structure of this sentence event is a 'simultaneous grafting of the performative and the reportive'.[9] This same configuration can be discovered in the Aristotle quote. Friends are addressed, spoken to, 'Oh my friends . . .' only to be told that they don't exist, 'there is no friend'. The performative and the reportive are grafted into one sentence, and they are contradictory. A radical dislocation takes place functioning as contradiction and logical necessity. To make sense of this, imagine that the party for whom our message is intended can only receive it when we address them with a term they identify with, yet one which we must later disavow. The logic of this teleiopoesis aims at the presupposition of the ontological and injects a temporal dislocation into the very sentence, it functions like a 'boomerang that . . . relentlessly pursues its progress towards changing the place of the subject'.[10] The performativity of the teleiopoetic sentence involves the reader, who at the end of the sentence may have 'already become the cosignatories of the addresses addressed to you'.[11] Teleiopoesis opens up the discourse to a 'perhaps' which permits Derrida to execute two crucial procedures of philosophical analysis.

1. The first move is to recall 'the acquiescence more originary'[12] to any question. This inquiry into foundations also occurs in other strands of Derrida's texts, such as: 'Signature, event, context' where he writes about a '[graphematic] system of predicates in the structure of locution (thus before any illocutory or perlocutory determination) [that] blurs all the oppositions which follow'.[13] In the *Politics of Friendship* this approach leads Derrida to philosophically interrogate foundations and presuppositions which structure our understanding of the political. This is where he discovers a Ciceronian–Aristotelian model of friendship at work, a model relying on presence and sameness.
2. The second move suspends the 'thesis of existence' by repeatedly saying 'if there is one'.[14] This angle lets one attempt to think of friendship without the assumption of presence. Or in Greek terminology to be revisited further below: it lets us imagine a 'philia without oikeiotes'.[15] When the initial acquiescence of the first move is a system which relies on presence, the second move of the suspension of the thesis of existence is a suspension of the very foundation of that system.

These two approaches outlined above structure our writings on the theorists below. The [acquiescence more originary] is recalled and the exemplar located within the text, whilst the second part of each section sets itself the cumulative task of suspending the thesis of existence and working towards a problematisation and possible deconstruction of the exemplar.

The quotation attributed to Aristotle, which Derrida employs as an undulating theme in the *Politics of Friendship*, can be read through both the approaches outlined above. In the first instance, 'Oh my friends, there is no friend' points to the originary acquiescence at work in friendship – the assumption of presence, whilst the second half of the sentence suspends the thesis of existence. In a similar vein it is possible to read the entire *Politics of Friendship* as a teleiopoetic event. Teleiopoesis is labouring throughout the text: grafting the performative and the reportive, opening up the thematic of politics, pointing to a foundation of a certain model of friendship at work in the political, and suspending the model whilst involving the reader in an intimate fashion. In summary, whilst Derrida's text is definitely not teleological it can easily be read as teleiopoetical. To observe the model of friendship which Derrida uncovers and suspends in his text, the Ciceronian concept of the exemplar must be introduced.

The exemplar is Cicero's response to 'what is the friend?'. In Derrida's words the exemplum means 'portrait but also, as the exemplum, the duplicate, the reproduction, the copy as well as the original, the type, the model'.[16] Derrida's lengthy quotation from Cicero's Laelius de Amicitia is worth reproducing in full at this point.

> For the man who keeps his eye on a true friend, keeps it, so to speak, on a model of himself (tamquam exemplar aliquod intuetur sui). For this reason, friends are together when they are separated, they are rich when they are poor, strong when they are weak (et imbecilli valent), and – a thing even harder to explain – they live on after they have died (mortui vivunt), so great is the honour that follows them, so vivid the memory, so poignant the sorrow. That is why friends who have died are accounted happy (ex quo illorum beata mors videtur), and those who survive them are deemed worthy of (vita laudabilis).[17]

The exemplar gives us the explanation and possible horizon for friendship. The friend is our duplicate, reproduction, type, and model. He or she is not simply one of us, he or she is one of me. Derrida points out that this model of friendship prefers the same to the other – the friend is the same and not the other in this philosophical tradition. Since the friend is a 'model' of the self, friendship (philia) actually has a structure. The friend is the reflection of what he desires, but, since he can only desire things which he lacks, which he has been deprived of, then before that privation friendship must have been linked to what is oikeios (familiar).[18] Oikeios is an adjective which means that 'which is one's own, personal, even intimate and interior, as well as that which is close, from the parent or the friend or the compatriot',[19] it stems from the Greek noun oikos, which means the hearth, the familial lodgings, the home. The logic and the structure of the exemplum tell us that philia relies intimately on oikeios, oikeiotes and the oikos, all concepts based on the presence of the familiar. The Ciceronian model of friendship, the exemplar, gives us the structure for a relationship of the one and the other, the original and the copy. The friend is our ideal image and he resides close to the hearth.

Now, important for Derrida's work and this paper's theme is that the structure of friendship is both 'acknowledged and unrecognised'[20] by Aristotle. His argument is that analysis will never be able to account for the actual event of friendship. Friendship can not be reduced to the theoretical possibility of friendship. All our writings on the friend are simply models of a friendship, which cannot restrict the radical potentiality of a hitherto unseen friendship. This works as a suspension of the structure before the structure, it injects a perhaps into all of our thinking.

The Aristotelian tradition which Derrida develops does recognise a structure to friendship, but it does not contain the possibility of friendship to this structure. The Ciceronian tradition, on the other hand, accounts for the possibilities of friendship. It gives a definition and a model of the friend, the exemplar. This model of the friend, the other that is the self, is the model of friendship which this chapter will problematise in the three IR texts.

SAMUEL HUNTINGTON

Samuel Huntington is a figure of great academic distinction within the International Relations Community. He is currently the chairman of the Harvard Academy for International and Area Studies, founder and co-editor of *Foreign Policy*, and the president of the American Political Science Association. His work has often been described as influential and path-breaking within the United States. Whilst he was already an established academic authority before its publication *The Clash of Civilizations* has made him famous, even infamous, in some parts of the world.

Huntington's stated aim for writing *The Clash of Civilizations* is to construct a viable political model for what he terms the 'new era',[21] by which he means the post-Cold War world. Through a procedure of exclusion he first considers a number of options before proposing the model of clashing civilisations for the 'new era'. Amongst different para-digms of the world which he considers is the idea of one world, where the fall of the Berlin Wall marked the end stage of humanity's ideological development. According to Huntington this idea, whose most famous exponent is Francis Fukuyama, is 'clearly far too divorced from reality to be a useful guide to the post-Cold War world'.[22] Huntington also devotes space to discussing the model of an international system of states. He concludes that this model, which Kenneth Waltz utilises, 'suffers from severe limitations' because 'state borders have become increasingly perme-able'.[23] The inability of these and other models to account for world affairs leads Huntington to propose what he perceives as a Kuhnian paradigm change in IR. The model which he advocates is one of a multi-civilisational world in which the major conflicts are inter-civilisational. Huntington proposes eight major civilisations for the world: Sinic; Japanese; Hindu; Islamic; Orthodox; Western; Latin American; and (possibly) African.[24.] To define what a civilisation is Huntington invokes the authority of Herodotus. The text features the Athenians pledging to the Spartans that they will not betray them to the Persians. The logic of the exemplar is so prominent in this section that it deserves to be quoted in the full:

> For there are many and powerful considerations that forbid us to do so, even if we were inclined. First and chief, the images and dwellings of the gods, burnt and laid ruins: this we must needs avenge to the utmost of our power, rather than make terms with the man who has perpetrated such deeds. Secondly, the Grecian race being of the same blood and the same language, and the temples of the gods and sacrifices in common; and our similar customs for the Athenians to become betrayers of these would not be well.[25]

For Huntington this is a clear indication that shared blood, language and religion are what constitute and justify a civilisation. It is apparent from this text that Huntington views the friend, our political ally, as the exemplar. The friend shares blood, language and religion: *oikeios*, he is a model of the self. Because this is the case, and has been the case, because this is an 'old truth', Huntington proposes that westerners should, 'accept their civilisation as unique not universal and unite to renew and preserve it against challenges from non-Western societies'.[26] This model of friendship, which Derrida would call homophilia, is at once the experience structuring the political and the foundation for the categorisation of political entities. Its logic permits Huntington utterances such as, '[w]hile Muslims pose the immediate problem to Europe, Mexicans pose the problem for the United States'.[27]

This logic of the *exemplar* manifests forms of what Plato and Carl Schmitt would call *stasis*, *polemos*, *hostis* and *inimicus*.[28] Enemies in this paradigm fall into two different orders: public enemies who are *hostis* (not of the same people); and private enemies who are *inimicus* (of the same people). The quarrel with *inimicus* is a mere *stasis*, whilst conflict with *hostis* is a full out *polemos*. In Huntington's text *stasis* represents the superfluous intra-civilisational conflict and *polemos* the appropriate inter-civilisational clash, *hostis* refers to inter-civilisational enemies, whilst inimicus are intra-civilisational enemies. The enemy is also a type of exemplar. This is not apparent at first, one expects the Muslim to be quite distinct from the Westerner, and yet there is an exemplar at work in Huntington's text. The enemy is an exemplar in *The Clash of Civilizations* because he represents a civilisation, just as the friend does. The identities of each civilisation share the same form (shared language, religion, etc.), they merely carry different contents. The other is the same as the self within the confines of what constitutes a civilisation, the other is a brother. The rest of this section returns to some of Derrida's writings on fraternity.

What Derrida has to say on the homophilic discourse of the Greeks applies just as much to Huntington, 'everything seems to be decided where the decision does not take place'.[29] By linking the political to a perceived natural biological order the entire horizon of the political; the friend, the enemy – are all determined before anybody ever makes the decision to do so. Or differently, it is because our politics link the isonomic and the isogonic[30] that political configurations are constructed before the political decision to do so occurs. And yet, according to Derrida this does not absolve us from the responsibility of accounting for this decision, as 'responsibility must imperatively answer for itself before what is, at birth and at death'.[31] Derrida's response to this type of thought is simple, yet profound. He asks if anyone has 'ever met a brother?'[32] The crucial point is that whilst Huntington's politics relies on the symbolic projection of a fraternity, this fraternity in itself is never natural or neutral, but a political construction. The discourses of nationalism and racism that rely on this construction are repeatedly engaged with a 'renaturalization[33] of this myth'.[34] This myth of the fraternal brother produces a politics that is determined before it takes place. Furthermore, the isogonic–isonomic link, this homophilia, forms the condition of political freedom for the Greek people and residents of Huntington's world. The Greeks are bound in their relations to each other and to the barbarians, just as Huntington's civilisations are bound in their relations to each other. The political horizon is constructed and determined by discourse before politics actually occurs.

This section has illustrated the prevalence of the exemplar in Huntington's discourse, the categories of *stasis* and *polemos* which it leads to, and the suitability of a Derridean critique for *The Clash of Civilizations*. The next section looks at a thinker whose work is related to Huntington's, Kenneth Waltz.

KENNETH WALTZ

This section gives an outline of Kenneth Waltz's systemic approach, traces the exemplar, *stasis* and *polemos* at work in his writing, and returns to a Derridean critique of the exemplar. More than any book in IR Kenneth Waltz's *Theory of International Politics* has been treated as the seminal text of neo-realist thought. Waltz's stated aim in the work is none other than to 'construct a theory of international politics that remedies the defects of present theories'.[35]

To do this he devises a systemic approach to IR, one which views the system as a permissive cause for all occurring politics. Waltz claims that a system is 'composed of a structure and of [atomistic] interacting units'.[36] According to him, to define a structure requires 'ignoring how units relate with one another (how they interact) and concentrating on how they stand in relation to one another (how they are arranged or positioned)'.[37] This arrangement of units is not a property of the units but a property of the international system. As one might have suspected, these atomistic units of the international system are states, and whilst Waltz does concede that states 'never have been the only international actors' he justifies restricting the category of the unit to the state because they are the 'major' players.[38] His main argument at this juncture is that whilst the internal structure of a state is hierarchic (government decides) the order of the international system is anarchic, and will remain so until one 'of the competing units is able to convert the anarchic international realm into a hierarchical one'.[39] The hierarchy/anarchy distinction in Waltz's work is the *stasis–polemos* dichotomy in a different manifestation, symptomatic of the logic and the function of the exemplar.

A preliminary remark on Waltz's exemplar: because Waltz does not find the need to account for the origin of the atomistic units of his system his discourse does not utilise the theme of natural blood ties, as do Schmitt's and Huntington's. Instead his proto-scientific discourse tends to treat the units as a natural order, which he is simply describing. None the less: the logic of the exemplar is at work in his text, it exists on two levels. The fault line to his thinking can be found in the hierarchy – anarchy distinction. In the first instance the exemplar defines the unity of a state, a coherent hierarchical order, which is contrasted to the international sphere, the anarchic order. On the level of the state, the political friend is defined by an equal subjection to the hierarchy (he is a member of the same coherent hierarchy), in the international we find that the enemy is also given to us through the exemplar, the enemy is a state, like ourselves. What we find in this section is that the binding function of blood ties has been replaced with the master-signifier of 'hierarchy'. Through a conscious or sub-conscious act of catechresis Waltz has exported the structure of orgiastic discourses engaged in a renaturalisation of the myth of the brother to the domain of systemic scientific thought. His structural approach stratifies the logic of the exemplar to such an extent that it does not even find the need to account for the origin of its units of analysis; in this respect it takes all of the constructions of fraternity and difference as given and merely devises a system to account for their actions. Inadvertently or not, this move continues to depoliticise and renaturalise the primacy of the exemplar and the preliminary distinctions of *stasis* and *polemos*. The logic of the exemplar at work in Huntington's and Waltz's discourse permits each of them to paint coloured political maps of the world, in which there is a finite number of peoples contained to a given number of *oikos*: this model conflating the topographical with the ontological is ontopological.[40] The rest of this section returns to a Derridean critique of the exemplar.

Up until this juncture our Derridean critique has claimed that the brother is a type of legal fiction, that the enemy is given by the exemplar as well, that this political configuration takes place before any decision, and that the logic of the exemplar gives a people the horizon of their political freedom (Greeks bound in their actions to each other, as they are in their actions to the barbarians). What is missing from this line-up is Derrida's use of 'unheimlichkeit'. 'Unheimlichkeit' is what describes the lodging of the enemy at the heart of the friend and the friend at the heart of the enemy, which we have witnessed in the inversion of the exemplum above.[41] The German word *unheimlich* is a fine choice to describe this slippage of friend and enemy. *Unheimlich* means spooky, but it is based on the noun *Heim*, which means home, the *oikos* – the word describes that which is spooky, but also un-homely, unfamiliar. At the same time the word trembles with the possibility of another prefix, *ge-heim*, meaning secret in German, giving testimony to the inherent relation of the *oikos* to the secret. In a move which dislodges the structuring force of the territory, which questions the basis for all ontopology, Derrida proposes that the friend should be thought of as 'One soul in twin bodies'.[42] Since the friend would thus have more than one place, he would never have a home of his own. Moreover, the body of the friend could always become the body of the other. This understanding of friendship, circumventing the category of the home, that which is familiar, that which is suitable, poses an alternative to a *philia* based on *oikeiotes*. The next section analyses the writings of one renowned IR academic who might argue that his model does away with Huntington's and Waltz's categories of difference and overcomes their spatial mapping of being, Francis Fukuyama.

FRANCIS FUKUYAMA

This section introduces Fukuyama's writings and works out a strand of the exemplar in his work which is slightly different from that of the preceding theorists. The section closes on a return to a Derridean critique of the exemplar.

Francis Fukuyama achieved international notoriety through the publication of a journal article entitled 'The end of history?' in the summer of 1989. His thesis was that history, understood as a struggle of competing ideologies, might have ended with the collapse of the Soviet Union. Liberal democracy had emerged triumphantly from a dialectical interplay of competing ideas and was laying the foundation for a world civilisation and history. According to him, 'what is emerging victorious . . . is not so much liberal practice, as the liberal idea'.[43] What Fukuyama required for the validity of this thesis was a holistic understanding of universal history. Through a very particular, some would say peculiar, reading of Hegel and Nietzsche he defines universal history as 'an attempt to find a meaningful pattern in the overall development of human societies generally'.[44] The central law which Fukuyama assumes in our universal history is an 'interrelationship between modern natural science and modern social organization'.[45] In simplistic terms, the argument is that only a certain type of social organisation is conducive to modern natural science. Since the advent of science is universal, it is only a matter of time until the political system which supports it best also becomes universal. As we can see, this position is opposed to Huntington's view of a clash of civilizations, where liberal democratic values are a unique aspect of Western society and not of society in general. Indeed, with regard to Islam, Fukuyama writes that 'the Islamic world would seem more vulnerable to liberal ideas in the long run than the reverse, since such liberalism has attracted numerous and powerful Muslim adherents over the past century and a half'.[46] The model of the world which Fukuyama sketches is a temporal one in which history and development are intricately intertwined. He gives an illustrative fable at the close of his book to summarise his argument on the teleology of human development. He says that with enough time, mankind will 'come to seem like a long wagon train strung out along a road'.[47] Some wagons will be getting lost, others will be attacked by Indians,[48] others will be bivouacked in the desert, but 'the great majority of wagons will be making the slow journey into town, and most will eventually arrive there'.[49] Translated back into IR, all nations and countries are developing on the same trajectory, they are simply at different places, at different times in their development. The exclusion at work in this model is the splitting of humans into 'first men' and 'last men', men who are in history and men who are at the 'end of history'.

Where in all of this could one find the exemplar at work? To be sure, Fukuyama's categorisation of the world does not rely on a spatial *oikos*, a home, or on blood lines as the preceding models do. His paradigm is not ontopological like those of Waltz and Huntington. This is because Fukuyama does not really view America or liberal democracy spatially as the other theorists do, instead he views it temporally as a stage in humanity's development – the final stage. His notion of being is thus not tied to the topographic, it is not ontopological, instead it is tied to the temporal, it is ontochronological.[50] Thus, whilst his *philia* and mode of political aggregation is without an *oikos*, without a home, it is not without *oikeios*. The exemplar in Fukuyama's model is present, he simply has a different understanding of the self which leads the exemplar to manifest itself in a different fashion. What we encounter in Fukuyama's text is an exemplar which is founded on a view of the self that is temporal, people are the same when they are in the same stage of humanity's development. The political other, in this model, is an older model of the self, he or she is an exemplar as well, but an exemplar from the past.

All of the discourses above share the logic of the exemplar. Huntington is aware of it and affirms it as the only proper politics, Waltz cements it into his systemic theory without even addressing it, and Fukuyama translates the exemplar of blood lines, of biological fraternity, into a temporal one – into an order of sequential exemplars. A question which Derrida asks that applies to all these thinkers, is what is meant when one says the brother?[51] For our political analysis, what are Huntington, Waltz and Fukuyama talking about when they devise their political systems, when they inadvertently use a model of the friend which is the, natural or spiritual, brother? And if the friend is really given to us through what is *oikeios*, which is based on the *oikos*, how then can we think of the friend in a globalising world in which it is becoming increasingly difficult to locate and define one's true home or time, to point to the place of one's being? How can friendship exist, be true to its spirit, if it is based on a schemata of the exemplar? How are we supposed to understand the emphasis on difference in these various approaches to IR when all of them have a model of the friend that is based on exemplarity? And is there a different way of thinking the international, the global and the political other than through the structure of the exemplar? Or put differently:

> [When will be ready] for an experience of freedom and equality that is capable of respectfully experiencing that friendship, which would at least be just, just beyond the law, and measured up against its measurelessness?[52]

This section located a different manifestation of the exemplar in Fukuyama's work, one that defines itself temporally and not spatially. It then returned to the cumulative Derridean critique of the exemplar. The conclusion returns to the debate at hand and attempts to dispatch our current thinking towards current events.

Supplement: By Way of Conclusion

Attempting to spare the reader a reiteration the conclusion realigns our three theorists, inquires into how our political practice in the 'War on Terror' might be haunted by theory, and calls for an IR *à venir* to circumvent these difficulties. Having traced one manifestation or another of the exemplar through all of them, a certain non-identity of the texts with themselves becomes apparent; there is a coherence and unity of the exemplar which simply does not permit the radical scansion IR courses perpetuate when they teach us contending approaches and great debates. Continuing along the theme of the exemplarity of the IR theories, one might be compelled to propose that our three IR theories represent the same structural framework of the exemplar implemented into three different modalities of time; they are exemplars of each other. Huntington works with a civilisational model which he justifies through its historical significance, he calls for a 'renewal' of Western civilisation.[53] This is a model of the exemplar that is couched in writings on blood and lineage, harking back to the natural biological order of the political world it is an exemplar that recognises itself as an exemplar of the past reasserting its relevance today. Waltz, on the other hand, focuses entirely on the present world system, finds no need to account for the origin or the disappearance of states, but simply desires to formulate a rational model of contemporary IR. He believes that this model, where the binding function of blood ties is replaced with hierarchy, is a justified abstraction of the present world – an exemplar of the present. As one might have suspected, Fukuyama's exemplar is an exemplar of the future. He looks forward and beyond genealogical blood ties of the past, to an exemplar that is temporal and based on a society's progress. Throughout the course of his text he constantly refers forwards, to the 'end of history' that is coming. At the two extremes of this spectrum, Huntington and Fukuyama, we find the two great myths of politics at work: the one stating that everything was in a good state, one which needs to be sustained or returned to, and the other exclaiming that everything will be in a good state, one which needs to be worked towards. One thing this chapter has attempted to demonstrate is that these two oppositional poles are structurally identical, they have the same form.

The question of the exemplar is crucial in IR because it gives us the foundation for *stasis* and *polemos*, and thus also the foundation for 'human' and 'not-so-human' categorisations in the political sphere. Exemplarity works as an ordering principle in IR. The presence of this exemplar leads to exclusion and gives us the distinctions of *stasis* and *polemos*, which represent the fault line of legitimate and illegitimate targets in IR. Dominant American 'War on Terror' discourse signifies targets that are acceptable: Iraqi civilians; and targets that are not: Spanish civilians. Yet this is not where the distinction ends. The recent pictures of the torture taking place at Abu Ghraib prison leave one dumbfounded at how such an atrocity could be committed, how people could stand and smile next to it, have trophy shots taken as souvenirs. One can not help but notice an uncanny resemblance to pictures taken from big game hunts, where the hunter stands smiling next to the animal, the non-human he or she has killed. Whilst the crime itself does not necessarily prove that some American forces are viewing their Iraqi inmates as subhuman, the trophy photography does. One should not believe that our theme of the exemplar, of *stasis* and *polemos*, that then translates into legitimate and illegitimate targets is not intimately related to the current 'War on Terror'. The modes of objectification and exclusion which these acts and pictures are based on are connected to our understanding of the friend as exemplar. Disturbingly, the Abu Ghraib atrocities can be justified by various modes of exclusion and distinction which exist in the above analysed theories:

1. These people are of different blood ties, they are not they same as our civilisation, this engagement does not take place within the confines of one civilisation's moral code, but functions as sheer war, as *polemos*.
2. These acts of war are committed in an international sphere of anarchy. Our internal organisation of hierarchy does not apply to this state of war.
3. These people are first men, they represent a different type of man, one that is caught within the past and forms the last obstacle to the 'end of history'.

All of these three theories produce categories of legitimate and not-so-legitimate subjects. Singularly, but particularly when combined, this structural bifurcation permits horrendous acts of war, because in all of our theoretical alternatives other is produced as an other with which friendship is categorically not possible. Friendship with the other is never possible for Huntington; only possible for Waltz when *one* state converts the international anarchy into a hierarchy, when the other is subjected; and only possible for Fukuyama when the other evolves or is colonised into the same. Furthermore, in the 'War on Terror' the enemy can be regarded as radically other: terrorists are signified as false representatives of Muslim civilisation, the terrorist is not a state, the terrorist is a hurdle to universal progress. The friend in each and every one of these traditions is always the same, never the other. But why, Samuel, Kenneth and Francis, follow in the footsteps of these annals of blood? Why not search for a different way of thinking the friend?

International Relations *à venir*: looking for where the blood tie or the spiritual tie might begin, and for where they might end, one discovers that this mode of distinction has nothing to do with actual biological or ideological connections, but much rather functions as a foundationless basis for the justification of our current modes of political aggregation and political procedures of othering. To avoid this limitation IR *à venir* must make the conceptual leap from thinking the somebody, a specific corporeal presence, to thinking the someone, a far more open entity of singularity. To avoid the exemplar's effect of exclusion as witnessed in the texts above, we need an understanding of friendship that is based on radical alterity and singularity, and not on the same. IR *à venir* would cease to distinguish between IR and ir, would recognise that the upper-case practice produces the lower-case category. It would be able to accept the perhaps, the radical uncertainty of knowledge, the 'coexistence of incompatible values'[54]. IR philosophers *à venir* would have to be 'friends of the truth'.

> But the friends of truth are not, by definition, in the truth; they are not installed there as in the padlocked security of a dogma and the stable reliability of an opinion. If there is some truth in the perhaps, it can only be that of which the friends are the friends. Only friends. The friends of truth are without the truth, even if friends cannot function without truth. The truth – that of the thinkers to come – it is impossible to be it, to be there, to have it; one must only be its friend.[55]

Most importantly IR must remain to come and never present closed, finished totalities and schemata in its representation of the world and must prepare itself for a responsibility it has not yet seen.

NOTES

1. Jacques Derrida, *The Politics of Friendship*, London: Verso, 1997, p. ix.
2. The upper-case lower-case distinction, commonly accepted in the literature, relies on a dichotomy of 'real world' and 'theory' – a distinction which is to be problematised in the course of this chapter.
3. Samuel Huntington, *The Clash of Civilizations*, New York: Touchstone, 1997.

4. Kenneth Waltz, *Theory of International Politics*, USA: McGraw-Hill, 1979.

5. Francis Fukuyama, *The End of History and the Last Man*, New York: Perennial, 2002.

6. Jenny Edkins, *Poststructuralism and International Relations*, London: Lynne Rienner, 1999.

7. For Derrida's critique of the teleological impetus of literary criticism see 'Force and signification' in Jacques Derrida, *Writing and Difference*, London: Routledge, 2002.

8. Derrida, *Politics of Friendship*, p. 31.

9. Ibid. p. 32.

10. Ibid. p. 42.

11. Ibid. p. 37.

12. Ibid. p. 38.

13. Jacques Derrida, *Limited Inc.*, Chicago, IL: Northwestern University Press, 2000), p. 14.

14. Derrida, *Politics of Friendship*, p. 38.

15. Ibid. p. 154.

16. Ibid. p. 4.

17. Ibid. p. 5.

18. Ibid. p. 154.

19. Ibid. p. 169.

20. Ibid. p. 16.

21. Huntington, *The Clash of Civilizations*, p. 20.

22. Ibid. p. 32.

23. Ibid. p. 35.

24. Ibid. p. 47.

25. Ibid. p. 42.

26. Ibid. p. 21.

27. Ibid. p. 204.

28. Carl Schmitt, *Der Begriff des Politischen*, Berlin: Duncker & Humblot, 2002, p. 29.

29. Derrida, *Politics of Friendship*, p. 99.

30. Isonomic is the making equal of individuals in front of the law, whilst isogonic is a term from geometry meaning to have or make equal angles. Our equality before the law is traced back to a racial equality.

31. Derrida, *Politics of Friendship*, p. 99

32. Ibid. p. 93.

33. Derrida's term of 'renaturalization' is similar to Jenny Edkins's use of 'depoliticization'. See Jenny Edkins, *Poststructuralism and International Relations*, London: Lynne Rienner, 1999.

34. Derrida, *Politics of Friendship*, p. 93.

35. Waltz, *Theory of International Politics*, p. 1.

36. Ibid. p. 79.

37. Ibid. p. 80.

38. Ibid. p. 93.
39. Ibid. p. 66.
40. A neologism by Derrida.
41. Derrida, *Politics of Friendship*, p. 58.
42. Ibid. p. 177.
43. Fukuyama, *The End of History and the Last Man*, p. 45.
44. Ibid. p. 55.
45. Ibid. p. 82.
46. Ibid. p. 46.
47. Ibid. p. 338.
48. The choice of the American 'Push West' and 'Indians' for this fable is crass in its colonial implications.
49. Fukuyama, *The End of History and the Last Man*, p. 339.
50. The neologism is arrived at through combining ontology with chronology.
51. Derrida, *Politics of Friendship*, p. 304.
52. Ibid. p. 306.
53. Huntington, *The Clash of Civilizations*, p. 301.
54. Derrida, *Politics of Friendship*, p. 34.
55. Ibid. p. 42.

7

Ethical Assassination? Negotiating the (Ir)responsible Decision

Dan Bulley

McGarry [Chief of Staff]:	This is the most horrifying part of your liberalism. You think there are moral absolutes.
Bartlet [President]:	There are moral absolutes.
McGarry:	Apparently not. He's killed innocent people; he'll kill more; so we have to end him. The village idiot comes to that conclusion before the Nobel Laureate.
Bartlet:	*El Principe* has justified every act of oppression.
McGarry:	This is justified. This is required.
Bartlet:	Says who?
McGarry:	Says me, Mr President. You wanna ask more people, they'll say so too.
Bartlet:	Well, a mob mentality is just –
McGarry:	Not a mob. Just you. Right now. This decision . . .[1]

It is notoriously difficult to pinpoint the moment of decision in foreign policy. Graham Allison's analysis of the United States administration's decisions in the Cuban missile crisis shows three different ways one can study these decisions, none of which can ultimately specify when and why decisions were taken.[2] The foreign policy situation quoted above appears in *The West Wing*, an American television series following the Democrat President Bartlet and his senior staff. President Bartlet holds a strong Catholic faith and is greatly troubled by his disillusioned Chief of Staff's desire to assassinate the known terrorist Abdul Shareef, a thinly veiled Bin Laden, from Qumar, the barely disguised Saudi Arabia. The dilemma, however, is that while Shareef is the Qumari defence minister, there is overwhelming evidence that he is also a leader of the Bahji terrorist network (read Al Qua'eda), guilty of terrorist attacks on the United States, including a recent attempt to blow up the Golden Gate Bridge. Using this situation provides a means of illuminating, albeit *in extremis*, the possibilities of a responsible decision and the ethical dilemmas of foreign policy. Although foreign policy is not 'made' solely by 'foreign policy makers' in any simple way, Bartlet, as McGarry points out, must assume the decision and responsibility, *at that moment*.

Traditional foreign policy analysts would almost certainly dismiss such an illustration because a fictional situation can tell us nothing about 'real life'. However, there are good reasons for not doing so. Firstly, as stated above, unlike 'real life' we *can* pinpoint the moment of decision and thus analyse the possibility of ethical negotiation. Secondly, and more importantly, we must call into question the status of this 'reality'. All foreign policy is interpreted, understood and relayed through discourse and language. There is no 'thing itself' of foreign policy, only its representation in discourse. In Derridean terms, experience can never consist of '*pure* presence but only of chains of differential marks'.[3] If there is no purely present foreign policy there can be no concrete distinction between 'reality' and 'fiction' – fiction is seen as a representation of reality, but 'reality' itself is always already a representation.

Not only is there no sure way of distinguishing fact from fiction, this play of representations means that all foreign policy can be treated as a text to be read and interpreted. Equally, however, there is no foreign policy text, or context, which can be exhaustively ring-fenced. We can never say a certain aspect of life, history or culture is irrelevant to a foreign policy decision. This is because every text, all experience, refers to, and is constituted by, other texts: all other cultural and historical life. Texts are always already *intertexts*, or spaces where representations overlap, blend and clash.[4] This does not mean that we can constitute the foreign policy situation to be discussed as real, and suspend all reference to what foreign policy analysts would call 'reality.' Rather, it increases our frame of reference, as all such 'reality' is constituted by a chain of allusions and traces which can never be totalised. A particularly fortuitous example can be taken from Peter Riddell's account of Tony Blair's foreign policy. Due to a complete inexperience of government before 1997, Blair and his team of advisers have, 'however subliminally, or even partly intentionally . . . copied the American television series *The West Wing*'.[5]

This chapter examines the links between Derridean negotiation and the apparent ethical impasse of his work, using the *The West Wing* as a constant reference and illustration. Derrida's thought shows how a future-oriented thinking of the 'ethical' can remain as open as possible, while acknowledging that the need for a decision necessitates closure. Choices must be made but must not have the character of an ultimate decision that one can be satisfied with, that one can claim was 'ethical.' Rather, to remain as open as possible, the choice must be made through *negotiation* and *invention*. Similarly, Derrida's legacy must always remain, like the decision, open, undecidable and uneasy. I will outline what I mean by negotiation, and then draw out five of its implications, in general and for foreign policy. While this will not give an 'ethical' decision, as this remains the (im)possible to-come, it crucially leaves us *open* to the 'ethical', while bestowing no 'good conscience' about our decision. To begin with, however, we must look at why Derrida's apparently debilitating philosophy[6] necessitates the making of the decision at all.

CALCULATING THE INCALCULABLE: AVOIDANCE OF THE WORST

Derrida deals with the making of decisions in his discussion of a justice beyond law in 'Force of law'. While declaring that justice exceeds law and calculation, he makes it clear that this 'should not serve as an alibi for staying out of juridico-political battles'. But why not? If our decision can never be just, what drives us to make the decision at all? If Bartlet's search for the just decision (whether or not to assassinate Shareef) can never be fulfilled, why bother with justice? His answer is worth extended quotation:

> Left to itself the incalculable and giving idea of justice is always very close to the bad, even to the worst for it can always be reappropriated by the most perverse calculation. It's always possible. And so incalculable justice *requires* us to calculate . . . Not only *must* we calculate, negotiate the relation between the calculable and the incalculable, and negotiation without the sort of rule that wouldn't have to be reinvented there where we are cast, there where we find ourselves; but we *must* take it as far as possible, beyond the place we find ourselves and beyond the already identifiable zones of morality or politics or law, beyond the distinction between national and international, public and private, and so on. This requirement does not properly belong either to justice or law.[7]

Crucially, an openness to justice cannot be an *a priori* good thing. Indeed, like the future, one can say it can only be 'anticipated in the form of an absolute danger'.[8] As incalculable and unknowable, an unconditional openness to the future-to-come of justice risks the coming of what he calls the 'worst'. By remaining absolutely open to the justice, what actually comes might be truly devastating. The most obvious figures of the 'worst', or, 'perverse calculation', are atrocities such as genocide, Nazism, xenophobia, 'ethnic cleansing'. These we can, and must, oppose or prevent. But why only these? Derrida states that what we can oppose is only those 'events that we think obstruct the future or bring death', those that *close* the future to the coming of the other.[9] We can oppose this future-present (a predictable future that will be present in time) coming then on the basis of *the future-to-come* (a future with no expectation of presence). Or, to put it perhaps too simplistically in terms of the other: we can oppose those others who prevent our openness to other others. We have a duty to guard against the coming of such a theory or idea.

But the question remains as to what makes us responsible to the other in the first place. Levinas suggests that our 'being-in-the-world', our being-as-we-are, is only conceivable in relation to, and because of, the other. Thus, the death of the other calls our very being into question.[10] Ethics in this sense precedes ontology as our responsibility to the other precedes our own being. We may say then that our commitment is to those that accept the other as other; others that allow the other to be. There is a danger, however, that this becomes foundational, treated as a grounding principle outside traditional modernist ethics on which we can build a new 'theory of ethics'. This is not the value of Derridean and Levinasian thought. They have not unearthed the absolute truth about the ethical, but rather, they take traditional ethical thinking to its limit. Whether or not a Jewish tradition is privileged over Greek, they remain within, but at the margins of, Western metaphysics. Derrida's 'responsibility [to the Other] without limits'[11] does not escape this; it does not establish itself unproblematically as a 'ground' or firm foundation outside traditional thought on which we can build a theory of ethics. Rather, his thinking of the ethical shows that we can think these things differently, while still accepting the exigency to prevent the 'worst'.

There can be no ultimate foundation for what we think is the worst. And such a foundation cannot come from outside Western metaphysics. Limit thinking is not an immovable basis for judgement of the worst, and this is why it is so dangerous and troubling. The non-basis of judgement is rather the desire to stay as open as possible while recognising that a judgement necessarily *closes*. The goal is for our closure to have the character of an opening. This opening would close to the future as *future-present*; a future that is predictable, that will come and be present, given time. But it aims to remain open to the *future-to-come*; the hopeful longing for the unpredictable, unprecedented future that can never be expected or presented. Nevertheless, every judgement remains a closure. And every closure is problematic.

While we can say that every closure is problematic, we can also *perhaps* say that not every closure is *as* problematic. The perhaps in this sentence is essential. While on the one hand, in an absolute sense every closure is as unjustifiable as any other, on the other hand, we have to make the decision, we *must* close in order to avoid the worst. Thus, while it is wrong to say that a closure is less problematic, *perhaps* some closures are more justifiable, if this is the right word. However, responsibility is not such a simple tale as this; there are further aporias (or further permutations of the same aporia). Problems rarely arise where one other simply seeks the complete annihilation of another other. President Bartlet is faced with Shareef who has killed, has been foiled in an attempt to kill, and has promised to kill more citizens.[12] Does this justify a decision to kill *him*?

Bartlet is a Catholic and believes strongly in the commandment, 'Thou shalt not kill'. He has an unconditional responsibility to his God *not* to kill Shareef. But he has a general responsibility not to allow the deaths of 'innocent' American citizens. Thus, Bartlet must make an irresponsible decision to remain absolutely responsible, or an absolutely irresponsible decision to remain generally responsible. The moral of such a tale of morality, Derrida tells us, is morality itself; that '[o]ne must behave not only in an ethical or responsible manner, but in a non-ethical, nonresponsible manner.'[13] In addition to this, of course, Bartlet retains a responsibility not just to God, but to Shareef himself *as other*. He has a general responsibility to Shareef because Bartlet's being, his being-as-he-is, is dependent upon Shareef – ethics, his responsibility to Shareef, precedes his ontology. In this way, the aporias are multiplied. There can be no simple responsibility to the other, as there is no ultimate way of judging between our responsibility for others, as '[e]very other (one) is every (bit) other'.[14] In this ethical/ontological sense, ties of nationality matter not at all; we are as responsible to every one (Shareef) as we are to every other (American citizens).

Even if Shareef did seek the annihilation of all Americans it would still be unjustifiable to kill him. After all, to return to the long quotation above from 'Force of law', whose calculation can we say is perverse, or the 'worst'? Why are we responsible to victims rather than the perpetrators of atrocities if both are equally 'other'? Who makes this decision and how can it be justified? Derrida says that incalculable justice gives us a duty to calculate, to form laws, which will always remain *different* and *irreducible* to justice itself, if there is any. The 'ethical', if by this we mean an incalculable openness to the other, contains a duty, a requirement to affirm moral norms (such as 'thou shalt not kill') but these moral norms are not the 'ethical' itself; the responsibility they enact is also irresponsible. The two (the 'ethical' and moral norms) are heterogeneous but they are linked in the same way as justice and laws, through the necessity of calculating the incalculable. However, these moral norms that we constitute cannot be anything other than context-bound affirmations *of the moment*. Ultimately, they have no transcendental foundation.

Any 'ethical' or 'just' decision, if there are any, must, through a double movement then, both refer to and suspend moral norms and laws. These norms must be conserved and destroyed.[15] The difficulty is that we must gesture in opposite directions at the same time, preserving our suspicion of existing norms and yet intervening to prevent the worst. 'Ethical' decisions cannot simply apply norms and laws as this would be to mechanically follow a programme, and not a decision at all. If Bartlet were to simply assert that it is wrong to kill under any circumstances he would not have made a decision; rather the decision was already made and he simply applied the rule/norm. But decisions also cannot entirely destroy such norms as this would beckon in the possibility of killing under any circumstances. Thus, each time a norm or law is affirmed, it must also be *reinvented*. One must re-justify its use each and every time *as if* the moral norm were invented then and there. Thus, we are not mechanically following a rule, rather we *invent* the rule, norm or law, each time.[16] We must also take this invention *as far as possible*, while always recognising the urgency of the decision. The just decision never waits for extended contemplation, it is always required immediately in its interruption of knowledge through openness to the other.[17]

NEGOTIATION AND ITS IMPLICATIONS

The last sentence of the long 'Force of law' quotation above says that this injunction to calculate the incalculable cannot properly belong to law or justice, norms or ethics. What can we name this non-space of invention between the two then, and what does it involve? Following Derrida closely we can call it a *negotiation*. The word 'negotiation' comes from the Latin *negotium*, 'no-leisure'. Derrida sees this '[u]n-leisure' as the 'impossibility of stopping or settling in a position . . . establishing oneself anywhere'. Its best figure is that of a shuttle, going back and forth between different positions.[18] This concept of the shuttle is that of the undecidable, but the undecidable is strictly *not* indeterminacy. Rather the limits of the shuttle are known, as undecidability is 'always a *determinate* oscillation between possibilities'.[19] In the foreign policy situation being discussed, the limits of the shuttle are between determinate options: the assassination of Shareef or not; the responsibility to Shareef and that to American citizens; the unconditional responsibility to God/moral norms and a general responsibility.

Of course, when one says 'negotiation' one thinks of compromise and impurity, and Derrida acknowledges this: 'Negotiation is impure'. Purity is, after all, an impossibility: any responsible decision is irresponsible; any moral decision immoral. Thus, the necessary contamination that results from negotiation is 'in the name of purity'.[20] The name of this purity, the duty of all negotiation, even its 'categorical imperative', is, of course, 'to let the future have a future, to let or make it come, or, in any case, to leave the possibility of the future open'.[21] Thus, negotiation must be 'everything but a position or an assurance', as these would close. Rather, negotiation is that which is left over after all knowledge, science and calculation have been exhausted.[22] After this cursory commentary on the word five far from exhaustive implications can be drawn.

Avoiding assurance

First, this un-leisure means that we can never make a decision that will satisfy or assure, that will allow us to relax. One can never know whether or not one has been responsible, whether one has made a responsible decision. If we did, this would be an assurance, a closing-off to the future. Our decision is always a closure, but never an unproblematic closure. Thus, 'one cannot have a good conscience'.[23] There is never a time when we can say with confidence, 'I have been just/responsible/ethical', only that we have acted in accordance with law, or moral norms whose very founding defer the problem of justice, responsibility and the 'ethical'.[24]

Good conscience merely denotes that we have acted irresponsibly and unethically by reducing such notions to that which they must exceed.[25] Bartlet's Chief of Staff, Leo McGarry, *appears* at least relatively sure of the responsible decision: the assassination of Shareef he says, is justified and required. But the only way of gaining such certainty is to ignore the excess of the concept of responsibility, that is, its irresponsibility. Our politico-ethical decisions must always then be surrounded by a 'perpetual uneasiness',[26] because negotiation is about gesturing in opposite directions at the same time; affirming both the absolute/unconditional *and* the conditional.

Negotiating the non-negotiable

Secondly, we can say that negotiation cannot be between things that can be negotiated.[27] If there is an easy resolution of two positions in a third, we are within the realm of dialectical reasoning and a privileging of presence; leisure, not un-leisure. The third position closes, it rests, it is satisfied. The double bind of deconstruction, on the other hand, is exactly a double duty to two incompatible imperatives.[28] Thus, it can never rest. Deconstructive negotiation can only happen between non-negotiables: 'negotiation is always negotiation of the non-negotiable'.[29] The *Oxford English Dictionary* confirms that if something is negotiable it is, 'open to discussion or modification', thus it is 'able to be traversed; passable'. But the problem of ethics and the 'ethical' is precisely that it is *impassable*. It is an aporia; a dilemma with an irresolvable, internal contradiction. We cannot justify our sacrificing of one other for other others, God for Americans, or Shareef for American citizens. Negotiation must negotiate the aporia, this is its 'aporetic fatality'.[30]

But crucially this fatality is not a fatalism. Fatalism would be to say that, due to this aporia, discussions of the 'ethical' have no place in foreign policy. Ethics demands the retention of the unconditional, foreign policy can only ever refer to the conditional; one is riven with paralysing paradoxes and ambiguities, the other must be certain and unequivocal. Thus, an 'ethical foreign policy', a truly responsible decision, is simply condemned to unconditional 'idealism' which can have no place in the real world. Deconstruction, on the other hand, negotiates precisely this which cannot be negotiated. For all those who would like to see discussions of the 'ethical' in foreign policy, who would like to hear a debate on making 'responsible' decisions, we can concur with Derrida: deconstruction is a 'stroke of luck for politics' and for 'all historical progress'.[31] Precisely because the duty of deconstruction is to negotiate the non-negotiable, deconstructive thought is precisely what the study of 'difficult cases', such as ethics and foreign policy, needs.

In the example from *The West Wing*, Bartlet must negotiate between the unconditional duty not to kill, and the conditional: the knowledge that obeying such an imperative would be sacrificing others. There is no third position; we cannot escape either responsibility. But he must also negotiate between what he knows and what he does not. This means bearing in mind what Donald Rumsfeld might call the known unknowns 'what we know we do not know', and potentially the unknown unknowns 'what we do not know we do not know':[32] what will this do to the moral standing of America? What will happen when Qumar finds out? How many will die if the assassination leads to war with Qumar? What will this do to Bartlet's electoral prospects approaching the Presidential election? As the fourth series unfolds some of these unknowns become known: Qumar accuses Israel of assassinating Shareef; this is used as an excuse to kill the Israeli foreign minister and to provoke a war with Israel; and Bartlet's daughter is kidnapped by a Bahji terrorist cell, leaving him to invoke the 25th Amendment and step down briefly as President.

All of these factors point to the fact that foreign policy is incalculable. The future cannot be known, it exceeds knowledge and scientific calculation.

Negotiation is *both* this need to calculate the incalculable, to try and prevent the coming of the worst (for Bartlet this would presumably be the detonation of a chemical/biological/nuclear weapon in the United States mainland), *and* that which exceeds calculation. Without reference to this latter, unknowable aspect there is no openness to the future and no responsibility taken (as the decision will be simply a calculation, a pre-ordained result of an applied rule). However, Derridean thought does not suspend all reference to these 'real' world conditions, but rather confirms that it is precisely between the two irreducible, but indissociable, poles of the unconditional and the conditional that negotiation, and thus the decision, must take place.[33]

Retaining risk

Thirdly, we can say that negotiation always retains an essential element of risk. Negotiation, I said, was the need to calculate, but also that which exceeds calculation. It is this excess, this necessary openness that contains the risk. As we have said, the future can only be anticipated as an absolute danger and our negotiation must always be future-oriented. In trying to think differently and retaining a reference to absolutes, one opens oneself up to risks, even to the worst. This danger must not be played down or deconstructive thought 'made safe'. A negotiated decision by Bartlet would not avoid the unknowns which then take place, and its openness allows the possibility of the worst. But if we take no risks then, as Derrida observes, 'we do nothing, and nothing happens'.[34]

The two non-deconstructive options appear less risky but are fundamentally negative: one could simply deny the aporia by artificially simplifying concepts such as the ethical (as either conditional or unconditional); or one could acknowledge the aporia and conclude that ethics and responsibility have no place in foreign policy. We must not deny the risk we run in negotiation, but without taking such risks things can get even worse. Worse still, says Derrida, this is 'the worst along with good conscience',[35] as one is satisfied that one has made the best decision with the second option, and/or acted ethically and responsibly with the first. The difference is that, with a deconstructive negotiation, the risk run can be experienced 'both as a threat *and as a chance*',[36] a chance of avoiding the worst.

Inventing the (im)possible

Fourthly, then negotiation is not just about oscillating between alternatives, it is about transaction and *invention*.[37] The openness to the future enabled by this unsatisfied oscillation between absolutes, between the singular and general, the unconditional and conditional, allows the possibility of an invention and thinking of what remains unthought. But both points must always be retained. Retaining what Derrida calls an unconditional 'hyperbolic' ethical vision of his concepts keeps us always 'torn' (always with a bad conscience, un-leisure, perpetual uneasiness), but allows the possibility to 'inflect politics', to change things, to think differently, to invent.[38]

Derrida observes that we cannot derive a politics from his unconditional hyperbolic principles such as justice, or ethical hospitality to the *arrivant*. But he goes on to say that what must be rethought is the traditional notion of politics.[39] The 'political' itself must be politically negotiated and invented. Negotiation is about maintaining the space for the play of *différance*, for play as *jeu*. This *jeu* is not complete freeplay of undecidability, but an inventive space which can lead to change, to creation. The invention will not, however, be of the same order as a dialectical resolution. There will be no third term presented which settles opposition. Rather such an invention of *différance* must itself preserve the space of play for new inventions. What Derrida tries to think then is the risk-ridden *unprecedented*. Of course, there can be no *absolute* unprecedented, as everything is formed by repetition and iterability, but it is only by confronting this paradox that one can 'think the unthought'.[40]

This is all rather abstract, but it can be helpfully illustrated by Derrida's thinking on international institutions, and the invention of the new International. International institutions are obviously imperfect, but this does not mean they should be abandoned. Rather they must be rethought, negotiated, even *re-invented*. Derrida begins to do this through a thinking of a new International, where we can see him actively negotiate the very terms of its coming. Words such as 'solidarity' and 'community' between 'citizens', 'political subjects' or 'human beings' are avoided because of their connotations – what they differ/defer back to. Instead, he aspires to a *bond* between *singularities* all over the world, which extends beyond the very concepts of nation and state. If we feel a bond to a singular Croat, Bosnian, Ukrainian and so on then, it is neither that of one citizen to another, or between two 'citizens of the world':

> No, what binds me to these people is something different than membership in a world nation-state or in an international community . . . there is a bond, but this bond cannot be contained within the traditional concepts of community, obligation, or responsibility – is a protest against citizenship, a protest against membership in a political configuration as such. The bond is, for example, a form of political solidarity opposed to the political *qua* a politics tied to the nation-state.[41]

Such a 'bond' he says elsewhere can only be one without name, co-ordination, party or institution.[42] This 'New International' is exactly what 'demands thought and negotiation'.[43]

A 'New International' will always be improvable and perfectible. This (im)possible invention through negotiation is not simply a resolution or a closure, but a remaining open. Derrida's language in the long quotation above exhibits the necessarily pained and awkward nature of his negotiation. It is as tortured as any 'policy' that can result from it. A foreign policy that negotiates and remains open to the ethical can never be present, 'set in stone', or a set of rules to be applied to situations as they arise. But, equally, it cannot be a constantly deferred decision, a waiting for a possible future-present.

The (un)ethical and the (ir)responsible

Fifthly, the final implication I wish to draw is that, as implied above, even a foreign policy that resists programming, that negotiates and remains open to the 'ethical' is not, and can never be, an ethical foreign policy. Whether the decision to assassinate Shareef is negotiated or not, whether it remains open, never satisfied and invents itself in that moment or not, it will never *be* ethical or responsible. This is because negotiation is not *the ethical*. The relation between the two is, says Derrida, very complicated.[44] Negotiation can be conceived as an *ethos*, a manner of being, a 'moral tyranny' weighing down upon one. But it is not the 'ethical' *itself*. This is because, firstly, while negotiation must retain the reference to the 'ethical', the 'ethical' itself must remain of the order of the un-presentable, like justice, democracy and hospitality. Secondly, this is because negotiation always contains calcula-tion. It partakes of the duty to calculate the incalculable, but cannot itself be of the order of the incalculable, *because it calculates*. While negotiation necessarily *exceeds* calculation,[45] thus allowing space for *différance* and the play of invention, it none the less must calculate in order to avoid the worst. Neither can negotiation be termed a 'provisional morality' as this has the danger of becoming a traditional interpretation of the 'ethical' and implies a waiting for the 'fully ethical' decision.[46]

Rather the place of negotiation is the proper place of the *political*, which must both calculate and exceed calculation, must both strive for presence and remain unpresentable.[47] John Caputo observes that politics 'will never be what Levinas calls ethics' and what Derrida calls unconditional hospi-tality, or justice. This is because 'what he calls ethics does not exist but is a kind of hyperbolic demand on existence'.[48] While Caputo is right, I would maintain that a rethought, deconstructive concept of the political is not wholly separable from the 'ethical', because it always retains a reference to it. Thus, we can see why the term 'ethico-political' is so useful. Negotiation is properly the place of the ethico-political.

CONCLUSION: NEGOTIATING ASSASSINATION

This chapter has pulled together Derrida's thinking on the (im)possible ethically responsible decision through the notion of negotiation. Far from leaving us to 'wait and see', the messianic incalculability of justice and the 'ethical' commands us to decide, to calculate and negotiate against the worst outcome, though we can never be sure in our judgement of the worst. Several implications of negotiation must be kept in mind. The concept means avoiding all assurance and 'good conscience' as it seeks to paradoxically negotiate the non-negotiable and invent the (im)possible unprecedented decision. These paradoxes mean that one can never escape risk with negotiation and show that any decision, even a negotiated determination, will always be unethical as well as ethical, irresponsible as well as responsible. Negotiation is, therefore, the place of the ethico-political, and suited to the (im)possible decisions of foreign policy.

But what does this mean for Bartlet's decision: whether or not to assassinate Shareef? Chief of Staff, Leo McGarry, gives the traditional view of foreign policy. He has abandoned notions of an unconditional morality and presents the decision as simple (a decision the 'village idiot' makes before Bartlet, the 'Nobel laureate'). For McGarry, it is a matter of the application of knowledge, a programmed response. Bartlet, on the other hand, affirms moral absolutes. He alone must make the decision, as McGarry points out, but he also is the only one capable of negotiating the aporia of the 'ethical', due to his retained reference to absolutes.

None the less, McGarry is himself correct in observing that Bartlet's liberalism is truly 'horrifying'. Simply put, retaining these unconditionals could well usher in the 'worst' – the deaths of thousands of 'innocent' Americans. This is reminiscent of the scandalous story of Abraham, who sacrifices his responsibility to his son Isaac to be absolutely responsible to God. In doing so, as Derrida observes, Abraham is at once the most immoral and the most moral of men, the most responsible and the most irresponsible.[49] Bartlet spends the following twenty-four hours in pained, tortuous negotiation, shuttling between the unconditionals and conditionals, the known and the unknowns, the calculable and the incalculable, none of which he can fully satisfy.

Finally, two minutes before the decision has to be taken, the following exchange ensues:

Bartlet:	It's just wrong. It's absolutely wrong.
McGarry:	I know. But you have to do it anyway.
Bartlet:	Why?
McGarry:	Because you won.
	[Long pause]
Bartlet:	Take him.[50]

In the end, the decision has to be made. Bartlet calculates the incalculable, even though it is 'absolutely wrong', in order to guard against the worst. He remains deeply troubled, and cannot settle to having made the 'ethical', responsible, just decision. While we, like Bartlet, cannot say he has acted 'ethically' (he has always already acted unethically) in assassinating Shareef we can say that he alone in this situation has truly sought a negotiation and invention. He alone remains open to the 'ethical'.

Using The West Wing has partly been a matter of cheating the foreign policy analysts. It has given us a key into what many traditional analysts would love to know – the minds of the foreign policy makers. It has allowed us to see what this un-leisure of negotiation might look like, what it is to be 'torn' by two imperatives. Crucially, however, even in this situation, one can never know whether a negotiation has taken place. But does this matter? The aim of this chapter, and of all Derrida's work is not to accuse, judge and punish. Unlike so many of Derrida's critics when he was alive, and now that he is dead, deconstructive thought contains a generosity which seeks to avoid Nietzschean ressentiment. It does not matter that we cannot 'know' whether an ethico-political negotiation has taken place in the minds of real statesmen, because we are not trying to accuse them or hold them responsible. Rather this chapter enacts a negotiative ethos, both with foreign policy and with Derrida's legacy: shuttling, remaining uneasy and searching for the invention of new possibilities.

NOTES

1. 'We Killed Yamamoto', The West Wing, Series 3, Episode 21, written by Aaron Sorkin, directed by Thomas Schlamme, USA: Warner Brothers, 2001-2.
2. G. Allison and P. Zelikow, Essence of Decision: Explaining the Cuban Missile Crisis (2nd edn), New York: Longman, 1999.
3. J. Derrida, 'Signature event context', in Derrida, Limited Inc, Evanston, IL: Northwestern University Press, 1988, p. 10.
4. J. Der Derian, Antidiplomacy: Spies, Terror, Speed and War, Oxford: Blackwell, 1992, p. 27.
5. P. Riddell, Hug Them Close: Blair, Clinton, Bush and the 'Special Relationship' (Revised edn), London: Politico's, 2004, p. 9.

6. See S. Critchley, *The Ethics of Deconstruction: Derrida & Levinas*, Oxford: Blackwell, 1992, pp. 189–90.
7. J. Derrida, 'Force of Law: "The mystical foundations of authority"', in D. Cornell, M. Rosenfeld and D. G. Carlson (eds), *Deconstruction and the Possibility of Justice*, London: Routledge, 1992, p. 28.
8. J. Derrida, *Of Grammatology*, Baltimore, MD: Johns Hopkins University Press, 1976, p. 5.
9. J. Derrida, in J. Derrida and B. Stiegler, *Echographies of Television: Filmed Interviews*, Oxford: Polity Press, 2002, p. 11.
10. E. Levinas, 'Ethics as first philosophy', in S. Hand (ed.), *The Levinas Reader*, Oxford: Blackwell, 1989, pp. 82–3.
11. J. Derrida, 'Force of Law', p. 19.
12. This intelligence is ascertained earlier in the episode of this chapter's opening exchange.
13. J. Derrida, *The Gift of Death*, Chicago, IL: University of Chicago Press, 1996, pp. 67–8.
14. Ibid. p. 68.
15. Derrida, 'Force of law', p. 23.
16. Ibid. p. 23.
17. Ibid. p. 26.
18. J. Derrida, *Negotiations: Interventions and Interviews 1971–2001*, Stanford, CA: Stanford University Press, 2002, p. 12.
19. Derrida, *Limited Inc*, p. 148.
20. Derrida, *Negotiations*, p. 14.
21. Derrida, *Echographies*, p. 85.
22. Derrida, *Negotiations*, p. 195.
23. Ibid. p. 232.
24. Derrida, 'Force of law', p. 14.
25. Derrida, *The Other Heading: Reflections on Today's Europe*, Bloomington, IN: Indiana University Press, 1992, p. 81.
26. J. Derrida, in 'Dialogue with Jacques Derrida', in R. Kearney, *Dialogues with Contemporary Continental Thinkers: The Phenomenological Heritage*, Manchester: Manchester University Press, 1984, p. 120.
27. Derrida, *Negotiations*, p. 304.
28. Ibid. p. 13.
29. Ibid. p. 304.
30. Ibid. p. 304.
31. Derrida, 'Force of law' p. 14.
32. Cited in J. Edkins and M. Zehfuss (2003), 'Generalising the international', *Review of International Studies*, 31:452 (note 3).
33. J. Derrida, *On Cosmopolitanism and Forgiveness*, London: Routledge, 2001, p. 45.
34. Derrida, *Negotiations*, p. 238.
35. Ibid. pp. 178–9.

36. Derrida, *Echographies*, p. 65, [emphasis added].

37. Ibid. p. 81.

38. Derrida, *On Cosmopolitanism*, p. 51.

39. Derrida, *Echographies*, p. 17.

40. Derrida, *Negotiations*, p. 238.

41. Ibid. p. 240.

42. J. Derrida, *Specters of Marx: The State of the Debt, the Work of Mourning & the New International*, New York: Routledge, 1994, pp. 85–6.

43. Derrida, *Negotiations*, p. 241.

44. Ibid. p. 15.

45. Ibid. p. 13.

46. J. Derrida, ' "Eating well," or the calculation of the subject: an interview with Jacques Derrida', in E. Cadava, P. Connor and J.-L. Nancy (eds), *Who Comes After The Subject?*, New York: Routledge, 1991, p. 117.

47. Derrida, *Negotiations*, pp. 178–9.

48. J. D. Caputo, *Against Ethics*, Bloomington, IN: Indiana University Press, 1993, p. 120.

49. Derrida, *The Gift of Death*, p. 23.

50. 'Posse Comitatus', *The West Wing*, Series 3, Episode 22, written by Aaron Sorkin, directed by Thomas Schlamme, USA: Warner Brothers, 2001–2.

8

Exploiting the Ambivalence of a Crisis: A Practitioner reads 'Diversity Training' through Homi Bhabha

April R. Biccum

INTRODUCTION

Couched in a theoretical trajectory from Derrida to Homi Bhabha, this paper makes a case for the knowing and purposeful exploitation of ambivalences in the public discourses and spaces of authority. My intention in this chapter is to negotiate the legacy of Derrida through his inflection in the scholarship of post-colonial theorists, in particular Gayatri Spivak and Homi Bhabha. Using my own experience as a 'diversity trainer' in the voluntary sector as a case study, I propose a pedagogical and political strategy which is inflected and made possible by Derrida's legacy. In the ambivalent national scene of a liberal democracy forced to legislate for legitimacy's sake against its own institutional racism, the chapter will read, through Homi Bhabha, a pattern of responses of participating members of British civil society to 'anti-racist' training. The chapter contends that this is an example which shows both how certain ambivalences in the workings of civil society and public discourse *can be* exploited (in this case through the use of pedagogy and compliance with new race relations legislation) and suggests that exploiting ambivalences is a political strategy particularly appropriate for this historical moment. Thus, contrary to claims regarding the dearth of politics in post-structuralist thinking, this might be a way of negotiating Derrida's legacy and reorienting it towards praxis.

Allow me first to begin by contextualising what I regard as the British national scene. There is a profound and ambivalent slippage in the question: what does it mean to be a British citizen[1] when it connotes not only the politico-socio-legal context for the current moment, but carries within it the haunting spectre of Britain's colonial past, of which the issue of migration, migrant communities, multi-culturalism, community cohesion and race relations is a pesky and continuous, if perpetually suppressed, reminder. Global citizenship has been included as the newest thread in PSHE education, promoted by the Department for International Development (DFID), at the same time that the nation's borders are closing down for the rather more specific citizenships of people from countries like Iraq and Afghanistan. Development Education has been introduced via the proliferation of Development Education Centres around the United Kingdom and a guidance for educators has been produced by DFID titled 'The Global Dimension' (replete with web-based resources) which encourages the education of Britain's ethnically diverse youth to value the 'global interconnectedness' of today's global society in a way that reifies neo-liberal forms of global governance and simultaneously celebrates 'British' heritage in a way that is silent around the legacy of colonialism.[2]

There is a deep ambivalence (in Bhabha's sense) for a liberal democratic nation state forced to legislate, for legitimacy's sake, against its own institutional racism. There is an even deeper ambivalence around the ways in which an institutionally racist society enforces its own legislation against the racism of its institutions. The current paradoxical climate of border paranoia, global migration and foreign intervention has sharpened the ambivalence of public spaces and created, I would argue, unique opportunities for their exploitation for the purposes of creating spaces amenable to the production of what Gayatri Spivak has formerly called 'transnational literacy'.[3] The possibility for exploiting ambivalent spaces in an educational context occur both in the form of changes to the national curriculum with the introduction of a 'global dimension', in the proliferation of Development Education, and in public sector responses to changes in the Race Relations (Amendment) Act 2000. Compliance to the latter is often being sought, in Arun Kundnani's words, with 'the same old palliative measures' in the form of diversity, anti-racist or awareness raising training.[4] This chapter, therefore, is a practitioner's exploration into and reading of 'diversity training' as an ambivalent space in this current and paradoxical context of minority rights and immigration crises, international security, terror wars and millennial development. I will read my own experience of 'diversity training' through the theoretical tools provided by Homi Bhabha, exploring by way of this example the implications for bringing national narratives and subjectivities to crisis, and showing both the way that the ambivalence of pedagogical, political spaces and rights-based discourse can be exploited, and also the *necessity* of their exploitation as a (and note the singular) political strategy predicated upon a post-structuralist epistemology.

POST-COLONIAL THEORY AND THE LEGACY OF DERRIDA

Broadly speaking, post-colonial theory is what has happened, as the result of the post-war migration, when 'Third World' intellectuals entered metropolitan academies and began to alter traditional fields of study around literature and culture. What occurred was a simultaneous reconsideration of the subject matter, perspective and assumptions of conventional European and American disciplines in the study of literature and the human sciences, in tandem with the introduction of perspectives and literatures of the 'post'-colonial diaspora and South. A shift in the study of literature occurred, along with a whole host of studies looking at colonial discourse and culture, starting with Said's now notorious *Orientalism*.[5] Edward Said, Homi Bhabha and Gayatri Spivak, dubbed by Robert Young the 'Holy Trinity',[6] are not only the three most well known post-colonial scholars, they are also largely responsible for the 'turn to theory' of the 1980s[7] and the taking up of the work Foucault, Derrida and Lacan for informing their analysis of colonial culture and discourse.

My approach and analysis in this piece has been influenced by two members of the 'holy trinity', Homi Bhabha and Gayatri Spivak. Bhabha is not as closely associated with the work of Derrida as Gayatri Spivak, who has written the introduction to the English translation of *Of Grammatology* and has made a career of employing deconstructive reading. Nevertheless, for my purposes, Homi Bhabha provides highly useful and easily applicable analytical tools that are inflected by Derrida's notions of the other/alterity, duality and double gesture and the time/space dimension of deferral,[8] which means that despite the authoritative attempt to iterate a logocentre and make it stick there is always a slippage and a deferral of fixity and meaning, always the potential within colonial discourses for disruption within its own 'logic'. Bhabha's theorisation of colonial discourse is in fact and more importantly a theorisation of the operation and discursive functioning of colonial power and culture. For Bhabha, the inflection of Derrida can be read in his foregrounding of ambivalence in the culture and discourse of empire, and the ambivalence and instability of public and national narratives and discourses of authority. Part of Bhabha's work is attendant on the discursive structure of colonial culture, and the other part is attendant on the instability of national narratives which of necessity will unravel as they are rewritten from the margins by post-colonial migrants. Bhabha makes use of popular cultural artefacts such as the film *Handsworth Songs* and the novels of Salmon Rushdie as moments which illustrate how the narrative of the United Kingdom as nation-state are interrupted by narratives which reinscribe colonial history in the cultural production of its post-colonial migrants. The memory of colonial history undergoes a desperate disavowal in public consciousness, and this is integral to what Spivak has famously called 'sanctioned ignorance'.[9] It is this disavowal in the national narrative which for Bhabha belies the structural incompleteness of 'White' British national culture, an idea which maps onto Derrida's notion of deferral and closure,[10] and it is this structural incompleteness which bears the potential for disruption through the cultural production of post-colonial migrants.

In *The Location of Culture* and his edited anthology *Nation and Narration*, Bhabha plays on all of these themes of nation, narrative, location, home and domesticity, focusing both on how these narratives function and on the ways in which they are disrupted. For Bhabha these narratives are not fixed or intransient but rather are in continual and repetitive (re)production and circulation, and this movement and transience is both the source of their power and the source of their fissure and ambivalence. Taking his inference from Derrida, there is for Bhabha no fixed presence behind the practice of colonial authority, rather, like Derrida's notion of the 'supplement', there is a double gesture of staging and framing the repetitive iteration of presence, originality, supremacy, which is perpetually threatened with its own exposure as text, as construction, in the very act of attempting to fix its own authority. Thus, the narratives which make the colonial relation possible, such as teleological narratives of history and modernity, the notions of supremacy which underpin the idea of development-cum-civility, repeat, Bhabha says, furiously, uncontrollably.[11] For Bhabha, just as for Derrida, there is a contradictory duality or ambivalence around which colonial discourse is conceptually organised and which both enables it to signify and is the point of fissure at which it can be deconstructed. If we apply Bhabha's conceptual framework to development discourse, by way of example,[12] we can see that the idea of development-as-civility is a narrative which inscribes the British national narrative, and must enunciate itself in the ambivalent scene of development education and signify according to the articulation of its opposite, un(under)developed, developing or poor nations. Thus, two terms, two narratives, development-as-civility and poverty-as-degeneracy, must be paradoxically articulated simultaneously and yet kept structurally separate while at the same time there is a need within development education to promote the idea of interconnectedness as an inevitable result of globalisation. What I describe here, therefore, is an ambivalent national scene rife with possibility for the exploitation of what is an unavoidable ambivalence, a space in which the development education practitioner can force the two terms to collide, revealing their structural link, belying their staging as narrative, producing a space in which a connection can be made between the poverty of the global South and the 'development' of the global North. Thus, Gyan Prakash in 'Postcolonial criticism and Indian histor-iography' provides a useful summation of Bhabha's approach:

> Bhabha's analysis of colonial discourse at the point of its stress departs from the strategy of reversal practised by previous criticism. For, at these moments of indeterminacy, when the discourse can be seen to veer away from the implacable logic of oppositionality, the critic can intervene, and using historical work as a licence for a strategy of critical reading, re-negotiate the terms of the discourse . . . Bhabha reads this heterogeneity in the native re-writing of the colonial text, in those 'hybrid' moments when the colonised produce not a copy of the original but misappropriate it, thereby re-formulating the master text, exposing its ambivalence and denying its authority. From this point of view, categories of racial, class, ethnic, gender and national difference arise not as the result of a well-intentioned liberal gesture but as social identifications found at the point of colonialism's conflictual and contingent mode of functioning.[13]

My suggestion is that Bhabha's Derridean inflected emphasis on colonial discourse at its point of fissure provides moments not only for subaltern reappropriation, but also for the conscious exploitation of ambivalence by those in public spaces with a post-structuralist sense of how the discourse functions. Therefore, by providing analytical tools which signal how colonial power and subjectivity operates, Bhabha and Spivak (and Edward Said, though I won't discuss his contribution here) have done something potentially dangerous. The danger, for colonial subjects, in knowing how colonial power operates and how colonial subjectivity is produced is that *we might recognise ourselves in it*.

One of the many differences between Bhabha and Spivak is that while Bhabha has implied that his privileged position is interchangeable with the position of all 'post-colonial' migrants, Spivak has attended to her position as migrant intellectual as one of privilege.[14] Following Spivak then, my contention with respect to Bhabha's reading strategies is that the cultural artefacts which Bhabha celebrates as 'new', hybrid, incommensurate and disruptive, are themselves commodities produced for the very system of circulation and exchange which is productive of the violence in the first place. Moreover, the stratified politics of post-colonial migration is largely absent from Bhabha's analysis. In fact, it could be argued that the radical or disruptive potential of cultural production such as film and literature is always already mitigated by the commodification of narrative of which they are an expression. In this sense capitalism quite literally *houses*, as a metaphor for containment, the possibility of its own dissent. Also contentious in Bhabha is that the cultural products he celebrates as inherently disruptive are produced by and large by middle-class post-colonial migrants and they most likely appeal to educated bourgeois sections of the United Kingdom populace already celebratory of a liberal multiculturalism and that they don't necessarily reach a popular consciousness in the United Kingdom. Therefore, these supposed disruptions in the fabric of British national narrative and public life in the form of cultural production by post-colonial migrants do not do the work which Bhabha ascribes to them in the popular consciousness. Rather, they exist alongside national narratives, as various commodified narratives appealing to different sectors of the market. Hence, there is a need for a more active rewriting of the nation from within pedagogical/public spaces in which colonial history can be reinscribed and the British national narrative can be called into question. This is why I suggest that the conscious exploitation of ambivalence is also a necessity.

In contrast to Bhabha, Spivak places an emphasis on complicity as a place from which to develop a more responsible intellectual practice, one which questions the authority of the investigating subject because it is always and ever alert to the relationship between knowledge, discourse, material relations and power. Thus, one of Spivak's many Derridean inflections is the idea that we are 'obliged to inhabit that which we critique',[15] and that there is no outside, a-institutional space from which to critique the colonial text. The critic's attention should, therefore, be not only on the material and discursive function of power, but also on the critic's own locus of enunciation within the very apparatus of knowledge production.[16] Thus, Spivak insists that instead of speaking for 'the oppressed', that those in a position of power should learn to learn from the other,[17] and her work takes on a more explicitly pedagogical tone. In Spivak's project of 'unlearning' she has articulated a pedagogical praxis aimed at challenging the 'sanctioned ignorance' of Western academic paradigms and regimes of knowledge production. Her emphasis is on recognising how dominant representations in world history, literature and media encourage people to forget about the 'Third World', and on a strategy of using privilege against itself.[18] This 'sanctioned ignorance' or 'blindspot'[19] is what the field of post-colonial studies loosely terms an elision, or writing out, or what Bhabha terms a split and doubling, or a distancing and differentiation of the binary couplet. From the perspective of a critical pedagogy, unlearning in Spivak's sense keeps the investigating subject from universalising her own subject position and is, therefore, strategically/methodologically counter to the imperial project which functions according to the logic of the (imperfect, incomplete and perpetually deferred) universalisation of a specific – Western, rational, (white) – subjectivity.

Thus, a kind of post-colonial pedagogy emerges in Spivak's work that gestures towards a critical pedagogy in that it takes as its starting point an attention to 'self' as a site of knowledge production. This is a kind of pedagogical and political praxis explicitly taken up in the 'new' culture of politics at the World Social Forum.[20] In her discussions of the 'open space' methodology in a pedagogy inspired by the radical democracy of the World Social Forum, Vanessa Andreotti describes a post-colonial pedagogy as a praxis which is inflected by the work of Spivak, Foucault, Bhabha, Said, Derrida and the later work of Paolo Freire.

> This pedagogical strategy implies a recognition that the 'Empires' we would like to change do not exist only outside of us – their violence operates in a complex way and is reproduced on a daily basis even by the people who see themselves as the ones who are challenging them. These empires have historically shaped the way we see the world, the way we think and the way we relate to others. In a pedagogical process, this recognition demands a productive acknowledgement of complicity with 'the system' and shifts the focus of the intervention from a politics of hostility (of 'us versus them') towards a politics of 'friendship to come' (or 'us all').[21]

Andreotti argues that this set of skills and knowledge about oneself, one's narrative production and a relativisation of narratives which attempt to account for how and why the world is the way it is and how and why it should remain or be organised otherwise is called 'transnational literacy'. This recognition that 'teachers and learners have and construct their own knowledge and that all knowledge is partial and incomplete'[22] is the necessary first step in Spivak's pedagogical strategy of learning to learn from below, and it is this strategy I attempted to employ in my work as 'diversity trainer' which produced 'mixed results' as I shall explore below.

THE CONSCIOUS EXPLOITATION OF AMBIVALENCE – READING DIVERSITY TRAINING THROUGH HOMI BHABHA

My example of the conscious exploitation of ambivalence comes from three years' work in a black voluntary sector organisation. This organisation occupied precisely the sort of ambivalent and divisive position that the government funding of grass-roots politics effected throughout the 1980s which is described by Arun Kundnani in 'The death of multi-culturalism'.[23] That is, by way of a progressive process of submitting grass-roots activity on the part of migrant communities to an enclosure into civil society funding schemes, the voluntary sector comprises a sanctioned elite claiming to speak on behalf of diverse communities and a 'social exclusion industry' that functions largely according to a logic of assimilation and capacity building. My job as 'diversity trainer' was to facilitate the responses of public and voluntary sector organisations to new race relations legislation which anxiously owned up to the existence of 'institutional racism'. My job, as I read it, therefore, was to engage directly with the creation and interpolation of British national narratives in varying degrees and to prompt the kind of transnational literacy described above. My intention was to employ as far as I was able the critical pedagogical, or 'open space' methodology described above in reference to the World Social Forum, and to exploit this ambivalence in the same way I described is possible for development education. These were my ambitious and idealistic aims, which were perpetually complicated and perhaps mitigated by the desires and expectations of soliciting organisations, who most often wanted quick-fix formulae which would extricate them from any future accusation of institutional racism while changing their working practices and organisational structure and culture as little as possible. It was this ambivalence I worked at 'pushing' or exploiting, even if only with limited and incalculable success or failure.

Some of the training occurred in the north of Nottinghamshire, which is dominated by mostly white, former mining communities, disenfranchised and where there is strong nationalist and far-right activity. When not in these localities, my participants were largely white, educated members of civil society at both service and management levels. My pedagogical methodology frequently centred around the use of images as a way of taking the onus off my participants, providing a stimulus and an opportunity to begin to use latent critical reading skills. The image I would most often show and which elicited the strongest reaction, the reaction I would like to interpret here, is a Pear's soap advert from the nineteenth century.[24] It consists of two panels, one in which a 'black' baby is in the process of being cleansed by Pear's soap with the help of a white child standing over him, and one in which the 'black' baby emerges from the bath having been washed white, for which the white child holds up a mirror to show the *difference*. The inference Anne McClintock draws from the advertisement has to do with imperial notions of commodity fetish through which the colonies will be civilised and which have attached to them racialised tropes which associate whiteness with cleanliness as civility and blackness as unclean barbarity.[25]

I used this image to demonstrate how a representative imperialist attitude was propagated and disseminated through advertising throughout the nineteenth century. I showed it to make the point that advertising and media images are not innocuous, that advertising in particular has colonial origins and to get participants thinking about twenty-first-century British cultural inflections in nineteenth-century colonial history, and the popular narratives which they see around them everyday and to prompt a critical engagement with those narratives. What I began to notice persistently and consistently over the three years that I did this training, was that this image (and the few others I have which are similar) would elicit a very particular and repeated response from my participants across a variety of contexts, when they were asked 'what narrative, or what is the story you read from this image?'. And while alert to the risk of being reductive in relation to, or the impossibility and ethicality of claiming to apprehend anyone's sub-jectivity, it is the persistent and consistent pattern of responses that these images elicited that I would like now to read and interpret through Homi Bhabha.

There were, of course, many and varied responses, but inevitably one particular response repeated itself in virtually every session over three years. That response was that whatever the narrative of the image, the image my participants would insist *is not racist*, or less directly some participants would assert that the child in the image is not black, he's dirty. Please note that no reading of the image was offered in advance and this response would often come before a reading of the image attendant on race was offered by another participant. In this view the participants were adamant, even when shown other examples of similar narratives in other images.[26]

Interpreting this response, I would argue first that it comprises a form of denial that is bound up in the pervasive elisions (in culture, education, media and politics) of the colonial moment. What I consistently witnessed over three years is the performative 'playing out' of what Bhabha has called the writing out of the colonial moment, and what Spivak calls 'sanctioned ignorance'. Most of my participants in over three years training have confessed and demonstrated in abundance to having absolutely no knowl-edge of British colonial history and ignorance of the reasons for migration and the experiences of migrant communities in this country. My point with regard to the consistently enunciated denial on the part of my participants (and not just to images but to numerous examples and personal testimony) is that it is symptomatic, which is to say, there is something at stake in it.

Bhabha theorises the elision of the colonial moment as 'a conspiracy of silence around the colonial truth, whatever that might be', and he notices that 'around the turn of the century [twentieth] there emerges a mythic, masterful silence in the narratives of empire . . .'.[27] But this elision is not merely *symptomatic* of Eurocentric narrative construction, it is *operative and enabling* of such a construction, because as Bhabha puts it, the 'disavowal is not merely a privilege of negation or elision; it is a strategy for articulating contradictory and coeval statements of belief'.[28] Thus, it is the persistent writing out of the colonial moment that makes the narrative of civility, modernity and development possible and produces two coeval terms (development-as-civility and poverty-as-degeneracy) as described above. Even as disavowal 'negates the visibility of difference', it nevertheless 'produces a strategy for the negotiation of knowledges of differentiation'.[29] Difference is simultaneously present and absent when articulating a position constructed as the normalised but invisible point of departure. Thus, at the risk of foreclosing on, speaking for or claiming to know the minds of my participants, I would *read* that what is really at stake in their responses is a formulation such as the following: *I had better deny this narrative as racist, less I am exposed as racist.* I would read these as the implicit subtexts behind the enunciation in my training sessions (at least one in every session), that 'it's not racist' or 'the baby isn't black.' Once again, I never offered a reading of the image, so the differentiated term is never introduced before my participants deny it, and their denial – *that's not racist, the baby isn't black* – implies knowledge of, and what is more the authority to say, what racism actually *is*, and the bizarre double think that would deny difference as blackness, even before that differentiated term has been introduced.

While facilitating the ensuing and often charged discussion, I never in any of my sessions foreclosed on the alternative reading that the child in the image is not 'black' but rather a 'white' child who is dirty as the result of the common nineteenth-century practice of employing child labour in the sweeping chimneys or in factories and so on. This reading is as potentially valid as any other, but complicated by the fact that this image (and the trope of washing whiter than white as endemic to the narrative of civility) proliferates and has currency throughout nineteenth-century advertising and has its origins in eighteenth-century anti-humanist propaganda, and can still be found in circulation. This reading is further complicated, and still inscribed by the colonial narrative, when it is remembered that the process of racialisation enabling the narrative of white supremacy in the European family of man in the nineteenth century affected the Irish, women and the working class, who were also 'racialised' within that narrative. Thus, reading the child in the image as dirty due to child labour is still immersed in the construction of 'race' in colonial Britain's domestic divisions of labour.[30]

Bhabha speaks of the construction of the colonial subject as 'the effect of power that is productive', in order to understand this construction, 'one has to see the surveillance of colonial power as functioning in relation to the regime of scopic drive',[31] that is, *seeing and being seen.* Bhabha points out that in order to operate as a signifier of discrimination, skin must be produced or processed as visible.[32] In order to do that, white skin, constructed as the sight of purity, origination, wholeness, must be made *invisible*, the unseen *measure of difference*, and yet, as Bhabha would point out, the ambivalence lies in the fact that the process of rendering all other skin types visible, itself threatens to expose the process of differentiation, that there needs to be white for there to be non-white. Discrimination is authorised in the 'occlusion of this preconstruction of differentiation'.[33] The cultural effect of this pervasive elision says Bhabha is paranoia:

> What emerges in these lies that never speak the 'whole' truth, come to be circulated from mouth to mouth, book to book, is the institutionalisation of a very specific discursive form of paranoia, that must be authorised at the point of its dismemberment.[34]

Thus, the anxious subscript of the anomalous assertion in my example is belying a paranoia which *might* read, '*please don't expose me as racist*', or worse yet, '*please don't force me to admit it to myself*'. This anxiety is produced by the same ambivalence which Bhabha theorises in 'enlightened' nineteenth-century discourse on the despotic rule of India by a 'free' people. It amounts to the ambivalence of a *liberal whiteness*, and returns us to the paradox of a 'multicultural' liberal democracy which is institutionally racist. For how can we possibly live in a free and democratic society in which racism is endemic? If racism is institutionally endemic then it is possible I might have to address how my own identity has been racialised in order to comprehend the process by which racial differentiation is produced. My whiteness is no longer invisible, *the images I'm seeing, therefore, must not be racist, the baby can't be black and the testimony I'm hearing must be false*, and notice that even in denial, the differentiation is produced. What I am describing, therefore, is a moment in which, confronted by an image which suggests the construction of racialised identities as endemic to British national culture, participants were invited to see themselves, perhaps for the first time, as 'white'. The pattern of responses from some of my participants was denial and refusal.

Part of what my anti-racist or 'diversity training' attempted (and probably failed) to do, therefore, was to invite my participants, in a facilitated discussion about race and racism, to interrogate their own identity as 'white' through a narrative of history and a knowledge of the nation which is nominally excluded from the narratives they have used to inform how they understand themselves in the world. The follow-on step would have been an acknowledgement or recognition that in a liberal democratic nation-state that constructs racialised identities (indeed functions on the construction of racialised identities),[35] the identity racialised 'white' becomes the most economically, politically and socially *privileged.*

The emphasis in my pedagogical experiment was that this is not an entrenched subject position, it is learned and, therefore, *unlearnable.* Unlearning one's privilege *as a loss* is precisely for Spivak how one works against a subject position constructed and operating as dominant and/or privileged in which one might find oneself.[36] Unlearning 'white' privilege *might*, therefore, take the form of a double gesture of learning and unlearning what it means to be white in the British national context, how whiteness has been constructed historically and operates contemporaneously in hegemonic fashion in the nation space and the degree to which these narratives have been interpolated. Learning and unlearning can take the form of a recognition of counter-narratives, or becoming aware of, taking *responsibility* for one's privilege in the world, but never as a loss that one should mourn. Rather, it can take the form of a recognition of the racialised narratives of authority and taking the courage and responsibility to say: *I'm not, or I won't be that kind of 'white'.* Unlearning ('white') privilege can take the form of producing other or alternative subjectivities resistant to, because they are analytically aware of, narratives of authority and their various subject producing apparatuses.

Taking up Bhabha then, unlearning white privilege could potentially produce *(an)other knowledge of the nation*, one all the more effectively disruptive because it comes from a variety and diversity of subject positions and is not necessarily caught up in the process of cultural commodification and, therefore, becomes one that might seek solidarity across difference with others articulating a position of resistance. The unrealistically ambitious aim of this kind of pedagogy then, was the dissemination of a kind of praxis, skills and analytical tools that are attendant of the production of self and knowledge, a kind of praxis that *might* result in the use of one's privilege to undermine the structure of privilege and inequality, a praxis of using ambivalence against itself.

CONCLUSION

Bhabha has theorised the 'unhomely' or the colonial 'uncanny' which creeps up upon us, when we might find ourselves 'a la Isabelle Archer', regarding our dwellings in 'incredulous terror'.[37] This, I would argue is what is at stake in unlearning ('white') privilege, this moment in which you uncannily recognise the colonial subject in yourself. Reading this crucial moment, therefore, when I confronted my participants with images that *recalled* colonial history and the racialised narratives that made it possible, the white liberal looks upon her/his implicit racism in 'incredulous terror' and either denies it and retreats to the safety of the colonial world view (in which, thankfully, you do not have to see), or lets it in and allows it to disrupt how one thinks about oneself in the world, and in this way might be prompted to begin to take responsibility for something which is not entirely their fault. Taking responsibility for something which is not entirely your fault (acting because you believe there to be something at stake) is the beginning of a political ethics, a 'new culture of politics';[38] 'For the critic must attempt to fully realise, and take responsibility for, the unspoken, unrepresented pasts that haunt the historical present.'[39]

The kind of pedagogy I have described, therefore, I offer by way of example of a kind of political praxis or form of resistance which, informed by a post-structuralist epistemology, attempts the exploitation of ambivalent spaces to move the possibility of alternative knowledges and epistemological skills beyond the realm of the 'already converted'. Reaching a popular consciousness (in one sector and with very limited success) is part of what my work as a 'diversity trainer' and my strategy of exploiting the ambivalence of that particular practice was aimed at directly. If ambivalence is inescapable, then our political praxis must be one that resists the temptation to melancholically mourn that loss, but rather must be aimed at its exploitation in a struggle for a different set of knowledges.

Such a praxis, however, is not itself devoid of ambivalence but contradictorily caught within it. A post-colonial pedagogy, for instance, does not escape the risk of pastoralism inherent in critical pedagogies.[40] No pedagogy can deny its desire for the creation or the positing of an ideal subject which is its aim,[41] and given this, any self-proclaimed ethical pedagogy must recognise that its success is also a failure. My example demonstrates both the need for the exploitation of ambivalences in this curiously crisis ridden moment and suggests through a post-colonial pedagogy *an example* of how it might be done. By inviting my participants to examine racism in the context of the epistemological construction of race as such, there is the suggestion that I was asking of my participants the impossible – their own 'white death'.[42] Just as a critical pedagogy has the potential to produce a 'transnational literacy', there is also the risk of rejection and failure. Here, therefore, there is an inference that 'open space' or critical pedagogies provide a methodology through which essentialised, unexamined subject positions, or fundamentalist world views cannot survive. The result for participants is that they are confronted with a choice of submitting to the methodology and relinquishing their subject commitment (even if for a moment) or refusing the process altogether.[43]

In *Aporias* Derrida describes a 'certain experience of hospitality as the crossing of the threshold by the guest who must be at once called, desired and expected, but always free to come or not to come'.[44] In this sense, and within the economy of Derrida's possibility as the expectation of the absolute *arrivant*, my participants were my guests, and I was theirs. The *arrivant* in this sense makes the ultimate border most difficult to delineate because it has always already crossed it: 'The arrivant makes possible everything to which . . . it cannot be reduced, starting with the humanity of man.'[45] To extend this logic of the possibility of the impossible, one must acknowledge with this sense of 'absolute risk', that there may not be an originary which engenders and makes possible. The idea that there is no foundation, or ordering of meaning, ultimately no explanation is the greatest source of anxiety, the idea that is most threatening to a 'Western' metaphysics. So that within this same logic, the hospitality that Derrida prescribes toward the event, in the face of the *possibility* of the arrivant, may be in vain. The *expectation* must entail in its possibility that one may be waiting for nothing, in the double sense that nothing will come and there is *no reason* for waiting. Moreover, there is the possibility in an expectation of disappointment. It is within this schema that even the ambivalence of a conscious exploitation of ambivalence must be recognised. That the event, if there is one, may contain nothing new, or nothing at all, an empty vessel, the guest may arrive empty handed, a circumstance which the *hospitable* must be prepared to accept, graciously and without malice. These are the risks, as I see it, of the conscious exploitation of ambivalence as *a* strategy, *for the moment*. Speaking only for myself inasmuch as that is possible, I think it's a risk worth taking.

NOTES

1. See DFID, 'Spreading the word, building support for development', *Developments: The International Development Magazine*, 2000.
2. Ibid.
3. Spivak herself no longer uses this terminology but it has been widely taken up by educational practitioners utilising a critical pedagogy as political praxis. For more on the trajectory of the idea of 'transnational literacy', see Diana Brydon, 'Postcolonialism Now: Autonomy, Cosmopolitanism, and Diaspora'.
4. A. Kundnani, 'The death of multi-culturalism', *Independent Race and Refugee News Network*, Institute of Race Relations, 2002.
5. E. Said, *Orientalism*, London: Penguin, 1995.
6. R. Young, *Colonial Desire: Hybridity in Theory, Culture and Race*, New York/London: Routledge, 1995.
7. J. McLeod, *Beginning Postcolonialism*, Manchester: Manchester University Press, 2000.

8. J. Derrida, *Margins of Philosophy*, trans. Alan Bass, Brighton: Harvester Press, 1982; and J. Derrida, *Of Grammatology*, trans. Gayatri Spivak, Baltimore, MD: Johns Hopkins University Press, 1976.

9. G. C. Spivak, *The Postcolonial Critic: Interviews, Strategies, Dialogues*, New York: Routledge, 1987. Spivak has recently distanced herself from this term as well.

10. Derrida, *Margins of Philosophy*; and Derrida, *Of Grammatology*.

11. H. Bhabha, *The Location of Culture*, London: Routledge, 1994, pp. 55–9.

12. Elsewhere I have made the case, using post-colonial theory, for a direct line of continuation between colonial and development discourse.

13. G. Prakash (1992), 'Postcolonial criticism and Indian historiography', *Social Text*, 31/32: 8–20 at 17.

14. Spivak, *Outside in the Teaching Machine*, New York/London: Routledge, 1993; and S. Morton, *Gayatri Chakravorty Spivak*, London: Routledge, 2003.

15. Spivak, *The Postcolonial Critic*.

16. Spivak, *Outside in the Teaching Machine*; G. C. Spivak, Landry and MacLean, *The Spivak Reader: Selected Works of Gayatri Chakravorty Spivak*, New York/London: Routledge, 1996; and Spivak, *The Postcolonial Critic*.

17. Morton, *Gayatri Chakravorty Spivak*, p. 43.

18. Spivak, *The Postcolonial Critic*; and Spivak, *Outside in the Teaching Machine*.

19. Derrida, *Of Grammatology*.

20. T. Ponniah, 'The World Social Forum: the revolution of our time', interviewed by A. Biccum (2004), in *Situation Analysis: A Forum for Critical Thought and International Current Affairs*, 4: (Autumn), 7–15; and C. Whitaker, 'The World Social Forum: recovering utopia', interviewed by V. Andreotti (2004), in *Situation Analysis: A Forum for Critical Thought and International Current Affairs*, 4: (Autumn), 111–21.

21. V. Andreotti (2005), 'The other worlds educational project and the challenge and possibility of "open spaces"', *Ephemera: Theory and Politics in Organisation*, 5: 102–15 at 106.

22. Ibid. p. 109.

23. Kundnani, 'The death of multi-culturalism'.

24. A. McClintock, *Imperial Leather: Race, Gender and Sexuality in the Colonial Contest*, New York: Routledge, 1992. All images referred to come from McClintock, *Imperial Leather*, pp. 213, 218, 221, 224 and 225.

25. McClintock, *Imperial Leather*, pp. 212–13.

26. McClintock, *Imperial Leather*.

27. Bhabha, *The Location of Culture*, p. 123.

28. Ibid. p. 132.

29. Ibid. p. 132.

30. For elucidation and evidence for this argument see McClintock 1992.

31. Bhabha, *The Location of Culture*, p. 76.

32. Ibid. p. 79.

33. Ibid. p. 79.

34. Ibid. p. 80.
35. For an argument to this effect in the context of the United States see J. Olson, *The Abolition of White Democracy*, Minneapolis, MN: University of Minnesota Press, 2004. In it, Olson shows that in the context of the United States democracy is always/already paradoxical and citizenship in this context is always/already racialised.
36. Spivak, *Outside in the Teaching Machine*.
37. Bhabha, *The Location of Culture*, p. 9.
38. For a description of the 'new culture of politics' as it manifests itself in the anti-globalisation movement and the World Social Forum, see Sen et al., 'Challenging empires' and the special edition of *Ephemera* devoted to social forums at www.ephemeraweb.org.
39. Bhabha, *The Location of Culture*, p. 12.
40. For a description of pastoralism as a risk in critical pedagogies see C. Menezes (2004), 'Thinking critically of critical teaching: critical pedagogies revisited', *Situation Analysis*, 21–31.
41. Menezes, 'Thinking Critically of Critical Teaching'; and P. Sherman Gordan and C. Albrecht-Crane (2005), 'Critical pedagogy in conservative contexts: introduction', *Cultural Studies*, 19:407–14.
42. I am indebted to Dylan Rodrigues, whom I recently encountered at the University of California Humanities Research Institute's Summer Seminar in Experimental Critical Theory, for this phrase.
43. I am grateful to my colleague Andrew Robinson for a succinct clarification of this idea.
44. J. Derrida, *Aporias*, Stanford, CA: Stanford University Press, 1993, p. 19.
45. Ibid. p. 34.

III

Following/Breaking

9

Sartre and Derrida: The Promises of the Subject
Chaque fois unique, la fin du monde

Christina Howells

One should not develop a taste for mourning, and yet mourn we must. We must, but we must not like it, mourning that is, mourning itself, if such a thing exists.[1]

Derrida's death has necessarily brought us face to face with mortal questions, questions which preoccupied him increasingly in his own writings and reflections, especially, but not exclusively, since 1990. This volume, devoted to Derrida's legacy, gives us an opportunity to think afresh about these questions within the context of the Janus-face of all such memorials: looking back at the work which always feels cut short by death, and simultaneously looking forward to discover where we can go from here, mindful once more of our own vulnerability and mortality. This chapter deals with the relations between Derrida and Sartre, whose death in 1980 gave rise to a similarly memorable occasion of mourning amongst those interested in the French philosophical tradition, and the centenary of whose birth in 2005 has been marked by an extraordinary world-wide plethora of conferences and memorial events.

The subject of Derrida's relations with Sartre has preoccupied me for around twenty-five years, since I first discovered Derrida's work in fact, in 1980, the year of Sartre's death, and felt certain he owed an enormous amount to the patterns of thinking, if not necessarily the conclusions, of his philosophical predecessor. Derrida himself, though initially sceptical, came increasingly round to this view, and was always immensely generous when discussing the question with me. I remember one of my first real conversations with him, in Cerisy-la-Salle in the 1980s, when I had given him a copy of an article I had written on his unacknowledged debt to Sartre. 'Sartre and Derrida: loser wins'. He made an appointment to discuss it with me. The appointed time arrived and I approached him, as he sat waiting on one of the many benches in the beautiful Normandy gardens. '*C'est très beau*', he said. 'It's very beautiful'. 'And very true?', I asked nervously, holding my breath. 'And very true', he replied, with a kind, if ironic, smile. Since then my work on Derrida and Sartre has continued to read them in conjunction with each other, even, and perhaps especially, in areas which might seem at first sight least promising, such as those of subjectivity and freedom, where many critics have been content simply to oppose them. The present chapter will continue this kind of double reading, in connection in particular with the questions of promises, subjectivity, responsibility and decision-making.

Derrida's first published references to Sartre date, I think, from 1962, in *The Origin of Geometry*, where Derrida explores Husserl's phenomenological conception of the imagination. Husserl, he claims, never interrogated the imagination with sufficient rigour, and it retains in his work an ambiguous status, being 'a derived and founded reproductive power on the one hand, and, on the other hand, the manifestation of a radical, theoretical freedom'. Sartre, Derrida claims, went much further in his analyses:

> It is because he starts by thematising imagination directly as an original, situated *vécu*, with the help of the imagination as the operative instrument of any eidetics, it is because he freely describes the phenomenological conditions of fiction, that the Sartrean [philosophical] breach has so profoundly unsettled, indeed disrupted the whole landscape of Husserlian phenomenology and abandoned its horizons.[2]

In 1962, then, Derrida described Sartre as a destabilising force, a breach in the phenomenological landscape, shattering Husserlian certainties, just as Derrida himself was to do soon afterwards. But only a few years later, in 'The ends of man', a conference paper that Derrida delivered in New York in 1968, Sartre has become, it seems, a metaphysical humanist, author of a 'phenomenological ontology' which is described by Derrida as a form of 'philosophical anthropology'.[3] Sartre's ironic demolition of humanism in *La Nausée* has been relegated to a footnote:

> It's in the discussion with the Autodidact that Roquentin takes humanism most severely to task, dismissing all the different styles of humanist, and, at the very moment when nausea is rising up slowly in his throat he says to himself: 'I don't wish to be assimilated, nor for my good, red blood to fatten up that lymphatic beast: I shan't be so stupid as to call myself an "anti-humanist". I *am not* a humanist, that's all there is to say.[4]

What then may we conclude from this about Sartre's philosophy? If Derrida acknowledges that Roquentin dismisses humanism, this does not stop him accusing Sartre of being profoundly marked by it, and of never questioning 'the history of the concept of man'. This is quite simply false. Not in the sense that Sartre questions the *history* of the concept – he rarely examines conceptual history – but rather in the sense that, precisely, it is man who is in question for Sartre: his unity which does not exist, his essence which IS not, and his contradictions which make of him a 'useless passion'. If it is true, as Derrida argued in his own defence in 1989, that questioning concepts such as 'man', 'democracy', and 'responsibility' does not make one either anti-humanist, anti-democratic, or irresponsible;[5] similarly, and *a fortiori*, this questioning certainly does not make its author a defender of the old concepts he is attempting to interrogate. As Derrida is certainly aware. It is, of course, in Derrida's own texts that I learnt to make these judgements that I am now using to try to demonstrate that Sartre's philosophy is not metaphysical in the humanistic sense of the word. For it is, of course, in the same article, 'The ends of man', that Derrida contends that metaphysical discourse is unavoidable, even for those such as Heidegger who attempt to deconstruct it. And Derrida recognises that Sartre's intention was certainly to oppose 'the substantialist temptation', and to 'think afresh . . . the meaning of man'. However, in his view, Sartre did not manage to escape from classical anthropology: 'despite this claimed neutralisation of metaphysical presuppositions', he writes, 'we must still recognise that the unity of man is never itself put in question'.[6]

Let us examine the question a little more closely. One of Derrida's most precise claims is that, for Sartre, 'being in itself and being for itself were both being'. This is certainly correct in a narrow sense, but Derrida is not taking seriously the fact that if the for itself is being, it is in the mode of not being. 'The for itself has no being because its being is always at a distance'.[7] It is true that another footnote to Derrida's article alludes to the non-self-identity of the Sartrean subject, but no consequences are drawn from the observation. This will no doubt astonish lovers of Sartre's paradoxes. In his first published writings, such as *The Transcendence of the Ego* in 1936, consciousness is described as impersonal, or at least pre-personal. The 'I', in Sartre's account, is not a unifying force; on the contrary it is the act of reflection that confers existence on the 'I'. 'There is no "I" on the unreflective level.' And the subject itself is entirely absent from Sartre's text, except for a brief moment when it appears as a negated trace, only to be immediately denied: 'This absolute consciousness, when it is purified of the "I", has nothing more of a subject about it.'[8]

My title promises to speak of promises, the promises of the subject.

Perhaps I will keep my word. For the moment I hand over to Derrida who is an expert in how not to speak ('*Comment ne pas parler*'):

> Discourse about promises itself anticipates the promise: *in* the promise . . . As soon as I open my mouth I have already promised, or rather, in the first place, the promise has captured the 'I' who promises to speak . . . This promise is older than I am.[9]

To keep my commitments, if not my promises, I come back to the subject. First of all to the Sartrean subject. In *Being and Nothingness* Sartre defines for the first time what he understands by subjectivity: it is 'consciousness (of) consciousness',[10] and 'the instantaneous cogito'.[11] That is to say, subjectivity arises from the reflexivity of consciousness, and is non-positional and non-thetic. It is the reflexivity of consciousness that constitutes the for itself and prevents consciousness from remaining 'a transcendental field without a subject'.[12] In one sense Derrida is right when he maintains that 'as consciousness, the subject has never been able to manifest itself except as self-presence'.[13] But this self-presence is itself paradoxical, for it is precisely what prevents self-identity. The term 'self' (*soi*), from the for itself, is grammatically a reflexive, it indicates a relationship between the subject and itself, but the subject can never 'be' itself, because if it were there would be no more reflexivity, and the self itself would disappear in identity and self-coincidence.[14] The self can never inhabit consciousness, it is rather an ideal and a limit. So the for itself is only a self in an unrealisable sense, 'over there', 'out of reach'.[15] We will return to this 'over there' when we come back to look again at Derrida's texts. That's a promise. Will I be able to keep it? I do not know.

Let us stay for a moment longer with Sartre. We are close now to the heart of the question, to its navel (ombilic).[16] Will it resist our analysis? We have just seen that it is the self-presence of the for itself that founds its negation of its own identity:

> Self-presence . . . is a way of not being self-coincidence, of escaping identity.[17]

> If it is present to itself, that is because it is not entirely itself.[18]

As I have argued elsewhere, Sartre's analysis of the self-presence of the for itself, and in particular the way he uses Husserl to demonstrate the impossibility of escaping from reflexive division, prefigures Derrida's deconstruction of Husserl's *Logical Investigations* in *Voice and Phenomenon*.[19]

Derrida shows how Husserl's analyses undermine his own insistence on the very notion of self-identity, especially in his discussions about temporality and interior monologue. This is precisely Sartre's argument in the first chapter of the second part of *Being and Nothingness*. Derrida was doubtless well aware of this since he was very familiar with Sartre's text. But did he have it in mind when he wrote his own critique of Husserl? I doubt it, and he suggested as much himself in 'Il courait mort', a rich and moving essay in which Derrida discusses Sartre for the fiftieth anniversary issue of *Les Temps Modernes* in 1996. Referring to Sartre's critique of the ideology of fraternity, described by Sartre as the 'defensive arm of bourgeois democracy' in so far as it invokes a merely passive link between distinct molecules, Derrida admits:

> Recently, in the *Politics of Friendship*, when I repeatedly questioned the authority of the fraternalist schema and all it implies in our culture, I had forgotten . . . that Sartre had already challenged the rhetoric of fraternity. This forgetting, which must happen to me more often than I realise afterwards, constitutes the fundamental theme of this letter: a strange transaction between amnesia and anamnesia [forgetting and remembering] in the heritage which makes us what we are and which has already invited us to think what we have not yet thought, as if our heritage was always a spectre still to come, a ghost running ahead of us, after whom we race, running in our turn towards death and till we are out of breath.[20]

And Derrida revisits *La Nausée* in a renewed attempt to decide the vexed question of Sartre's humanism: at times the most ferocious anti-humanist, at others its most infamous firing target; at times the exponent of commitment, deliverance and salvation, at others the philosopher who reminds us that commitment may be unavoidable, but we can only ever make our choices against a backdrop of undecidability. There is no evidence here of an heroic decisionism based on free will. No wonder Derrida's feelings about Sartre were, to say the least, ambivalent, writing at one moment: 'Nothing is more unstable, divided, uncertain, antinomic than my friendship for Sartre and *Les Temps Modernes*', but immediately afterwards speaking of a 'passion for Sartre that, to tell the truth, I still sometimes feel'.[21] It is, of course, the Sartre of non-coincidence who attracts Derrida, as he attracts me too: 'It is with the Sartre who is in disagreement with himself', he says, 'that I feel myself most in agreement'.[22] And he quotes one of several extraordinary moments when Sartre seems to anticipate the deconstruction of presence:

The epoch . . . always goes beyond itself, in it we find a rigorous coincidence between the concrete present and the living future of all men who constitute it . . . even if it is true that this future has never become a present. [23]

And Derrida comments as follows:

Here is a contradiction or a non-coincidence (for when Sartre says 'rigorous coincidence' he is designating in a strange way the rigour of a non-coincidence of the present and the future, and of self-presence in so far as it must 'return to itself from the starting point of that future'). Here is a dehiscence or a discordance with which I feel myself even more in accord today, precisely because it is a question of a disjunction in the self-identity of the epoch or of the present.[24]

And this 'future which has never become a present' of which Sartre speaks has, as we shall see, the structure of a promise: it is marked by the dehiscence which, for Derrida, could perhaps constitute a 'subject which would not be pre-deconstructive'. For Derrida is deeply interested in a subject of this sort. If in 1968 Derrida defined the subject in terms of a negation of sovereignty, and as a 'system of relations between the layers',[25] in 1980 he was more interested in the ethical importance of rethinking the notion of man, not so much ontologically (What is man?) as in the terms of the Heideggerian reformulation of the question 'Who is man?'. And ten years later, in 1989, he is explicit in his defence of current studies of the subject as forming part of the deconstructive enterprise:

We were speaking of dehiscence, of intrinsic dislocation, of difference . . . Some people might say, but precisely, what we call the 'subject' is not absolute origin, pure will, self-identity or the self-presence of consciousness, but rather this non-self-coincidence . . . I am thinking of those who wish to reconstruct today a discourse which is not pre-deconstructive about the subject, about a subject which no longer has the form of self-mastery, of self-adequation, centre and origin of the world etc., and who would define the subject as the finite experience of non-self-identity, of the underivable call which comes from the other.[26]

I don't know who Derrida was thinking of when he spoke of these attempts to re/deconstruct a subject today – of Levinas, perhaps, or of Philippe Lacoue-Labarthe, or of Jean-Luc Nancy himself, who was interviewing him at the time – but I know that he was not thinking of Sartre. None the less, everything he says about the non-self-identical subject applies precisely to the Sartrean subject. In a sense, one might say that Derrida was well aware of this. In the interview with Nancy he insists on the non-homogeneity of the 'classical subject', and on the fact that at the heart of Husserl's transcendental idealism, for example, there is 'a horizon of questioning which is not overseen by the egological form of subjectivity or intersubjectivity'.[27] But although he recognises the complexities and contradictions at the heart of the classical subject, be it Cartesian or Husserlian; and although he recognises that the precursors of the deconstruction of the subject, such as Nietzsche or Heidegger in their mistrust of substantialist or subjectivist metaphysics, never went through to the logical conclusion of their own thinking and remained firmly attached to the question 'Who?' that they managed to protect from deconstruction; and although he examines seriously the possibility of reconstituting or reconstructing the subject today, Derrida never makes a single reference to Sartre. However, the Sartrean subject is so far removed from self-adequation that Sartre can speak of it as a monster. In his reflections on Jean Genet, for example, Sartre writes: 'Today it is a matter of revealing the subject, the guilty one, the monstrous, miserable beast whom we risk at every moment becoming'.[28]

The absence in Derrida's work of any serious discussion of the Sartrean subject, so far removed from the self-mastery of the mythical classical subject, can doubtless be explained by what he said in the article for the anniversary issue of *Les Temps Modernes* concerning his mixed feelings about Sartre and his divided and antinomic friendship for him. But this explanation must not stop us from pursuing our analysis, and it is time now to turn more directly to Derrida, and to his promises and responsibilities. Already back in 1964, Derrida took it on himself to emphasise the limitless importance of philosophical questioning, and of the community of the question, and the decision: it is in the community of the question, he maintains, 'that take refuge and are resumed today a dignity and an untouchable duty of decision. An untouchable responsibility'.[29] It is to this community, and its responsibilities and decisions, that Derrida returns twenty-five years later in 1990, when he argues that without being 'intersubjective' it nevertheless has 'a memory, a genealogy and a project: a "project" before the "subject"'.[30] A project before the subject: what can this mean? It is at this point that we must return to the promise, for it is precisely the structure of the promise which serves to explain these apparent paradoxes. This is what Derrida has to say on the matter:

> The self (soi), the *autos* of the legitimate auto foundation (self-grounding) is *still to come*, not as a *future* reality but as that which will always retain

the essential structure of a promise and can only come about in this way, as *to come*.[31]

The self, then, is still to come. That is to say, it will never arrive. But this is not a matter of failure: on the contrary, it is precisely this structure which renders decision-making and responsibility possible:

> The relation to the self can only be . . . one of *différance* . . . Not only is obligation not thereby attenuated but it is there, on the contrary, that it finds its unique possibility.[32]

> We were asking *ourselves* the question: what is a decision, and *who* decides? And whether a decision is, as we are told, active, free, conscious, voluntary and sovereign. What would happen if we kept the word and the concept but changed these latter determinants?[33]

What Derrida wants to demonstrate is that the classical concept of the subject is strictly incompatible with responsibility and decision-making; for the self-identity of the subject would make the change required for any decision impossible: decision-making becomes:

> impossible and accessory as soon as a subject is what it is, indivisible and self-identical, subject to everything *except* to the possibility that something should ever really happen to it and affect it.[34]

> Doubtless the subjectivity of a subject never really decides anything: its self-identity and its calculable permanence render every decision an accident which leaves the subject intact. *A theory of the subject is incapable of accounting for the slightest decision.*[35]

These paradoxes should not surprise us. We have been prepared for them fifty years earlier by Sartre. He is no more of a voluntarist than Derrida:

> Voluntary deliberation is always rigged. How, in effect, can I weigh up motives and reasons on which I have already conferred a value before any deliberation, and by my very choice of my self? When I deliberate, the die is already cast.[36]

> When . . . we showed . . . that my possibilities aroused anguish because it depended on me alone to maintain their existence, this did not mean that they derived from a me who, at least, would have a prior existence and who would pass, in the temporal flow, from one state of consciousness to another state of consciousness.[37]

And again:

> It is not *because* I am free that my act escapes from the determination of motives, but, on the contrary, the structure of motives as inefficient is the condition of my freedom.[38]

As Derrida argues:

> At a certain point, the promise and the decision, that is to say responsibility, owe their possibility to the test of undecidability which will always be the condition of their existence.[39]

The paradoxes of the Derridean promise have also been, to a certain extent, preceded and foretold by Sartre's own paradoxes of temporality:

> The future is *what I have to be* in so far as I cannot be it.[40]

> The future is the ideal point.[4]

> It is the very nature of the For itself to have to be 'an always future hollow'. For this reason it will never have become, in the Present, what it had to be, in the Future. The whole of the future of the present For itself falls into the past as future along with the For itself itself. It will be the past future of a certain For itself, or a future anterior. This future is never realised . . . the future cannot be reached . . . hence the ontological disappointment which awaits the For itself at every outlet into the future: 'How beautiful the Republic was under the Empire'.[42]

What Derrida encountered when he reread *What is Literature?* in preparation for his essay in *Les Temps Modernes* about a future which never became a present was neither unique nor untypical. On the contrary, the whole philosophy of Being and Nothingness rests on the double impossibility of self-coincidence and self-identity in the present as in the future. The paradoxes of a future which will always be to come, and of a subject which never coincides with itself in the present, nor, *a fortiori*, in the future, these paradoxes have antinomic ethical implications: they have the structure of the promise, as Derrida has described it. 'The time is out of joint', and 'inadequate to itself'; 'it is the non-contemporaneity to itself of the living present' which makes the question possible.[43] 'There is a need for disjunction, interruption, heterogeneity.'[44] 'The necessary disjunction . . . is here that of the present.'[45]

So evil saves us from the worst (*le pire*).[46] This is what Sartre argues too:

'In the case of impossibility, the choice of Good leads to a reinforcement of the impossible; we must choose Evil in order to find Good'.[47] Or again: 'Good without Evil is Parmenidean being, that is to say Death'.[48] The subject may have the structure of a promise, we can agree on that, but what we have been hiding from ourselves until now is that the promise was a promise of Evil. Evil, inadequation, disjunction, are all necessary for us. Necessary evils, if freedom is to be preserved and promoted.

Notes

All translations from the French are my own unless otherwise indicated.

1. Jacques Derrida, *Chaque fois unique, la fin du monde*, Paris: Galilée, 2003, p. 141.
2. Edmund Husserl, *L'Origine de la géometrié*, trans. and introduced by Jacques Derrida, Paris: PUF, 1962, p. 135, note 1.
3. Jacques Derrida, *Marges de la philosophie*, Paris: Minuit, 1972, p. 137.
4. Ibid. p. 137.
5. Jacques Derrida, *Memoires pour Paul de Man*, Paris: Galilée, 1988, p. 224.
6. Jacques Derrida, *Marges*, pp. 136–7.
7. Jean-Paul Sartre, *L'Etre et le néant*, Paris: Gallimard, 1943, p. 167.
8. Jean-Paul Sartre, *La Transcendance de l'ego*, Paris: Vrin, 1972, p. 78.
9. Jacques Derrida, *Psyché: inventions de l'autre*, Paris: Galilée, 1987, p. 547.
10. Jean-Paul Sartre, *L'Etre et le néant*, p. 29.
11. Ibid. p. 83.
12. Ibid. p. 291.
13. Derrida, *Marges*, p. 17.
14. Sartre, *L'Etre et le néant*, p. 119.
15. Ibid. p. 148.
16. Jacques Derrida, *Resistances de la psychanalyse*, Paris: Galilée, 1996, p. 14.
17. Sartre, *L'Etre et le néant*, p. 119.
18. Ibid. p. 120.
19. See 'Conclusion: Sartre and the deconstruction of the subject', in *The Cambridge Companion to Sartre*, Cambridge: Cambridge University Press, 1992, and *Derrida: Deconstruction from Phenomenology to Ethics*, Cambridge, Polity Press, 1998.
20. J. Derrida, 'Il courait mort', Les Temps modernes, no. 584, Sept.–Oct. 1995, p. 11. (This text was reprinted in No. 629 of *Les Temps modernes*, March 2005, in hommage to Derrida.)
21. Ibid. p. 14.
22. Ibid. p. 32.
23. Ibid. p. 32.
24. Ibid. p. 32.
25. Jacques Derrida, *L'Ecriture et la différence*, Paris: Seuil, 1967, p. 335.

26. Jacques Derrida, 'Il faut bien manger, ou le calcul du sujet', interview with Jean Luc Nancy, in *Confrontations*, no. 20, 1989, p. 98.

27. Ibid. p. 97.

28. Jean-Paul Sartre, *Saint Genet comédien et martyr*, Paris: Gallimard, 1952, p. 662.

29. Derrida, *L'Ecriture et la différence*, p. 118.

30. Jacques Derrida, *Du Droit à la philosophie*, Paris: Galilée, 1990, p. 28.

31. Ibid. p. 41.

32. Derrida, 'Il faut bien manger', p. 95.

33. Jacques Derrida, *Politiques de l'amitié*, Paris: Galilée, 1994, pp. 15–16.

34. Ibid. p. 268.

35. Ibid. p. 87.

36. Sartre, *L'Etre et le néant*, p. 527.

37. Ibid. p. 72.

38. Ibid. p. 71.

39. Jacques Derrida, *Spectres de Marx* (Paris: Galilée, 1993), p. 126.

40. Sartre, *L'Etre et le néant*, p. 170.

41. Ibid. p. 172.

42. Ibid. pp. 172–3.

43. Derrida, *Spectres*, p. 16.

44. Ibid. p. 65.

45. Ibid. p. 56.

46. Ibid. p. 57.

47. Jean-Paul Sartre, *Cahiers pour une morale*, Paris: Gallimard, 1983, p. 420.

48. Sartre, *Saint Genet*, p. 211.

10

What It Is To Be Many: Subjecthood, Responsibility and Sacrifice in Derrida and Nancy[1]

Jenny Edkins

I can respond only by sacrificing ethics, that is, by sacrificing whatever obliges me to respond, in the same way, in the same instant, to all the others.

Jacques Derrida

We have not even begun to discover what it is to be many.

Jean-Luc Nancy

INTRODUCTION

In his photographs of children in displaced persons' camps, Salgado takes each subject seriously. His images dis-place us through their dignity and presence. We are no longer spectators but engaged: each gaze demands a response and produces the self as exposed. Pictures of prisoners from Tuol Sleng in Cambodia take the same form: a single figure facing the camera. Here, however, we are caught in an additional and irresolvable aporia: we are faced with thousands to whom we cannot adequately respond. As Derrida argues, responsibility is only possible by sacrificing ethics: we can respond to one only by sacrificing whatever obliges us to respond to others.

The Salgado pictures were taken in response to the curiosity of the subjects and their desire to be photographed, whereas the prisoners, many of them also children, were photographed before they were taken to be tortured or shot. Salgado's children are so utterly distinct one from the other and yet in some sense the same, and the same as each of us as children. In the Cambodia photographs, we are faced with the absolute singularity of not one or a number but of thousands in the face of death; each photograph is a call to an impossible responsibility, repeated inexorably. These photographs bring home in all its difficulty the problem of responsibility and sacrifice; they present the dilemma of singularity and plurality in all its tragic paradox. In both collections we find people posed in front of the camera, one by one, and yet as compilations the photographs expose existence as multiplicity.

Photographs such as these are in their different ways a challenge to notions of community as agglomerations of individuals, and in our response to them not only are we brought face to face with absolute singularity and the impossibility of responsibility – in that, as Derrida puts it, 'I can respond only by sacrificing ethics, that is, by sacrificing whatever obliges me to respond, in the same way, in the same instant, to all the others';[2] but we are also, and perhaps more importantly, reminded that 'we have not even begun to discover what it is to be many',[3] or what a politics that takes as its starting point being-in-common might be. I will argue that, if the focus is on singularity in the way that a close reading of Derrida's thinking in *The Gift of Death* seems to me to entail,[4] then we are faced with the conclusion that community can only work by sacrificing ethics. However, if singularity is achieved – out of plurality, perhaps – or, rather, if multiplicity or more accurately 'multiple singularity' arises as a result of being-with, then ethics and politics must be rethought with a focus on being-in-common. Such a thinking demands a careful examination of the relation between Derrida's investigation of singularity and Nancy's concept of the singular plural. In this essay I propose, and make a first move in, such an exploration.

Salgado's children

The moment you enter the room Salgado's children look directly, disconcertingly, straight at you. The youngest must only be around three or four years old, maybe less, but their eyes follow you around, their gaze expressionless, composed, unwavering, still. What is perhaps most surprising is the dignity: such youth – and yet such candour and such poise, with no sign of self-consciousness or awareness of the regard of the other. An amazing openness is backed by a challenging assumption of self-worth and integrity.

The detail catches your eye. The clothing is other people's cast-offs by the look of it: sandals in snow, girls' dresses on young men, babies' dresses worn as blouses. Clothing that is too large, falling off the shoulders, or too small, fastened tightly across the chest. It is incongruous. Knitted jumpers worn in hot climates. Traditional Tajik dress combined with an anorak. Fashion clothes reduced to their function, with style and label long forgotten. Clothes that don't matter.

The older children are wistful, grimmer, somehow determined. All places and all 'races' are represented: blue eyes and brown eyes alternate. Grubby faces from all continents clutch school-books in different languages. There is a boy with one arm, another with his ribs sticking through. They are almost all straight-faced and impassive, but you only realise this when you come across one girl who is weakly smiling.

Each individual has been taken seriously by the photographer. These are portraits, not the snatched images of news photography. The subjects are composed, calm, looking directly at the lens. They stand or sit in a temporary space of stillness, holding themselves upright, dignified. The photographer's fullest attention has been paid to lighting, surroundings and composition, even though the setting may be a wall riddled with bullet-holes rather than picturesque scenery or a neutral backdrop. The clothes are what they happened to be standing up in.

This traversing of genres is perhaps what challenges the visitors' expectations so much. We enter the exhibition of photographs of 'the displaced' as potential voyeurs, there to stare furtively at other people's misery, drawn by the title 'Children of Exodus' and its evocation of migrant populations around the world. We perhaps expect to show our sympathy and concern, or maybe to criticise the sentimentality or patronising attitude of the images. But it is not like that. On the contrary, we find *ourselves* immediately the centre of attention, the focus of the gaze that confronts us. We are the ones who are dis-placed by these solemn-faced children. We are no longer in control, no longer the omniscient benefactor or sentimental bystander. The scene is not one of wretchedness or abjection. We are moved, but in a different, more literal way: we are de-centred, thrown off balance.[5] Who are we? Who are these children? So utterly distinct one from the other, are they in some sense the same? The same in their difference perhaps? What is it about them that challenges us to rethink our expectations so much?

PORTRAITS

In the exhibition I have just described, the photographer has produced a series of images in the traditional genre of portraiture.[6] The power and address of the photographs derives not from the situation of the children as refugees or as homeless, or even as children, but largely from the form of the portrait itself and its gaze.[7] And from the multiplicity of such gazes repeated over and over again that out-face, out-stare and dis-place the visitor to the exhibition.

What is it about the portrait that makes its appeal so powerful? Why are Salgado's children so demanding of us? And so striking? In large part this force could be said to be one that has been inherent in the portrait since its inception. Jean-Luc Nancy argues that the portrait as a rendering in paint on canvas, or light on photosensitive paper, brings with it the many questions of personhood and subjectivity, or, as Nancy puts it, 'the entire philosophy of the subject'.[8] A portrait is said be a representation of a person for him- or herself, and not for their attributes or actions or connections. We have seen this in the case of Salgado's children: what we are shown in these portraits is not children of this or that religion or this or that country, migrants or outcasts, but children each in themselves present to the photographer as individuals, as '*quelqu'un*' – as someone – not '*quelque chose*' – something. But this leaves aside questions of what we might mean by a person in themselves, questions that the philosophy of the subject addresses, and that, Nancy argues, portraiture does too.

Importantly, the portrait is not just an image organised around a face, 'the face itself must be arranged around its gaze – around its seeing or its vision.'[9] The look is not to do with the eye alone, however, but concerns the whole face.[10] A portrait works, as a portrait of some*one*, an image organised around a face, not merely in revealing an identity, a '*self*.'[11] This is what is sought, no doubt, and a photograph succeeds, as in Roland Barthes' 'Winter Garden Photograph' of his mother, when something like the quintessence of the individual appears in the image.[12] As Barthes puts it, the 'Winter Garden Photograph' achieved '*the impossible science of the unique being*'.[13] Nevertheless, Nancy argues, for that to happen what is going on is more complex than imitation of features or form.

The portrait succeeds when it lets us see the 'self' (and ourselves) outside or alongside itself, dis-placed, taken from the place where its subjectivity or thrown-ness can be concealed. In the portrait what we call the self is *exposed* in its *ex-position*, and its intrinsic displacement revealed.[14] The portrait exposes or 'produces' the subject: according to Nancy, it is in the portrait that what we call 'the subject' is produced or made present and visible. The 'subject' is not something that is there prior to the making of the image. The work of painting or of photography is a work that produces the thing we call subject. In a sense the subject is contained within in the thickness of the canvas.[15]

The subject, then, is neither internal nor external, but is found in the relation between internality and externality. What the portrait does is produce, or ex-pose, the subject as precisely this relationality. Though purporting to represent a likeness or a resemblance, or to bring to light a deeper personality, the portrait in fact reveals an absence: the portrait is to do rather 'with drawing presence not outside of an absence but on the contrary right up to the absence which brings it in front of "itself" and exposes it to the relation to self in exposing it to "us".'[16] It does not engage us because it represents a likeness but because it makes plain our relationality: the portrait 'is the carrying out of ex-position, that is to say of *our* ex-position, that is, of our being-in-front – and therefore merely inside – of ourselves.'[17]

In the Salgado exhibition, the children face us with their gaze, their expressions mute, their clothes and their backgrounds neutral and inconsequential. We are given nothing in the photographs that might allow us to escape from the impact of the images as portraits. We are left face to face with the children as people, as subjects not objects. It is difficult to observe them dispassionately and sympathise with their poverty or dejection or their straightened circumstances. We cannot easily retreat into an abstract moral stance, or just agree that 'something should be done'. The children appear before us, produced as exposed subjects, but this simultaneously exposes our own subjectivity. The portraits are uncanny: they summon us, they do not remain separate. We are involved. We are moved: dis-placed, ex-posed in our own presence/absence, our own uncomfortable inside/outside dis-position.

Unlike traditional photojournalism, where we are invited to look – at people in different places, involved in lives we do not know in circumstances we cannot imagine – where 'we' gaze at 'them', Salgado's children gaze at us. Or rather through us: their gaze crosses us, interrupts us.[18] This gaze unsettles; it politicises; it throws into question the comfortable stabilities of everyday existence.

CHILDREN IN CAMBODIA'S S-21 PRISON

I want to turn now to another set of photographs, those taken of the inmates at the Tuol Sleng prison in Phnom Penh, Cambodia between 1975 and 1979. Many of these are pictures of children, but children less fortunate than those queuing up in front of Salgado's camera. Children in Cambodia's S-21 prison were photographed for a different purpose: as part of the administration and control of the prison and its prisoners. The photographs as they appear today in the Tuol Sleng Museum of Genocide Crimes in Phnom Penh, Cambodia, in exhibitions and on various web sites, including those of Cornell and Yale universities.

It is not easy to examine the photographs on their own terms, because before we encounter them we already know that these are pictures of people who were tortured and shot by the Pol Pot regime. We know that those who appear in the photographs are dead, and that they were executed.[19] In this sense, then, one of the features of the portrait that Nancy draws attention to is absent: we are painfully aware of the attributes and the circumstances of the people portrayed, and these portraits are already given a particular meaning by that context. When we come to look at them, our viewing is coloured. We are inclined, even more than with the Salgado exhibition, to see the people portrayed as objects (of our pity etc.).

The faces do not seem expressionless either. We detect a certain closure of the gaze, a blanking of the regard that faces us. The photographer taking these photographs was part of the torture machine: these children were likely to be aware of what the future held. We can see their fear and apprehension: their brows are puckered, their mouths tense and down-turned.

Or can we? Are we reading too much into the images? Some of the photographs do not seem very different from the Salgado portraits. One girl is almost smiling, and another looks unperturbed.

When the S-21 prison was taken over by the new authorities in Cambodia, the documents and photographs it contained were seen as important evidence of atrocities committed by the previous regime. The photographs appear today in displays on the walls of a section of the former prison. The images are on the whole nameless, having become separated from the files to which they relate. Occasional photographs were annotated with names by visitors who recognised relatives, but this practice has now been stopped. The collections have attracted much attention from outside Cambodia, from those concerned to preserve the records for future prosecutions as well as those wanting to make other uses of the material.[20]

When the photographs are presented in this way, there are no longer any victims. These are people, individual people, who appear one by one, each a person in their individuality, their difference. Each commands a response, and no response is adequate to the situation. We wonder whether some were guilty in some way – no doubt some indeed were – but this does not help. We are still faced with the absolute injustice of their situation, as they face death unknown, alone and unmourned.

In these images we are faced with the absolute singularity of not one, or a number, but of thousands of others, as they face the moment of their imprisonment, the moment of torture, of indescribable horror, of death. We cannot cope, except by irresponsibility. Each photograph we look at, each time there is no name, we are called upon to help. Yet to help is impossible. We can do nothing: these people are already dead, and in that sense perhaps beyond help. Putting that to one side, we cannot in any case help so many: we are each one person, with limited resources, what can we do? How could we intervene? Would we not be killed if we were in a position to try?

Obligation and Response

As we have noted, Derrida reminds us that

> as soon as I enter into a relation with the other, with the gaze, look, command, or call of the other, I know that I can respond only by sacrificing ethics, that is, by sacrificing whatever obliges me to respond, in the same way, in the same instant, to all the others.[21]

The Cambodian photographs present that dilemma in all its tragic paradox. They confront us and we have no response. We are bereft of any possibility of adequate action. Even, or perhaps especially, our feeling of shame and anger is inadequate.

Though this situation, looking at these photographs, brings home in all its impossibility the problem of responsibility and sacrifice, importantly this sacrifice is not something that only happens here, in this context. Following his discussion in *The Gift of Death* of Abraham raising the knife to sacrifice his son Isaac on Mount Moriah, Derrida reminds us that it happens 'day and night, at every instant, on all the Mount Moriahs of this world':[22]

> There is no language, no reason, no generality or mediation to justify this ultimate responsibility which leads me to absolute sacrifice; absolute sacrifice that is not the sacrifice of irresponsibility on the altar of responsibility, but the sacrifice of a most imperative duty (that which binds me to the other as a singularity in general) in favour of another absolutely imperative duty binding me to every other.[23]

There is no way out of this and it happens all the time and everywhere. Not just when we are faced with the horrors of the Cambodia photographs, or the challenge of Salgado's children.

Although certainly if Abraham attempted to sacrifice Isaac on Hampstead Heath, the strong arm of the law would soon put a stop to it, despite any possible protestations from a latter-day Abraham, this is not the end of the story. The same state that would insist that Abraham's sacrifice was murder is itself implicated, since as Derrida reminds us:

> that same 'society' *puts to* death or . . . *allows* to die of hunger and disease tens of millions of children . . . without any moral or legal tribunal ever being considered competent to judge such a sacrifice, the sacrifice of others to avoid being sacrificed oneself.'

Not only that, 'such a society . . . actually organises it'. Derrida goes on, and the anger in his text at this point is palpable:

> the smooth functioning of its economic, political, and legal affairs, the smooth functioning of its moral discourse and good conscience presupposes the permanent operation of this sacrifice. And such a sacrifice is not even invisible, for from time to time television shows us, while keeping them at a distance, a series of intolerable images, and a few voices are raised to bring it to our attention. But those images and voices are completely powerless to induce the slightest effective change in the situation, to assign the least responsibility, to furnish anything more than a convenient alibi.[24]

It is worse even than this. The state visibly organises the sacrifice of its military personnel in war, and then celebrates that sacrifice. Not only is the state implicated, it could be argued that the state as such, as an institution and a focus for loyalty and obedience, functions through such uses of sacrifice.[25]

MUG SHOTS

The involvement of the state – in this case the Pol Pot regime – in the production of the S-21 prisoner photographs is clear. In this sense, the images are not portrait photographs like the Salgado pictures but 'mugshots': the identity photographs taken of criminals, and indeed often of citizens too, as part of the procedures of control and administration of state bureaucracies. In a portrait, as Jean-Luc Nancy points out, identity is that given by the face itself. In identity photographs, on the contrary:

> when the portrait allows civil status to dominate it, when it becomes referential and descriptive (painted such that posterity, the people, the family, and even, as has sometimes occurred, the police, might be recognised, in every sense of the word), the identity of the person is found outside itself, and, in conforming to this other [identity], pictorial identity is lost.'[26]

In other words, the contrast is that:

> The identity image relates to its model. The portrait relates only to itself, because it bears relation only to the self: to the self considered as another, which is precisely, the sole condition under which there will be a relation.[27]

As we saw, it is the extent to which the portrait produces the 'subject' as ex-posed – the extent to which it exposes the uncanny relationality of subjectivity, as something that exists neither inside nor outside but that is produced on and through the thin line that supposedly separates the two – it is to this extent that the portrait engages our attention and challenges our self-hood and sub-jectivity. The mug-shot, in contrast, produces the subject as object: as bare life,[28] exposed only in its nudity and nakedness in the face of sovereign power. In the mug-shot relationality is denied and objectivity both asserted and produced: the person is detached and enclosed (boxed in, enframed), thrown out in front of us, exposed to our scrutiny. Our subjectivity (and theirs) remains concealed.

The question remains: to what extent are the Cambodia prisoner photographs, as they have come down to us, portraits? Are they nothing but the mug-shots of a genocidal regime? Do they show only scared children facing unknown – or indeed known – horrors? Certainly, they seem to prompt, in some viewers at least, a powerful response. The cynics amongst us could call this sentiment, or manipulation, and point to the way in which the response is prompted not so much by the images themselves as by the context, or surrounding text, in which they are inevitably embedded. Others could point to the way in which the response, though powerful, is one that constitutes the people in the photographs as mere objects of our sympathy: 'victims'. Do we respond only because we gain status from their victimhood: because we become the gallant rescuer?[29] Is that all that is going on?

CAMBODIA EXHIBITION 'MESSENGERS'

At this point it may be useful to consider another collection of photographs. In January 2000 an installation was shown by artist Ly Daravuth as part of a group exhibition in Phnom Penh entitled *The Legacy of Absence: a Cambodian Story*. The installation, called *Messengers*:

> comprised numerous photographic portraits of young Cambodians. The physical condition of the photographs, their colouring, composition and their subject matter – solemn, black-clothed girls and boys of various ages – are immediately recognised as S-21 prisoner portraits.[30]

The children stare out at us, some with furrowed brows, others looking detached. All mute and nameless, and all numbered. However, these children were not S-21 prisoners. These are portraits of 'messengers': children who were used to carry messages between officials in the Khmer

Rouge regime. Or at least some of them are portraits of these messengers. The historical photographs are interspersed with portraits of present-day Cambodian children taken by the artist. The photographs have been manipulated to mimic those of S-21 prisoners.

The artist is engaged in a double deceit. First, he exploits and then challenges our automatic reading of the photographs. Daravuth says of his installation:

> Because of the blurred black-and-white format and the numbering of each child, we tend to read these photographs first as images of victims, when they are 'really' messengers and thus people who actively served the Pol Pot regime. The fact that upon seeing their faces, I immediately thought of victims, made me uneasy. My installation wishes to question what is a document? What is 'the truth'? And what is the relationship between the two?[31]

Secondly, he lets images of contemporary Cambodians infiltrate the exhibition. These photographs have been posed and subsequently aged to mimic the 'messenger' photos and those of the S-21 prisoners. So, we first of all assume that we are in the presence of 'victims' of the genocidal regime, with whom we should sympathise; then we realise that, no, we are surrounded by those complicit, actively, with its 'perpetrators'. Finally, however, in the last overturning of our expectations, we realise that some of the pictures, and we do not know which, are of children who are only implicated, if at all, as the inheritors of the genocide. The web site of the exhibition tells us that:

> 'Messengers' leads us to admit that perhaps it is impossible to access any truth other than that once a child stood before a camera and was photographed. Who they are, what they did, and when they lived, is not revealed by the photograph which we still hold somehow to be the direct record of the truth. If upon entering we are seduced into easy sadness, we leave uneasy, recognizing the difficulties of ever discerning 'the truth' retrospectively.[32]

This final set of photographs does indeed throw into question important issues of 'truth' and the reliance that is placed on the photograph regarded as evidence, as an historical record. However, the most interesting aspect is perhaps what this deception does to us, and whether it is important – particularly in the context of the image as portrait and its appeal to responsibility.[33]

Can the possibility of deception, of a mistake, of an untruth, let us off the hook, as it were, as far as responsibility is concerned? Or is such a possibility always inherent in the very possibility of a distinction between perpetrator and victim, those with whom we should sympathise and those we should condemn? Can such distinctions ever be made with an easy conscience, to use Derrida's phrase This is not to say, of course, as Derrida is the first to emphasise, that distinctions should not be made, or decisions about culpability taken, in a court of law for example.[34] To rephrase the question, is our response or our response-ability to the subjects portrayed in the sets of photographs we have been considering here to do with 'what' they are – perpetrator or victim, refugee or impostor – or with 'who' they are, in their singularity (to use Derrida's phrase) or their sub-jectivity (to use Nancy's)? Do the portraits in Daravuth's installation, like Salgado's children, and indeed the Tuol Sleng photographs, bring us to face to face with what could be seen as the question of the 'who' rather than the 'what'? Is it enough that 'a child stood before the camera and was photographed'?

THINKING SINGULAR PLURAL

In this final section, I want to reconsider Derrida's discussion of responsibility and read it alongside Nancy's elaboration of ontology as 'being singular plural'. I shall argue that the question of responsibility entails the prior question of subjectivity and that a rethinking of subjectivity along the lines that Nancy suggests demands a re-figuring or a re-casting of the ethico-political.

Singularity

In Derrida's thinking the notion of responsibility is closely tied to that of singularity, a singularity that arises through death and finitude:

> Everyone must assume his own death, that is to say the one thing in the world that no one else can *either give or take*: therein lies freedom and responsibility . . . Thus dying can never be taken, borrowed, transferred, delivered, promised, or transmitted.'[35]

It is through the unsubstitutability of death that the identity or self-hood of the mortal self is given; subjectivity, or 'the identity of the oneself is *given* by death'.[36] This is the *gift* of death. Or as Derrida puts it also: 'responsibility demands irreplaceable singularity. Yet only death or rather the apprehension of death can give this irreplaceability, and it is only on the basis of it that one can speak of the responsible subject.'[37] But this leads to a paradox or an aporia:

> What gives me my singularity, namely death and finitude, is what makes me unequal to the infinite goodness of the gift that is the first appeal to responsibility . . . One is never responsible enough because one is finite but also because responsibility requires two contradictory movements. It requires one to respond as oneself and as irreplaceable singularity, to answer for what one does, says, gives; but it also requires that . . . one forget or efface the origin of what one gives.[38]

Responsibility relies on singularity, which itself demands an alone-ness:

> responsibility . . . consists in always being alone, entrenched in one's own singularity at the moment of decision. But as soon as one speaks, as soon as one enters the medium of language, one loses that very singularity. . . . Once I speak I am never and no longer myself, alone and unique.'[39]

So responsibility is not, cannot be, something public and accounted for. It cannot be expressed in a general code of ethics. On the contrary, and against common sense, 'far from ensuring responsibility, the generality of ethics incites to irresponsibility. It impels me to speak, to reply, to account for something, and thus to dissolve my singularity in the medium of the concept.'[40]

The concepts of responsibility and singularity, thought this way, lead to paradox and aporia, as we have already seen:

> What binds me thus in my singularity to the absolute singularity of the other, immediately propels me into the space or risk of absolute sacrifice. There are also others, an infinite number of them, the innumerable generality of others to whom I should be bound by the same responsibility. . . . I cannot respond to the call, the request, the obligation, or even the love of another without sacrificing the other other, the other others. . . . As a result the concepts of responsibility, of decision, or of duty, are condemned a priori to paradox, scandal, and aporia. Paradox, scandal, and aporia are themselves nothing other than sacrifice, the revelation of conceptual thinking at its limit, at its death and finitude.[41]

In Derrida's thinking the notion of singularity is what he is gesturing towards when he talks of the difference between the 'qui' and the 'quoi', the 'who' and the 'what'. For example, he talks of the difference between loving someone – the *qui* – for who they are, irreplaceably, and loving something about someone – the *quoi* – their attributes, their appearance, their personality, etc. Thus, the notion of singularity here is perhaps similar to the 'subject' produced in the portrait – as opposed to the identity attributed from outside to the mug-shot.

Singular plurality

I want now to consider Nancy's thinking of singularity and responsibility. According to Nancy, humanism is the bar to a thinking of community:

> it is precisely the immanence of man to man, or is it *man*, taken absolutely, considered as the immanent being par excellence, that constitutes the stumbling block to a thinking of community. A community presupposed as having to be one of human beings presupposes that it effect . . . its own essence.'[42]

In other words, once we start from the assumption that community has to be a collection of human beings, fused into a community, we have problems. The notion of the individual is equally problematic: 'The individual is merely the residue of the experience of the dissolution of community . . . It is another, and symmetrical, figure of immanence: the absolutely detached for itself, taken as origin and certainty.'[43]

What Nancy develops instead is an ontology of being singular plural or of being-with. Philosophy needs to begin again; against political philosophy and philosophical politics, it needs to

> think in principle about how we are 'us' among us, that is, how the consistency of our Being is in being-in-common, and how this consists precisely in the 'in' or in the 'between' of its spacing . . . it is necessary to refigure fundamental ontology . . . with a thorough resolve that *starts from the plural singular of origins*, from *being-with*.'[44]

In other words, it is necessary to reverse the order of philosophical speculation, so that the 'with' does not come second to some pre-existing consciousness, as it seems to perhaps in Derrida's thinking. This leads to a different understanding of singularity:

> a singularity is indissociable from a plurality . . . The concept of the singular implies its singularisation and, therefore, its distinction from

other singularities . . . The singular is primarily *each* one and, therefore, also *with* and *among* all the others. The singular is a plural.[45]

This means that '*not only must being-with-one-another not be understood starting from the presupposition of being-one, but on the contrary, being-one . . . can only be understood by starting from being-with-one-another.*'[46]

The ontology of being-with is not something that concerns human beings alone—they are not *alone*, but *with*:

> The ontology of being-with is an ontology of bodies, of every body, whether they be inanimate, animate, sentient, speaking, thinking, having weight, and so on. . . . Whether made of stone, wood, plastic, or flesh, a body is the sharing of and the departure from self, the departure toward self, the nearby-to-self without which the 'self' would not even be 'on its own' ['*à part soi*'].[47]

In other words, 'only a being in common can make possible a being-separated'.[48]

In Nancy's thinking, language, which for him appertains to human being, is central in the production or ex-position of the world and of meaning as singular plural:

> Language is the exposition of the world-of-bodies as such, that is, as originarily singular plural . . . Language is the exposing of plural singularity. In it, the all of being is exposed as its meaning, which is to say, as the originary sharing according to which a being relates to a being, the circulation of a meaning of the world that has no beginning or end. This is the meaning of the world as being-with, the simultaneity of all presences that are with regard to one another, and where no one is for one-self without being for others.[49]

Language is both what we speak to one another and what I speak to myself – since I am simultaneously 'us' and 'me':

> At this exact point, then, one becomes most aware of the essence of singularity: it is not individuality; it is . . . at one and the same time, infra-/intra-individual and trans-individual, and always the two together. The individual is an intersection of singularities, the discrete exposition of their simultaneity, an exposition that is both discrete and transitory.'[50]

This view of language perhaps distinguishes Nancy's thinking of singularity from Derrida's; in the latter, as we have seen, language, and the entry into language, speaking, brings about the loss of absolute singularity, the singularity that makes responsibility possible.

The ontology of being singular plural leads to a rethinking of community, not in terms of individuals brought together into a community, but in terms of being-in-common or being-with, before which or without which there are no 'beings'. The dimension of 'in-common' is one that is 'in no way "added onto" the dimension of "being-self" but that is rather co-originary and coextensive with it.'[51] The self is produced or ex-posed only through its being-in-common.

The question of death figures importantly here, as it does in Derrida's thinking of responsibility: 'Death is indissociable from community, for it is through death that the community reveals itself – and reciprocally.'[52] In other words:

> A community is the presentation to its members of their mortal truth . . . It is the presentation of the finitude and the irredeemable excess that make up finite being: its death, but also its birth, and only the community can present me my birth, and along with it the impossibility of my reliving it, as well as the impossibility of my crossing over into my death.[53]

What community reveals, in this presentation of birth and death, is the way existence is existence outside itself. This does not mean that we continue to live through a community: '*Community does not sublate the finitude it exposes. Community itself, in sum, is nothing but this exposition.*'[54] Death is not something that happens to an individual as such; it is not something we know ourselves, in ourselves, but only in others: 'One is born; one dies – not as this one or that one, but as an absolute "as such", that is, as an origin of meaning that is both absolute and, as is necessary, absolutely cut off (and consequently, immortal).'[55] Although one's death is one's own, and one cannot die in place of the other, as Derrida, following Heidegger, has reminded us, nevertheless:

> it is also true, and true in the same way, that the other dies insofar as the other is with me and that we are born and die to one another, exposing ourselves to one another and, each time, exposing the inexposable singularity of the origin.'[58]

Community then exposes finitude, or rather, community subsists in the ex-posure of the finitude of singular beings. Community is a sharing of this exposed finitude, a sharing that encompasses all beings, not just human beings or just the living. Community cannot be lost: it 'is given to us with being and as being' since being is only being-with or being-in-common.[57]

Responsibility

If community is thought this way, how then do we think responsibility? If all being is of necessity being-with or being singular plural, how do we re-think the aporia of responsibility?

That aporia, as Derrida presents it to us, arises from the impossibility of our responding to an other as singularity without the inevitable sacrifice of our response to all the other absolute singularities to whom we are similarly bound. Looking at the Cambodian photographs brought us face to face with the impossibility of responsibility to that singularity. There were just too many of them, we would have been powerless in the face of the Khmer Rouge authorities, and the children in the photographs were in any case already dead: there was nothing we could do. And yet we felt implicated. However, if community is nothing more or less than being-with, or being-ex-posed in our finitude, maybe there is another way of engaging with what is happening. Or indeed another way in which *we are inevitably already engaged* with what is happening or has happened.

We *are* implicated: we are *ex-posed*. Exposed as singularities in the face of other singularities to whom we are inevitably responsible in that 'we' are 'us' only in our being-with, a being with that is not an 'us' being-with a 'them', but a being-with that is only 'us', as the all of beings, alive or dead, animate or inanimate, perpetrator or victim. Responsibility is not something that can be sacrificed: response is an inevitability of our being-with. And in particular, in the case of the Cambodia photographs, our being alongside the exposure to death of other beings that we are being-with. We are ex-posed in our being outside ourselves, as singular beings: 'the singular being, because it is singular, is in the passion – the passivity, the suffering and the excess – of sharing its singularity'.[58]

For Derrida, also, we do have to respond, there is no choice in that regard. In that sense, for Derrida as for Nancy, we are already implicated in being-with: we inevitably compear. But we can only respond, for Derrida, 'by sacrificing ethics'. What does he mean here? On the one hand, 'sacrificing ethics' could be read as meaning sacrificing the comfort of knowing we are working within an ethical code, expressed in language, or in other words, giving up on the possibility of what Derrida calls elsewhere 'good conscience'.[59] Sacrificing ethics is not sacrificing responsibility. But on the other hand, he tells us specifically that by 'sacrificing ethics' he means 'sacrificing whatever obliges me to respond, in the same way, in the same instant, to all the others.'[60] In the passage quoted at length above, where Derrida discusses the impossibility of an adequate response to one that does not at the same time mean giving up on an adequate response to another, to whom, of course, we are equally responsible, he ends by emphasising that responsibility inevitably entails a conceptual dead-end or aporia. But that aporia is surely not a practical constraint, only a logical one. We still have, inevitably, in practice, to respond; it is only that we cannot do so in a way that we can justify, with a good conscience.

Thus, what we have then between Nancy and Derrida is perhaps more a difference in emphasis than a stark contrast. This difference comes from the insistence in Nancy on taking a specific ontological starting point. What Derrida does not do, at least in the text we have been discussing, is elaborate on how we might consider what it might be, other than an ethical code, that obliges us to respond 'in the same way, in the same instant' to all others. What is it that presents us with this impossible dilemma? Nancy's work gives us the suggestion of an answer. If our very being is already being-in-common, if we are already intimately involved with all others to the extent that they are not others but part of 'us', then it is a thinking (and a politics) that conveys and (re)produces an impression of separateness that is leading to our difficulty. And this, of course, is precisely what Derrida is saying when he argues that what we encounter in his aporia of responsibility is 'the revelation of conceptual thinking at its limit'.[61]

Although what we have identified is perhaps less a contrast than a difference of emphasis, it is nevertheless very significant, perhaps especially when we come to talk of the political and of community. Whereas with Derrida we are led to consider what binds us as singularities to other singularities,[62] in Nancy our attention is directed rather to the impossibility of being on our own without first being-with. Even as singularities, for Nancy, we are immediately in a relation of being-with other singularities: 'a singularity is indissociable from a plurality'.[63] Nancy's contribution, then, is to emphasise the necessity, politically, to focus *not* on how we might establish a bond between us, but *rather* on how it is that we have come to consider ourselves separate in the first place.

Conclusion

Derrida's aporia is only apparent if one takes existence as originally singular-being. If existence is singular plural then the question of responsibility, in the sense of the response of a singular being to another singularity at the expense of responses to other singular beings, does not arise in quite the same way. There is no way in which we *cannot* respond: existence *is* responsibility. To the extent that 'community is given to us with being and as being . . . we cannot not compeer'.[64] And there is no way in which our response can be judged inadequate: there is no transcendent or indeed immanent source for such a judgement. This is not a recipe for doing nothing. Although community is given to us, it is also 'a task and a struggle'.[65] The task is not to stop 'letting the singular outline of our being-in-common expose itself'.[66] The task is *to look at the photographs*, not look away, not assume the pretext of sentimentality or adopt the cynic's concern with authenticity or 'truth' as excuses for not looking.

We are not face to face with the multitude, as first appears when we look at the Cambodian prisoner photographs, but with ourselves as singularities. The task is to find a response that does not reinforce the purpose of inscription and subjectification that the photographs imply, as part of a genocidal state regime, but rather one that engages with the way we are all beyond and before ourselves. What the state attempts is the destruction of being-with or community, through the concentration camp, for example.[67] It is through exposing ourselves to the prisoner images that we can contest that destruction. Such ex-posure is uncomfortable, showing as it does our own finitude and being-with. It is not just that we recognise ourselves in these portraits (these people *could have been* 'us'), but that they *are* 'us':

> We are alike because each one of us is exposed to the outside that *we* are *for ourselves* . . . I do not rediscover *myself*, nor do I recognise *myself* in the other: I experience the other's alterity, or I experience alterity in the other together with the alteration that 'in me' sets my singularity outside me and infinitely delimits it.[68]

In the portrait photograph what we have is 'an exposition: finite existence exposed to finite existence, co-appearing before it and with it.'[69] This appears both in Salgado's children and in the prisoner photographs. In the case of the prisoners, we are distracted by the question of responsibility and the impossibility of both immanence and transcendence. An alternative would be to focus in the case of the second set of images, as in the first, on the way that, as portraits, they expose singularity, in all its limits, together with our inevitable engagement and ex-posure.

NOTES

1. Drafts of this chapter were presented at the Aberystwyth PostInternational Group Tenth Anniversary Conference, University of Wales, Gregynog, 6–8 January 2005 and the Centre for Security Studies Distinguished Speaker

Series, York University, Toronto, Canada, 24 February 2005. Thanks to participants at these meetings and to Martin Coward and Maja Zehfuss for their comments. I am very grateful to Lucie Dunn for her marvellous and timely translation assistance: she saved me from many mistakes. Errors that remain are, needless to say, my own. A longer version of the chapter appears under the title 'Exposed singularity' in *Journal for Cultural Research*, 9:4 (October 2005), pp. 359–86. Thanks to Blackwell Publishers for permission to reproduce extracts here.

2. Jacques Derrida, *The Gift of Death*, trans. David Wills, Chicago, IL: University of Chicago Press, 1995, p. 68.

3. Jean-Luc Nancy, *Being Singular Plural*, trans. Robert D. Richardson and Anne E. O'Byrne, Stanford, CA: Stanford University Press, 2000, p. xiv.

4. The reading of Derrida and responsibility is deliberately limited here to a close reading of one book, *The Gift of Death*.

5. I am, of course, making an assertion here about how people in general might respond to such an exhibition, and I have chosen to interpellate the reader into my interpretation. Clearly, the images could be read differently; there is no reason why visitors should not be bored rather than moved, for example.

6. Sebastiao Salgado, 'The Children of Exodus', Aberystwyth Arts Centre, 26 July–20 September 2003. The exhibition 'Exodus' was designed and curated by Lelia Wanick Salgado and produced by Marcia Navarro Mariano. Selected pictures from the exhibition appear in Salgado, *The Children: Refugees and Migrants*, New York: Aperture, 2000.

7. Notions of childhood are culturally and historically specific, but in many places relate strongly to the idea of 'innocence'; hence the widespread use of images of children in appeals for humanitarian assistance. See, for example, Erica Burman (1991), 'Innocents abroad: Western fantasies of childhood and the iconography of emergencies', *Disasters* 18:3, 238–53.

8. Jean-Luc Nancy, *Le Regard Du Portrait*, Paris: Galilée, 2000, p. 12. The translations are mine; I am indebted to Lucie Dunn for her help.

9. Nancy, *Le Regard Du Portrait*, p. 18.

10. Ibid. p. 18, n1.

11. Ibid. p. 13.

12. Roland Barthes, *Camera Lucida*, trans. Richard Howard, London: Vintage 1993, p. 67.

13. Ibid. p. 71.

14. Nancy, *Le Regard Du Portrait*, p. 16.

15. Ibid. p. 28.

16. Ibid. p. 51.

17. Ibid. p. 34.

18. Ibid. p. 86.

19. The Center for Holocaust and Genocide Studies web site (http://www.chgs.umn.edu) makes a point of telling us that none of the people shown in the photographs it presents were among the survivors.

20. Rachel Hughes (2003), 'The abject artefacts of memory: photographs from Cambodia's genocide', *Media, Culture and Society*, 25:23–44.
21. Derrida, *Gift of Death*, p. 68.
22. Ibid. p. 70.
23. Ibid. p. 71.
24. Ibid. p. 86.
25. Jenny Edkins, *Trauma and the Memory of Politics*, Cambridge: Cambridge University Press, 2003. As Nancy reminds us 'the modern age has struggled to *close the circle* of the time of men and their communities in an immortal communion which death, finally, loses the senseless meaning that it ought to have – and that it has, obstinately', Jean-Luc Nancy, *The Inoperative Community*, trans. P. Connor et al., Minneapolis, MN: Minnesota University Press, 1991, pp. 13–14).
26. Nancy, *Le Regard Du Portrait*, pp. 23–4.
27. Ibid. p. 25.
28. Giorgio Agamben, *Homo Sacer: Sovereign Power and Bare Life*, trans. Daniel Heller-Roazen, Stanford, CA: Stanford University Press, 1998.
29. In other words, are these photographs 'abject objects' as Kerwin Lee Klein characterises many contemporary memorial tropes? (Hughes, 'Abject artefacts,' p. 31).
30. Ibid. p. 33.
31. Ly Daravuth, quoted in Sarah Stephens, *The Legacy of Absence: Cambodian Artists Confront the Past*, Ly Daravuth. 'The Messengers', Reyum, 2000 www.asianart.com/exhibitions/legacy/messengers.html.
32. Ibid.
33. The Tuol Sleng photographs themselves also contain this ambiguity. Some of the people taken to S-21 prison were cadres of the Khmer Rouge regime. The prison functioned to manufacture difference and re-produce 'revolutionaries' as threats to the party (Alexander Laban Hinton, *Why Did They Kill? Cambodia in the Shadow of Genocide*, Berkeley, CA: University of California Press, 2005, pp. 223–9).
34. Primo Levi makes a similar point in his discussions of the Nazi concentration camps; he emphasises the 'grey zone' where the distinction between perpetrator and victim is unclear, but he is in no doubt that he wishes to see people held to account for their conduct (Primo Levi, *If This is A Man and The Truce*, London: Abacus, 1979 and *The Drowned and the Saved*, London: Abacus, 1989).
35. Derrida, *Gift of Death*, p. 44.
36. Ibid. p. 45.
37. Ibid. p. 51.
38. Ibid. p. 51.
39. Ibid. p. 60.
40. Ibid. p. 61.
41. Ibid. p. 68.

42. Nancy, *The Inoperative Community*, p. 3.
43. Ibid.
44. Nancy, *Being Singular Plural*, p. 26.
45. Ibid. p. 32.
46. Ibid. p. 56.
47. Ibid. p. 84.
48. Nancy, *Inoperative Community*, p. xxxvii.
49. Nancy, Being Singular Plural, pp. 84–5.
50. Ibid. p. 85.
51. Nancy, *Inoperative Community*, p. xxxvii.
52. Ibid. p. 14.
53. Ibid. p. 15.
54. Ibid. p. 26.
55. Nancy, *Being Singular Plural*, p. 89.
56. Ibid. p. 89.
57. Nancy, *Inoperative Community*, p. 35.
58. Ibid. p. 32.
59. For example, *Gift of Death*, p. 85.
60. Derrida, *Gift of Death*, p. 68.
61. Ibid.
62. He talks of 'a bond between singularities' (Jacques Derrida, 'Nietzsche and the machine', *Negotiations: Intervention and Interviews 1971–2001*, E. Rottenberg (ed.), Stanford, CA: Stanford University Press, 2002, pp. 215–56; p. 240).
63. Nancy, *Being Singular Plural*, p. 32.
64. Nancy, *Inoperative Community*, p. 35. The translation 'compear' here, which means in English appearing before a judge with another person, is an exact translation of 'com-parution'. Elsewhere, this is translated as 'co-appear' (Nancy, *Being Singular Plural*, p. 201, n. 55 (translator's note)).
65. Nancy, *Inoperative Community*, p. 35.
66. Ibid. 41.
67. Ibid. 35. Agamben's work on Auschwitz raises the question as to whether this optimism is justified (Giorgio Agamben, *Remnants of Auschwitz: The Witness and the Archive*, trans. Daniel Heller-Roazen, New York: Zone Books, 1999.
68. Nancy, *Inoperative Community*, 33–4.
69. Ibid. p. xl.

'Derrida's Theatre of Survival: Fragmentation, Death and Legacy'

Daniel Watt

> Who telleth a tale of unspeaking death?
> Who lifteth the veil of what is to come?
>
> Shelley, *On Death*

The domain of many of Derrida's writings have been philosophical texts, and whilst his works are variously 'used' in literature, the arts, architecture and other academic and creative disciplines, it is often with reference to the history of philosophy that Derrida is discussed.[1] Now within the previous sentence a number of problems and objections are already raised that Derrida has addressed in numerous essays: the concept of the work; distinctions between philosophy and other academic disciplines; the notion of beginning; property and ownership; and not least the legacies, obligations and rivalries within and between these disciplines. Derrida, in discussion about his role as a philosopher, offers this clarification of the orientation of his work:

> My central question is: from what site or non-site (*non-lieu*) can philosophy as such appear to itself as other than itself, so that it can reflect upon itself in an original manner? Such a non-site or alterity would be radically irreducible to philosophy. But the problem is that such a non-site cannot be defined or situated by means of a philosophical language.[2]

Such a 'non-site' seems familiar. It evokes the fragmentary project as inaugurated in *The Athenaeum*, within the context of literature; for that 'project' also concerns an identification (literature with literature, philosophy with philosophy, and each with the other) that cannot take place – a 'neutral manifestation' as Lacoue-Labarthe and Nancy put it.[3] In exploring this non-site, towards which philosophy is fascinatedly drawn and yet resistant too, Derrida articulates the difficulty of drawing boundaries and limits to the work of thought, be it philosophical, literary, historical, etc.[4] That Derrida rarely addresses fragmentation directly is an interesting issue, because so many of his texts have fragmentary modes, or aspects of the fragmentary form.[5] It is not my intention here to draw a totalising theory of the fragment around Derrida's work, or to apply 'Derrida' or 'deconstruction' to the fragment, instead I wish to explore what remains of the fragment in Derrida's texts – and consequently in the remainders of texts, from Heidegger, through to Levinas, Artaud, Barthes, Jabès and Blanchot, that he reads so carefully – and to suggest that the fragment and Derrida survive (on) each other.

What is affirmed in fragmentary writing is not the exclusivity of one particular genre, that of 'the fragment' occurring within a specific cultural and historical context, but the inclusivity of genres. In Derrida's work such an inclusivity is continually in operation drawing together apparently different and singular texts to demonstrate an interdependence of form and content, of argument and tonality, at the unapproachable centre of which is an obligation to keep the event of the future as an arrival, one always in deferral. Derrida's 'project' already includes the possibility of fragmentation at its outset, and this will always be a reiterative 'project' employing and discussing varied forms of fragmentation: ruin, dialogue, garland, chain (which appear throughout Schlegel's *Philosophical Fragments*). Yet it also includes a refusal of *fragmentation*, as it opens into systemisation and reflections on the absolute. In his interview with Henri Ronse Derrida says of his work:

> above all it is necessary to read and reread those in whose wake I write, the 'books' in whose margins and between whose lines I mark out and read a text simultaneously almost identical and entirely other, that I would hesitate, for obvious reasons, to call fragmentary . . .[6]

Hesitation before the programmatic fragmentation of the German Romantics perhaps, with a reference to an already fragmented double reading: Derrida and another. Derrida points his readers backwards to another author who it is necessary to re-read alongside Derrida's remarks, and Derrida is always indicating other writers and thinkers: Blanchot, Levinas, Heidegger, Deleuze. His statement to Ronse disrupts the reader's desire to move through, and beyond, a written work. Such a hesitation though does not carry the authoritarian 'not' of genre (which would exclude the purely sequential reading from beginning to end), Derrida instead defers the issue of the fragmentary, one which will surface in later works with reference to the visual, to art and the gaze. Fragmentary writing, although appearing to be a tightly defined mode of literature, actually bears many structural similarities to the aporias Derrida writes about and generates. However, it is not mere similarities that I wish to explore here, but the possibility that fragmentary writing describes the manner in which such aporias arise. Having said this though, it will become clear that neither the fragment, nor literature, will be easily assimilable into any recognisable critical perspective. The fragment is a work of the future and must remain so *and for no reason*, as Simon Critchley explains, echoing an earlier quotation from Wallace Stevens:

> The future is faced with fragments, with fragments of an impossible future, a future that itself appears fragmentary. And *this is the best*, and *for no reason*. Out of the bonfire of our intellectual vanities comes the ashes of compassion, of tenderness and generosity, and for no reason. After the unworking of human arrogance, we become 'the finally human natives of a dwindling sphere'.[7]

A LEGACY OF FRAGMENTS

Does the aphorism, which undergoes fragmentation, survive? Derrida's use of the aphorism is most clearly evoked in the dialogue between 'Fifty-two aphorisms' and 'Aphorism countertime', for they clearly treat the topic of the aphorism quite differently, drawing into question names such as Romeo (Montague), Juliet (Capulet), and 'deconstruction'. But after all, what's in a name? 'Aphorism: separation in language and, in it, through the name which closes the horizon. Aphorism is at once necessary and impossible'.[8] The naming of the aphorism begins to be drawn back inside a veil of language, into an obscure self-referentiality which is precisely the fascination of the fragmentary. But this is not a hall of mirrors, a narcissistic fascination. As Rodolphe Gasché describes, Derrida's relation to the Romantic abyss is firmly based on survival:

> The elaboration of this economy, which in traditional terms would amount to the thinking of the essence of the abyss, or the abyss in general, consists here, rather in the thinking of the general abysmal. Such thinking takes place, not by plunging oneself – romantically – into the abyss, but on the contrary, by saving 'oneself from falling into the bottomless depths by weaving and holding back the cloth to infinity, textual art of the reprise, multiplication of patches within patches.' In short, by constructing what I have termed the structural infinite. This is

the law that rules the interplay within the philosophical text between spurious infinity and true infinity, a law respectful of their radical difference, but capable also of formalizing these differents' interdependence as, precisely, differents. In thinking the economy of the abyss, deconstructive thought does without the abyss.[9]

There is no clear legacy from Romanticism to Derrida. He would not inherit the futurity (as teleology) of the fragment, or the edifying architecture of the aphorism. Instead the project, already interrupted with a commitment to fragmentation, is *perhaps* 'recast' and literature clearly supplements the philosophical agenda. Geoffrey Bennington, in 'Genuine Gasché (perhaps)', analyses the 'rephilosophising' of Derrida's work through Gasché's texts, finding in the event of a 'perhaps' the difficulty posed by Derrida's work to the hermetic environment of philosophy:

> Reading as such *always* engages a radical perhaps – and thereby a responsibility – insofar as it must *open* the book to get started. Gasché's rigorous insistence on philosophy as the true home of Derrida's work, his immeasurably helpful precision around the tradition Derrida reads, curiously refers us in its interstices to that 'perhaps'. A *certain* silence in Gasché calls irresistibly for our further unrepentant inventions of a still unread Derrida to come.[10]

Bennington continues to describe how Derrida 'frees up a non-traditional and essentially non-academic relation to tradition and its traditionality that is the chance of tradition's no longer determining what futures are now to come'.[11] Gasché's 'structural infinite' is certainly an excellent and clear demonstration of the non-abyssal nature of the philosophical slope of Derrida's work, however it fails to take account of the activity of interrupted, fragmentary infinity which opens the work outside of the philosophical space. Again Bennington shows how this 'vertiginous perspective' opened by reading (*perhaps* an always fragmented enterprise) 'cannot possibly "belong" to philosophy, and it is just the sort of thing that Gasché cannot but anathematise as "literary", though it cannot possibly "belong" to literature or literary criticism either'.[12]

Perhaps one difference between the aphorism and the fragment that should be emphasised is the name. An aphorism is authored, a fragment gestures towards the anonymous. Frequently the fragment fails at achieving anonymity, but the desire remains.[13] Derrida's paradoxical aphorisms, at once referring to each other, yet sufficient unto themselves and then continually undermining such definitions, are elaborately aporetic. Despite the complexities of property, ownership and authorship, we can still say that these belong to Derrida: his signature (re)marks them as aphorisms, they are not fragments, Derrida says as much: 'Despite their fragmentary appearance, they make a sign towards the memory of a totality, at the same time ruin and monument'.[14] However, here there is also confirmation of the impossibility of limiting the aphorism to a specific genre. The lure of the fragmentary is the simulacrum of the systematic, or the elaboration of micro-systems that can destroy their connecting macro-system. Such cancerous parasitism may seem horrific, but it is the force with which parts of a fragmentary system communicate with each other. Such a force is certainly present in Derrida's aphorisms, and it feeds from our desire to be taught, the didactic power of the aphorism is put to work by Derrida to evoke fragmentary dissemination: 'One expects the aphorism to pronounce the truth. It prophesises, sometimes vaticinates, proffers that which will be, stops in advance in a monumental form, certainly, but anarchitecturally: dissociated and a-systematic'.[15] Later though another tells us: 'Whether we like it or not the aphorism is irremediably edifying'[16] and the next in the series confirms the enlightening and structurally cohesive system of aphoristic foundation:

> There is nothing more architectural than a pure aphorism, says the other/so it is said [*dit l'autre*]. Architecture in the most philosophical form of its concept is neither a pure interruption, nor a dissociated fragment, but a totality which claims to be self-sufficient, the figure of a system (according to Kant the architectonic is the art of systems). It has the most authoritative, peremptory, dogmatic and complacently self-legitimising eloquence when it does everything to leave out a structural demonstration.[17]

Here, Derrida begins by offering a ghostly quotation, *dit l'autre*, with the otherness of a different voice. Such a voice, or the possibility of one, is the opportunity of every fragment, and of each aphorism as they appear here. The very specificity of these aphorisms would describe the limits of this fragmentary genre if it were not for the fact that their very 'architecture' is already founded on some loss, a ruination at the heart of the builder's enterprise.

Each aphorism in a series begins a manoeuvre, one that is completed once and for all within the confines of the aphorism, each one a preface towards the structure of their assembly. In each prefatory step something speaks, or opens the joining of architecture and signature, referring to all work by Derrida, from beginning to end, and both of these within each aphorism called to give account 'before the law', which is also this door. The 'speaking before' contained within the word preface will, therefore, become an account and legitimation of the urge to appear before the door of the law, and perhaps how one came – like a man from the country – to have such presumption. Bachelard writes: 'If one were to give an account of all the doors one has closed and opened, of all the doors one would like to re-open, one would have to tell the story of one's entire life',[18] including here the impossible paradox of concluding the story, the very narration of which would be the story of a life. The meeting of preface and aphorism perhaps opens too many doors and this is why Derrida emphasises the incompatibility of the aphorism with the preface: 'A preface reassembles, links, articulates, anticipates the passages, denies the aphoristic discontinuities. There is a genre forbidden to the preface, it is the aphorism'.[19] Yet, here it is, we are reading it, the forbidden genre applied. It may be protested that such reflexivity in the work opens an infinite void of disengagement with the work, an unbridgeable gap. There can be no critical purchase on such a blatant denial of the actual text, especially when followed by the particularly alarming: 'This is not an aphorism'.[20] Yet it is also because ordered and sequential, and conventionally read in series, that the aphoristic tendency to accumulate whilst dispersing is so appealing. It results in attracting the preface, including the preface within an (and all) aphorism, because each one systematically begins without building architecturally.

It is through quotation and repetition that the aphorism begins to acquire the power of diverse movement, stepping out beyond the confines of ordered reading, quotation disorders the event of the aphorism *fragmenting* it into a fragment.[21] This allows an interruption similar to the use of quotation in Benjamin's 'What is epic theatre?', where 'interruption is one of the fundamental devices of all structuring' and 'quot[ation of] a text involves the interruption of its context'.[22] Derrida also finds that, 'without interruption – between letters, words, sentences, books – no signification could be awakened'.[23] It would be easy to become misled here into an understanding of textual teleology as opposed to interruption. I think it is Derrida's claim that such interruption is already occurring even in a text with apparently solid origins and endings, and without interruption (even at the level of each letter) all would become homogenised. Interruption, through quotation, also reintroduces the legacy of thought and the survival of thinking back into the text; deferring the thought of the one who writes into the (fragmented) tradition of their own discourse.

The fragment, most deceptively as the broken fragment of antiquity, draws us towards the negative teleology of the ruin: as broken vessel tempting reassembly. The name of deconstruction also carries with it (an)architectural metaphors, that are certainly tempting but remain distanced by chains of metonymy such as hymen, différance, trace, pharmakon, etc. What remains of the force of interruption is an arena, or dramatic staging (a Brechtian Gest perhaps), of the desire to disperse whilst enjoining. Derrida describes this obligation – a particularly fragmentary obligation – early in 'Aphorism countertime':

> The impossible – this theatre of double survival – also tells, like every aphorism, the truth. Right from the pledge which binds together two desires, each is already in mourning for the other, entrusts death to the other as well: if you die before me, I will keep you, if I die before you, you will carry me in yourself, one will keep the other, will already have kept the other from the first declaration.[24]

This survival, or remembrance, is one beyond death or the dispersion inherent in the fragmentary temptation. It is this stepping beyond that characterises Derrida's relation to the theatrical, a space which is again a fragmentary one, as two conflicting desires (to perform and survive, but also to end and die) are maintained at once. Timothy Clark traces the theatre of impossibility that is played out so often in Derrida's texts:

> In almost any of those essays in which the question of literature is to the fore, th[e] theatrical model is one of Derrida's principal resources. It is prominent in the two essays in Antonin Artaud (especially 'The Theatre of Cruelty and the Closure of Representation' (WD, pp. 232–50)) as well as 'Dissemination' (Diss, pp. 289–366) and 'The Double Session' (Diss, pp. 175–286) and it is also implicit in Derrida's forceful versions of dialogue. The 'stage' becomes a philosophical and specifically a Heideggerian space. It engages with being in terms of its ambivalent status between appearing and signification, concerning as it does that 'presence (which) does not present itself . . . which disappears in the act of allowing to appear' (Diss, p. 314).[25]

Whenever there seems to have emerged a clear presentation of terminology, Derrida complicates the chain of signification, disrupting reading into the deferred (or ambiguous) space of the theatricality of language. Such an action is not to obscure the discussion, or simply to render indeterminate the issues at stake. Instead it is a strategic use of fragmentation, even at the level of denial of the preface, introduction, thesis and entire trajectory of an argument. In denying the totalised, or absolute, so much a part of many fragmentary projects, Derrida himself 'recasts' the fragment into the 'theatrical model' that Clark describes, where the work, again, disappears whilst appearing. It is a twisted path then, one which proceeds by arresting the arche-teleological momentum: a non-step, or 'certain step of the dance'.[26] What of all these non-steps, or possible steps trodden over, in the course of 'Fifty-two aphorisms for a foreword': *pas de préface* (aphorism 15), *pas de projet* (aphorism 38), *pas de l'habitat pour l'aphorism* (aphorism 41)? Derrida employs the metaphor of this movement with a similar effect to that of (an)architecture discussed above. This is a carefully structured fragmentary *step*, it operates the movement of an individual fragment (generating structure and dynamism), whilst withdrawing the power of each to be finally situated with reference to each other. Therefore, steps within the argument, and equally the preface, project and space of such an argument are deferred and returned to the pure kinetics of their event as fragments. And these again are recontextualised, as Clark states the 'theatre' of this dialogue is Heideggerian. Derrida seeks to repeat the traditional movement of a philosophical discourse, whilst at the same time resituating its main protagonists, be they Heidegger, Freud or Artaud, making their thought survive, but through a sort of oscillating space that neither advances nor retreats. Explaining this stepping back and forth Derrida writes of the steps taken in advancing a thesis concerning Freud's 'Beyond the pleasure principle':

> Now, if one attempts to make oneself attentive to the original modality of the 'speculative,' and to the singular *proceeding* [*démarche*] of this writing, its *pas de thèse* which advances without advancing, without advancing itself, without ever advancing anything that it does not immediately take back, for the time of a detour, without ever positing anything which remains in its position, then one must recognize that the following chapter repeats, in place and in another place, the immobile *emplacement* of the *pas de thèse*. It repeats itself, it illustrates only the repetition of that very thing (the absolute authority of the PP) which finally will not let anything be done without it (him), except repetition itself.[27]

Derrida allows his own work to undergo a process of dissolution, into repetitive structures, into performances which have vitality due to their detours, which are also immobile but demand to be repeated. It is an urge to perform with fidelity but also to deviate and innovate. Such a 'place' is the arena of fragmentary writing in which the form describes an apparent fixed and repeated structure, but the actual assembly (especially when reflected in a critical environment) is open to a different serialisation. Again the issue of movement, arrival and steps appear together, alluded to as a non-step of a thesis, but also a familiar step and one that Derrida has mentioned before especially in 'The time of a thesis: punctuations', concerning his thesis supervisor Jean Hyppolite who remarked that he was not quite sure where Derrida 'was going':

> I think that I replied to him more or less as follows: 'If I clearly saw ahead of time where I was going, I really don't believe that I should take another step to get there.' Perhaps I then thought that knowing where one is going may doubtless help in orienting one's own thought, but that it has never made anyone take a single step, quite the opposite in fact.[28]

Then later: 'this strategy is a strategy without any finality; for this is what I hold and what in turn holds me in its grip, the aleatory strategy of someone who admits he does not know where he is going'.[29] Derrida's work is infused with the dynamics of fragmentation, of a series of texts which do not simply recoup themselves into the 'edifying' discourse of a theory of 'deconstruction'. The movement of fragmentation will be one of chance then, of a connectivity which cannot be prescribed, but will be under the sway of a language that continually assumes a programmed system of reading. Derrida notes in 'My chances':

> We certainly count on the calculating capacity of language, with its code and game, with what regulates its play and plays with its regulations. We count on that which is destined to random chance (*ce qui destine au hasard*), while at the same time reducing chance. Since the expression '*destiner au hasard*' can have two syntaxes and therefore can carry two meanings in French, it is at once of sufficient determination *and* indetermination to leave room for the chances to which it speaks in its course (*trajet*) and even in its 'throw' ('*jet*'). This depends, as they say, on the context; but a context is never determined enough to prohibit all possible random deviation.[30]

So the destiny of fragmentary chance is to be both a calculation, part of the system of fragmentation, but also an abandonment to manifold random meanings, the *fragmentation* of the system. The chance of contextual randomness is not recouped by any arbitrary designation of limits, as Derrida states in 'Living on: border lines' where, 'no context is saturable any more. No one inflection enjoys any absolute privilege, no meaning can be fixed or decided upon. No border is guaranteed, inside or out'.[31] The potency of chance is also the issue of the final aphorism in 'Fifty-two aphorisms for a foreword' which describes the interruptive event of fragmentation (the potential of another reading) as the chance of the aphorism: 'Maintaining [*maintenir*], despite the temptations, despite the possible reapproriation, the chance of the aphorism, is to keep within the interruption, without the interruption, the promise of giving place, if it is necessary/if it is missing [*s'il le faut*]. But it is never given'.[32] This 'giving place' can refer to both the event of the aphorism – its actual statement – and the relinquishing of that event to the fragmentary chance of a different context. As Derrida mentions though, this is not simply given over to a different context without maintaining the possibility of another 'missing' context. Such fragmentation within Derrida's work is a step back, a re-reading, that explores a way of representing, or staging, the marginal without nostalgia. In a passionate entry in 'Biodegradable seven diary fragments' Derrida writes:

> One of the most necessary gestures of a deconstructive understanding of history consists rather (this is its very style) in transforming things by exhibiting writings, genres, textual strata (which is to say – since there is no outside-the-text, right – exhibiting institutional, economic, political, pulsive [and so on] 'realities') that have been repulsed, repressed, devalorized, minoritized, deligitimated, occulted by hegemonic canons, in short, all that which certain forces have attempted to melt down into the anonymous mass of an unrecognizable culture, to '(bio)degrade' in the common compost of a memory said to be living and organic. From this point of view, deconstructive interpretation and writing would come along, without any soteriological mission, to 'save', in some sense, lost heritages. This is not done without a counterevaluation, in particular a political one. One does not exhume just anything. And one transforms while exhuming.[33]

Not salvation, in terms of recovering what is lost for the reassembly of the fragments of a ruined past: a return to the eschatology of a dying culture. It is a stranger 'exhibition' that Derrida suggests, more like the salvage of flotsam from a wrecked ship. This also clearly explains Derrida relation to the thinkers and writers that he deals with so deeply: he has no mission of salvation, rather a task of transformation. The task of deconstructive thought would be to enable survival through transformation, rather than survival for the sake of 'going on'. Of course, in the above quotation Derrida is engaged with addressing criticism of his work on Paul De Man, and with the violence of quotation perhaps a certain displacement has occurred in its citation. This is also what is at stake in the fragment, its chances, how it easily doubles into both the ruination and achievement of an urge to be separate and connected. Early in the same work Derrida reflects upon the assembly of his thoughts: 'I will reassemble these remains while reflecting them a little. Filtering and ordering. We'll see what can be saved of them. But to float on the surface [*surnager*] does not necessarily mean to survive [*survivre*] . . .'.[34] As in 'Countertime 9' the question of survival appears, one that bears a complex series of problems in translation,[35] where each might precede another and destroy the entire edifice constructed by the series. 'Biodegradeables' maintains a fragmentary dialogue with other texts by Derrida and in raising the issue of survival again we find that this is one of his central concerns throughout many works.

'AS IF I WERE TWO': DERRIDA AND OTHER SPECTRES

In 'On a newly arisen apocalyptic tone in philosophy' many of the issues discussed with relation to the fragment are repeated with reference to 'tone' and philosophy. During the course of this essay it becomes clear that the tone of philosophy is not easily separable from the matter with which it wishes to deal. The structure of Derrida's essay is fragmentary, without expressing itself explicitly so. The gaps between each passage interrupt, separate and divide the discourse, they also perform the theatrical double space discussed earlier, and such theatricality becomes the subject of such importance within the essay itself, a cryptic dance of Isis, veiling and unveiling. Isolating one such fragmentary movement within the essay, bearing in mind the responsibility and infidelity of quotation previously explored, we read: 'This cryptopolitics is also a cryptopoetics, a poetic perversion of philosophy. And it is a matter of the veil and of castration'.[36] The cryptography of the 'mystagogue' (non-philosopher) becomes the subject of Kant's attack on what he views as an emergence of mysticism and pseudo-philosophy, embodied most dangerously in the person of 'a certain Schlosser'[37] whose translation of Plato's letters shows, for Kant, an increasing 'aristocratic esotericism' and 'idolatry of figures and numbers'.[38] Schlosser's very name allows a certain play around keys and castles, secrets and guardianship. Derrida presents Kant's objections to the emerging 'tones' in philosophy as a musical assemblage of fragmentary passages, indeed, he plays on the notion of musicality when addressing the delirium of the disordering of thought: 'The *Verstimmung* we are speaking about here is indeed a social disorder and a derangement, an out-of-tune-ness [*désaccordement*] of strings and voices in the head'.[39] Such a musical analogy also appears in 'Aphorism countertime', where the aphorism itself becomes an accidental musical derangement: 'An aphorism is exposure to contretemps. It exposes discourses – hands it over to contretemps. Literally – because it is abandoning a word [*une parole*] to its letter'.[40] The issue of being 'out of time' also bears on the apocalyptic because time is both running out but also the score of the apocalypse is, no doubt, of a 'time that is deranged and off its hinges'[41] as Blanchot has put it.

In such times, at the end of time, the obligation comes to speak with another voice, or at least admit the possibility of another tone of voice. That is precisely what Derrida does when he cites Holderlin, Heidegger, Blanchot and Nietzsche later in the essay. In a question concerning language and the last man (capitalised here to designate the last man of Nietzsche's 'Oedipus', and Blanchot's and Mary Shelley's fictions of the same title[42]) Derrida asks if all language is not that of the last man, and bearing in mind Kant's horror at the *castration* of philosophy at the hands of the 'mystagogues' it is important to bear in mind the double eschatology of this last man. A fragmentary doubling occurs here, where the voice returning to the last man is both his own but also that of another: ' "it forces me to speak as if I were two" '.[43] The fragment also speaks with such a voice, at once isolated and entirely contained, and at the next moment rhizomatically communicating with other fragments, constructing networks of association which then make the fragment alien and strange: a singular voice, off-beat, and fractured into exponential doublings. Derrida makes clear that such plurality is not decipherable, that is precisely the message it will deliver (but not in time, too late), because it is increasingly multiple, and not recoverable into an object of philosophical examination: 'it would be necessary to begin by respecting this differential multiplication [*démultiplication*] of voices and tones that perhaps divides them beyond a distinct and calculable plurality'.[44] Like the fragmentary series, which continually yields to different readings, so too the apocalyptic becomes 'the structure of every scene of writing in general'[45] and can only be enabled to occur, to be respected, as that which is promised to come.

Of course, this other that already dwells within philosophy, and is sent through language, is not simply literature, and neither is it *not* literature, to choose either of these possibilities would be to fail to heed what Bennington has already said of Gasche's 'anathematization' of literature. The relation of philosophy to literature is a complex one, a never resolved dispute of ownership and displacement. The fragment supplants conventional modes of textual and theoretical presentation, forming another pocket, or fold, of representation. The denial of the ideality of fragmentation is also an invitation in Derrida's work to read in fragments, to make a spectral guest of the fragment, which is already at the margins, ready to speak in another voice. In *Specters of Marx* an invitation is offered, the fragment invited as this 'unnameable and neutral power':

To welcome, we were saying then, but even while apprehending, with anxiety and the desire to exclude the stranger, to invite the stranger without accepting him or her, domestic hospitality that welcomes without welcoming the stranger, but a stranger who is already found within (*das Heimliche-Unheimliche*), more intimate with one than one is oneself, the absolute proximity of a stranger whose power is singular *and* anonymous (*es spukt*), an unnameable and neutral power, that is undecideable, neither active nor passive, an an-identity that, *without doing anything*, invisibly occupies places belonging finally neither to us nor to it.[46]

Interrupting so many of Derrida's texts, and especially in 'Fifty-two aphorisms for a foreword' and 'Aphorism countertime', is the work of Blanchot, never named in either, but surviving in the frequent use of '*arrêt de mort*' in the latter and the duality of the '*pas*' (step *not* beyond) in the former. In denying the ideality of fragmentation in German Romanticism, Derrida offers an aphoristic series that is similar to the fragment of Blanchot. Derrida's fragmentation is also a reading of Blanchot, one that survives the ruin because the work of death itself is postponed, 'arrested'. The fragmentary work offered by Derrida survives this arrest which separates each fragment from the title of each work, from the entitlement to belong to each work. It is a dubious immortality that the fragment offers: an undeath, or living on beyond the limits of an intact body. Such survival is the posthumous communication operating between Derrida, Blanchot, Heidegger . . . (and here it would be possible to insert all the names, of authors, artists, philosophers that Derrida has addressed), and between fragments.

The work of affirmation and fragmentation become so entwined, playing out the 'theatre of double survival' and other techniques or stagings of the desire to 'live on', and through such an affirmation of the future Derrida's work seems to speak of the fragment without directly addressing it. Lacoue-Labarthe and Nancy also find that 'Derrida's work on and around writing, the trace, and the dissemination of writing continues to proceed in the direction of this "thing" [the missing element that they describe as an "eclipse of the manifest in its manifestation"] – if indeed it implies a direction to take'.[47] They are careful with the word direction, for Derrida has been more than clear that he has no firm concept of the direction his work moves in. Equally the 'tradition' of such work, which includes Heidegger and Blanchot, has a difficult directionality, one that Derrida points out in *Aporias*:

When Blanchot constantly repeats – and it is a long complaint and not a triumph of life – the impossible dying, the impossibility, alas, of dying, he says at once the same thing and something completely different from Heidegger. It is just a question of knowing in which sense (in the sense of direction and trajectory) one reads the expression the possibility of impossibility.[48]

An invitation is opened to a sort of metastatic directionality enabling a reading of impossibility which, like the fragmentary, does not dispense with chance, misreadings and rewriting.

NOTES

1. See Jacques Derrida, *Positions*, trans. Alan Bass, Chicago, IL: Chicago University Press, 1981, particularly the interview with Henri Ronse pp. 3–14, pp. 42–3 and 93–5. Also Derrida's comments in an interview with Derek Attridge show the complex relationship that Derrida elaborates between philosophy and literature, and also his own reading of texts within each tradition. Derrida comments:

   Perhaps against the backdrop of an impotence or inhibition faced with a literary writing I desired but always placed higher up and further away from myself, I quickly got interested in either a form of literature which bore a question about literature, or else a philosophical type of activity which interrogated the relationship between speech and writing. Philosophy also seemed more political, let's say, more capable of posing politically the question of literature with the political seriousness and consequentiality it requires. ('"This Strange Institution Called Literature": An Interview with Jacques Derrida' in *Acts of Literature*. Derek Attridge (ed.), London: Routledge, 1992, pp. 33–75 at 39).

2. Richard Kearney, *States of Mind*, Manchester: Manchester University Press, 1995, p. 159.

3. See Phillipe Lacoue-Labarthe and Jean-Luc Nancy, *The Literary Absolute*, trans. Philip Barnard and Cheryl Lester, Albany, NY: State University of New York Press, 1988, p. 123. See also pp. 28–9 concerning the philosophical basis of German Romanticism.

4. On the subject of Derrida's relation to philosophy and 'the tradition' see Rodolphe Gasché's essay 'The law of tradition', in Gasché, Rodolphe, *Inventions of Difference: On Jacques Derrida*, London: Harvard University Press, 1994, pp. 58–81, especially pp. 59–62.

5. Most obviously these will be 'Fifty-two aphorisms for a foreword' and 'Aphorism countertime', but all of Derrida's work on some level disrupts the conventional presentation of philosophical and critical thought. Often this takes the form of parallel discussions, or texts that run alongside each other

down, or across the page, such as 'Tympan', 'Living on/Border lines' and *Glas*. The only texts, that I am aware of, to actually contain the word 'fragment' in their titles are 'Biodegradeables seven diary fragments' in *Critical Inquiry*, 15:4 (Summer 1989), 812–73 and 'Letter to Jean Genet (fragments)' in Derrida, Jacques, *Negotiations*, trans. Elizabeth Rottenberg, Stanford, CA: Stanford University Press, 2002, pp. 41–6.

6. Jacques Derrida, *Positions*, trans. Alan Bass, Chicago, IL: Chicago University Press, 1981, p. 4.

7. Simon Critchley, *Very Little . . . Almost Nothing*, London: Routledge, 1997, p. 138.

8. Jacques Derrida, 'Aphorism countertime', in Derek Attridge (ed.), *Acts of Literature*, London: Routledge, 1992, pp. 414–33, aphorism 22.

9. Gasché, *Inventions of Difference*, pp. 146–7.

10. Geoffrey Bennington, *Interrupting Derrida*, London: Routledge, 2000, p. 160.

11. Ibid. p. 161.

12. Ibid. p. 161.

13. Few fragmentary projects have ever achieved the anonymity that has been one of their principal aims. This is for a number of reasons, often through posthumous collection such as Benjamin's *Arcades Project*, or through academic curiosity such as the attribution of different *Athenaeum Fragments* to Friedrich and August Wilhelm Schlegel, Novalis and Schleiermacher.

14. Jacques Derrida, 'Fifty-two aphorisms for a foreword' in Papadakis et al., *Deconstruction: Omnibus Volume*, London: Academy Editions, 1989, pp. 67–9, aphorism 46 (future reference by aphorism number).

15. Ibid. aphorism 2.

16. Ibid. aphorism 42.

17. Ibid. aphorism 43.

18. Gaston Bachelard, *The Poetics of Space*, trans. Maria Jolas, Boston, MA: Beacon Press, 1994, p. 224.

19. Derrida, 'Fifty-two aphorisms for a foreword', aphorism 20.

20. Derrida, 'Fifty-two aphorisms for a foreword', aphorism 21.

21. This is a very literary event that Derrida describes with reference to Blanchot and Goethe, to death and reading, the fragment and totality, in *Demeure*, trans. Elizabeth Rottenberg, Stanford, CA: Stanford University Press, 2000, pp. 44–5.

22. Walter Benjamin, *Illuminations*, Hannah Arendt (ed.), London: Fontana Press, 1992, p. 148.

23. Jacques Derrida, *Writing and Difference*, trans. Alan Bass, London: Routledge, 1978, p. 71.

24. Derrida, 'Aphorism countertime', aphorism 17.

25. Timothy Clark, *Derrida, Heidegger, Blanchot: Sources of Derrida's Notion and Practice of Literature*, Cambridge: Cambridge University Press, 1992, p. 114.

26. Jacques Derrida, *Margins of Philosophy*, trans. Alan Bass, London: Harvester Wheatsheaf, 1982, p. 27.

27. Jacques Derrida, *The Post Card: From Socrates to Freud and Beyond*. trans. Alan Bass, Chicago, IL: Chicago University Press, 1987, pp. 293–94. See also notes 1 and 2 on these pages which emphasise the continued play on *pas*, throughout 'Freud's legacy', and also on *démarche* which unworks the thesis as it is advanced.

28. Jacques Derrida, 'The time of a thesis: punctuations', trans. Kathleen McLaughlin, in A. Montefiore (ed.), *Philosophy in France Today*, Cambridge: Cambridge University Press, 1983, pp. 34–50 at 36–37.

29. Ibid. p. 50.

30. Jacques Derrida, 'My chances/*Mes Chances*: A rendez-vous with some Epicurean stereophonies', in. J. Smith and W. Kerrigan (eds), *Taking Chances*, Baltimore, MD: Johns Hopkins University Press, 1984, pp. 1–32 at 4.

31. Jacques Derrida, 'Living on/Borderlines', in Bloom et al., *Deconstruction and Criticism*, New York: Continuum, 1979, pp. 75–176 at 78.

32. Derrida, 'Fifty-two aphorisms for a foreword', aphorism 52.

33. Jacques Derrida, 'Biodegradeables seven diary fragments', in *Critical Inquiry*, 15:4 (Summer 1989), 812–73 at 821.

34. Ibid. p. 812.

35. See Nicholas Royle's note number 3, accompanying 'Aphorism countertime' where he describes the multiple meanings of *Survivre*, surviving beyond, upon, despite, etc. One of the most forceful of these meanings, because it is also double is 'living on' which also directs the reader to 'Living on/Border lines'.

36. Jacques Derrida, 'On a newly arisen apocalyptic tone in philosophy', in P. Fenves, (ed.), *Raising the Tone of Philosophy*, Baltimore, MD: Johns Hopkins University Press, 1993, pp. 117–71 at 136.

37. Ibid. p. 135.

38. Ibid. p. 135.

39. Ibid. p. 132.

40. Derrida, 'Aphorism countertime', aphorism 4.

41. Maurice Blanchot, *The Writing of the Disaster*, Lincoln, NE: University of Nebraska Press, 1995, p. 78.

42. In 'The ends of the fragment, the problem of the preface: proliferation and finality in *The Last Man*', in Michael Eberle-Sinatra (ed.), *Mary Shelley's Fictions: From Frankenstein to Falkner*, Basingstoke: Macmillan pp. 22–38, Sophie Thomas explores the curious temporality of Shelley's preface in relation to Derrida:

> The preface thus makes present and absent what is to follow. Having anticipated everything, Derrida points out, it cancels the need for the main text. The difficult status of the preface, then, is both temporal and conceptual, and its difficulty is in no small part related to its status as a fragment in relation to the work it introduces. (p. 35)

43. Derrida, 'On a newly arisen apocalyptic tone in philosophy', p. 147.

44. Ibid. p. 156.

45. Ibid. p. 156.

46. Jacques Derrida, *Specters of Marx*, trans. Peggy Kamuf, London: Routledge, 1994, p. 172.
47. Lacoue-Labarthe and Nancy, *The Literary Absolute*, p. 124.
48. Jacques Derrida, *Aporias*, trans. Thomas Dutoit, Stanford, CA: Stanford University Press, 1993, p. 77.

Derrida vs Habermas Revisited

Lasse Thomassen[1]

INTRODUCTION: LET'S HAVE A 'DISCUSSION'!

Jürgen Habermas and Jacques Derrida, who are arguably two of the most important contemporary European philosophers, are typically taken as representatives of incommensurable approaches of modern and post-modern thought, and of critical theory and post-structuralism, respectively.[2] Over the years, Habermas, Derrida and their respective followers have viewed the other side as, at best irrelevant, at worst philosophically and politically dangerous. Yet, on 31 May 2003, Habermas and Derrida published an article together on the future role of Europe in *Frankfurter Allgemeine Zeitung* and *Libération*. Due to illness, Derrida was only able to write, together with Habermas, only a brief preface to the co-signed article. In it they write of the 'necess[ity] and urgen[cy] that French and German philosophers lift their voices together, whatever disagreements may have separated them in the past'.[3] This was a remarkable event in light of their earlier hostile exchanges in the 1980s. In 1985, Habermas published two chapters on Derrida in *The Philosophical Discourse of Modernity*.[4] The intellectual climate in Germany at the time was marked by an opposition between Enlightenment, reason and modernity, on the one hand, and what Habermas, among others, saw as the dangerous post-modern and neo-conservative critique of reason, on the other hand. If Habermas's reading of Derrida was unsympathetic, so were Derrida's responses to Habermas.[5] As he later noted, he had responded 'as far as possible with arguments, but admittedly a little polemical'.[6]

Initially, some commentators on the Habermas–Derrida debate divided themselves according to their allegiance to either Habermas and critical theory,[7] or Derrida and deconstruction.[8] However, a number of commentators, while no doubt more sympathetic to one than the other, argued that the opposition between Habermas and Derrida rested on misunderstandings. For instance, Christopher Norris argued that both Derrida and

Habermas work within the tradition of Enlightenment and Kant, and that Habermas's reading of Derrida as a total critic of reason was therefore misplaced.[9] Richard J. Bernstein and Richard Rorty, in different ways, argued that the two thinkers are complementary, asking different but equally important questions.[10]

More recently, commentators have argued that Derrida and Habermas are more or less complementary when it comes to ethics and politics, thus suggesting that even if *philosophical* disagreements remain, it may be possible for Derrideans and Habermasians to engage in a meaningful dialogue at the level of *ethics* and, especially, *politics*.[11] Likewise, others have argued that, while there are philosophical differences between Habermas and Derrida, one can supplement Habermas with Derrida,[12] or Derrida with Habermas.[13] This reflects Habermas's development of a discourse theory of law and democracy and Derrida's increased emphasis on political and ethical questions during the last two decades. It is in these areas that there has been a certain rapprochement between Derrida and Habermas during recent years. In the preface to their jointly signed article on Europe, Derrida writes that, '[d]espite all the obvious differences in their approaches and arguments', he 'shares [the] definitive premises and perspectives' of Habermas's views in the article:

> the determination of new European political responsibilities beyond any Eurocentrism; the call for a renewed confirmation and effective transformation of international law and its institutions, in particular the UN; a new conception and a new praxis for the distribution of state authority, etc., according to the spirit, if not the precise sense, that refers back to the Kantian tradition.[14]

Despite their differences, Derrida and Habermas are aligned against the same common enemies: inequalities arising from neo-liberalist policies, terrorism, including state-terrorism, nationalism and xenophobia.[15]

In a celebration of Habermas's seventy-fifth birthday in 2004, Derrida writes how, 'at a "party"' at the end of the 1990s, and '[w]ith a friendly smile, [Habermas] came up to me and proposed that we have a "discussion"'.[16] In *The Philosophical Discourse of Modernity*, Habermas had written that Derrida 'does not belong to those philosophers who like to argue'.[17] This view seems to have changed. Not only does Habermas now believe it is possible to discuss and argue with Derrida, but the gesture was mutual, and there was a new tone to Derrida and Habermas's comments on one another's respective works.[18] Although this is not the place to speculate about the reasons for this change, the change in intellectual climate from the 1980s to the late 1990s and today may not be without importance. In the 1980s, Habermas's reading of Derrida and deconstruction was cast in terms of either/or (either for or against reason, and so on). Today, with Derrida's explicit political writings, Habermas may acknowledge Derrida's allegiance to the ideals of the Enlightenment, even if he may be suspicious of his philosophical position.

These developments make it important to revisit and engage with the differences and affinities between Habermas's and Derrida's works. In light of new personal and political rapprochement, one must ask whether old philosophical disagreements remain. I will argue that the apparent rapprochement at the political level should not let us overlook the philosophical disagreements that remain, including disagreements over the nature and role of philosophy, to which I turn first. Of particular interest here is how one may or may not affirm the value of philosophy, and how Habermas and Derrida link philosophy to what Derrida calls an 'ethics of discussion'. In the subsequent section, I will consider Habermas's and Derrida's respective approaches to language and how they influence the ways they theorise.[19] As will become clear, my sympathies lie with Derridean deconstruction. Although I shall try to be fair to Habermas's position, the following is also (but not only) a defence of Derrida's work against the criticisms against it put forward from Habermas and other critical theorists.

The Initial Accusation: Subverting Philosophy

Habermas's *The Philosophical Discourse of Modernity* was one long defence of modernity, Enlightenment and reason and against what he saw as a post-modern and neo-conservative onslaught on those ideals. While Habermas's reading of Derrida in that book was perhaps not the most acute, it is none the less useful to take a second look at it here. In this section I shall consider his accusation that Derrida levels the distinctions between, primarily, philosophy and literature and, secondarily, logic and rhetoric. Because, as Habermas alleges, Derrida treats philosophy as literature, he undermines any appeal to reason and argument, and he treats argument and reasoning – including logic and philosophy – only in terms of rhetorical success. Thus, philosophical argument does not depend on logical criteria or the open exchange of reasons, but on the rhetorical use of words whose meanings are multiple.[20]

Habermas sees the levelling of these distinctions as Derrida's way of avoiding a performative contradiction. If Derrida were engaged in serious philosophical activity, Habermas argues, his absolute critique of reason would be caught in a performative contradiction because he would be appealing to what he was simultaneously criticising, namely reason. By levelling the distinctions and situating himself within a generalised literature and rhetoricity, Derrida is able to avoid a performative contradiction. However, avoiding the charge of performative contradiction comes at the price of blunting the force of critique.[21] According to Habermas, there is nothing left in Derrida or deconstruction with which to stand against unreason. Thereby Derrida – whatever his intentions – in fact plays into the hands of unreason and of conservative forces against emancipatory progress. This is the reason for Habermas's passionate defence of philosophical argument against what he sees as Derrida's subversion of the possibility of serious philosophy and, with it, the ideals of modernity, Enlightenment and reason.

In *The Philosophical Discourse of Modernity*, Habermas furthermore criticised Derrida for levelling the distinction between the two functions of language: problem solving and world disclosure. For Habermas, we can fall back on a number of idealisations that we make whenever we engage in communicative action. Once these communicative structures have been clarified, we can therefore proceed to solve problems of truth and normative rightness, whereas for Derrida, insight remains essentially shrouded in blindness. In Habermas's words: 'Derrida neglects the potential for negation inherent in the validity basis of action oriented toward reaching understanding; he permits the capacity to solve problems to disappear behind the world-creating capacity of language.'[22]

It is worth emphasising that Habermas does *not* argue that literature does not or should not play any role in our lives. It does, but one must distinguish literature from philosophy, and one must distinguish what literature can do (world disclosure) from what it cannot do (problem solving). Not everything can be rationalised in the sense of argumentation, but, to Habermas, that is all the more reason to distinguish things. Likewise, Habermas is not arguing that philosophy has no rhetorical or 'literary' elements. Not only does philosophy contain these elements, philosophy cannot do without rhetoric. Yet, the force of philosophy – and of argumentation, reasoning, and so on – stems from the partial bracketing of these rhetorical elements.[23]

THE RESPONSE: WHAT IS PHILOSOPHY?

In his replies to Habermas, Derrida appealed to what Habermas had accused him of undermining, namely philosophy, argument, an 'ethics of discussion', and truth as opposed to falsehood. Habermas's reading of his work, Derrida writes, 'is false. I say *false*, as opposed to *true*'.[24] With regard to philosophy and literature, he writes: 'I have never assimilated a so-called philosophical text to a so-called literary text. The two types seem to me irreducibly different. And yet one must realize that the limits between the two are more complex . . . and . . . less natural, ahistorical, or given than people say or think.'[25] Whether this distinction between philosophy and literature is really irreducible is questionable given, as we shall see, Derrida's view that the limits and identity of philosophy are inherently contestable.

Derrida's response to Habermas stressed an 'ethics of discussion', which includes certain academic and philosophical standards as well as the possibility of contestation, including contestation of those very standards. It is an appeal Derrida has made on several occasions of his polemics with other academics and in his writings on the institutions of philosophy and the university. In this context, the appeal to the ethics of discussion is not surprising given the connection Habermas himself makes between philosophy and serious argument and, in his theory of communication, between serious language and reason. In Derrida's view, Habermas in fact violated this ethics of discussion. He complains about:

> those who, if they are German . . . do not even read the French texts, but rely on American secondary literature . . . is that not what you call a 'permanent performative contradiction', when someone appeals to the authority of consensus and the ethics of scientific or philosophical communication without respecting their most basic rules?[26]

Moreover, Derrida claims, Habermas closed off discussion about the standards of philosophical inquiry. The problem with Habermas, in Derrida's view, is that he has a particular and limited view of what philosophy is and should be, and as a result he cannot see that Derrida is doing philosophy too, albeit in a different style. Habermas's rejection of Derrida's philosophy is imperialistic in the eyes of the latter, because it involves a sort of blackmail where one can only be either for or against reason, for or against modernity, for or against Enlightenment, and where Habermas can define what either alternative means. To Derrida, Habermas misunderstands the relevant alternatives, and he does not allow for different ways of doing philosophy.

On Derrida's view, philosophy is not a coherent whole with a determined identity and settled limits. Instead, it is internally divided: 'within ["philosophical discourse"] the regimes of demonstrativity are problematic, multiple, mobile. They themselves form the constant object of the whole history of philosophy'.[27] Thus, philosophy has no univocal answer to the question what philosophy is, what its object is, and how to do it. Indeed, were this not the case, philosophy would become stale, and there would be no *history* of philosophy. For Derrida, the condition of possibility of philosophy as a continued meaningful practice is that there is no single or final answer to the question 'what is philosophy?'. The argument here is both descriptive and prescriptive: 'what is philosophy?' is, as a matter of *fact*, part of the philosophical tradition, but it *ought* also, for Derrida, be part of that tradition as part of its self-reflective character.

Yet, making the question 'what is philosophy?' part and parcel of philosophical discourse destabilises the latter. On the one hand, Derrida's appeal to philosophical discourse affirms it as a ground on which we can proceed. On the other hand, emphasising the question 'what is philosophy?' as part of that discourse subverts the appeal to philosophy as a ground because it puts into question the very identity of that ground. Philosophy continues a tradition and a certain way of asking questions (including 'what is philosophy?'), yet this necessarily implies the possibility of discontinuing the tradition, of finding that what we used to think philosophy is, and should be, is no longer the case (and the possibility of discontinuation arises from within philosophy, from the latter's incorporation of self-reflection).

Moreover, while the appeal is to the presence of a philosophical discourse, the inclusion of the question 'what is philosophy?' propels that presence into the future, or more precisely, into a future 'to-come', to use a Derridean term from another context.[28] The affirmation of the value of philosophy becomes the affirmation of a 'philosophy to-come', a philosophy whose identity we cannot, by definition, pinpoint in any present, including any future present. The question ('what is philosophy?') cannot be raised from a point wholly within philosophy, because that would require that we had already determined philosophy's identity and limits, and that we had already answered the question. Insofar as it also deals with this question, philosophy is only possible in the future if it remains undecidable whether the question falls inside or outside the limits of philosophy. The condition of possibility of philosophy is, then, simultaneously the condition of impossibility of philosophy: we can only do philosophy insofar as it is undecidable what it is and how it should be defined. Or, in other words, the answer to the question 'what is philosophy?' must remain to-come. For Derrida, then, philosophy can only be affirmed as a value in the present in a way that postpones that affirmation into a future to-come.

This is the kind of philosophical writing that Derrida is engaged in:

'What is philosophy?' and 'What is literature?' More difficult and more wide open than ever, these questions in themselves, by definition and if at least one pursues them in an effective fashion, are neither simply philosophical nor simply literary. I would say the same thing, ultimately, about the texts that I write, at least to the extent that they are worked over or dictated by the turbulence of these questions.[29]

Are Derrida's writings philosophical? Yes, but . . . insofar as Derrida engages with the question 'what is philosophy?', there is an element of undecidability in them. Habermas is right to think that Derrida does not unequivocally affirm the value of philosophy and, beyond that, modernity, Enlightenment and reason. Derrida's affirmation of – or 'yes' to – those ideals are always followed by a 'but' or 'although', a doubt or qualification.

This also explains Derrida's 'interest in non-canonical texts that destabilize the representation a certain dominant tradition gave of itself'.[30] Looking at non-canonical texts is a way to put into question the tradition's self-description as (the only possible way to do) 'philosophy' and to stress the irreducible plurality of ways of philosophising. Derrida is suspicious of appeals to the tradition, and here one can include Habermas's appeal to the tradition in his critique of Derrida, when he writes that 'Derrida is particularly interested in standing the primacy of logic over rhetoric, canonized since Aristotle, on its head.'[31] For Habermas, the tradition of Western philosophy authorises the hierarchical distinction, which, in his view, Derrida merely wants to overturn. This may not be true, but the fact remains that Derrida cannot simply affirm the distinctions between philosophy and literature and between logic and rhetoric.

IMPLICATIONS: THE TASKS OF PHILOSOPHY AND CRITIQUE

The defence of philosophy must proceed in the name of a philosophy to-come, not just in the name of any present definition of philosophy. This is precisely why Habermas is sceptical of the critical force of Derrida's deconstruction: if the defence of, say, philosophy is marked by the structure of to-come, and if, as a result, philosophy cannot simply be opposed to something like 'non-philosophy' or 'literature' or 'unreason', then the value and rationality of philosophy can only be asserted against literature, and so on, through an ethico-theoretical decision. Where Habermas believes that Derrida is unable to engage in critique because he levels distinctions, Derrida believes that Habermas is uncritical because he takes these distinctions and the identity of philosophy as given. Since Habermas believes the answer to the question 'what is philosophy?' is given, according to Derrida, he forecloses any further argument and discussion about it. What we have here are two different 'ethics of discussion': one for whom such an ethics cannot simultaneously appeal to and put into question philosophical argument (Habermas), and one for whom such an ethics must do precisely that (Derrida). One for whom there can be no 'ethics of discussion' without some form of procedural foundation (Habermas), and one for whom there is no ethics without undecidability and decision (Derrida).

Both Habermas and Derrida are interested in limits. For Habermas, the purpose of philosophy is to get limits right. Derrida pursues a 'limit attitude' of a very different kind. He says about deconstruction and reason and, by extension, philosophy, that 'reason must let itself be reasoned with,' and that deconstruction involves 'an unconditional rationalism that never renounces . . . the possibility of suspending in an argued, deliberated, rational fashion, all conditions, hypotheses, conventions, and presuppositions, and of criticizing unconditionally all conditionalities, including those that still found the critical idea'.[32] Reason's or philosophy's self-reflection in part proceeds from itself, but it proceeds on the assumption that its self – its identity and limits – is part of what must be reasoned with. Or, in Derrida's terms, while philosophy's unconditional questioning must proceed from a certain tradition and conditioning, the latter cannot exhaust the unconditional questioning.

For both Habermas and Derrida, philosophy must be modest. According to Habermas, philosophy must restrict itself to rationally and critically reconstruct the immanent presuppositions of social practices. It may tell us how normative validity is possible, but it cannot give us any substantial norms that we must follow. For instance, in his discourse ethics, Habermas reconstructs the conditions of possibility of normative validity as a number of procedural requirements that must be followed if one is to be able to claim to have arrived at a right or valid norm. However, substantial values or norms must be decided among those affected by them, for instance by citizens in public deliberations. Derrida likewise refuses to give philosophy the role of giving authoritative answers to normative or political questions.

Yet, here we find a decisive difference between Habermas and Derrida over the task – and limits – of philosophy. It can be expressed as the difference between 'not yet' and 'to-come'. While Habermas stresses the fallible character of philosophy, he none the less works within the horizon of a not yet: it is, at least theoretically, possible to come up with the right answer. For Derrida, on the other hand, philosophical resolution or reconciliation will remain always to-come: it is not just practically but also conceptually impossible to solve – resolve and dissolve – the aporias of philosophical concepts, including the concept of philosophy itself. As a result, for Derrida, it is not enough for philosophy to come up with answers, to get distinctions right, for instance; it must simultaneously put these into question.

Different Styles of Philosophy: De/reconstructing Terrorism

In this section, I further examine how Habermas and Derrida go about doing philosophy by linking this to their respective conceptions of language. Although their conceptions of language are important for understanding their works, limitation of space only allows me to deal very briefly with these. I shall take Habermas's and Derrida's respective treatments of terrorism as my starting point.

In separate interviews in *Philosophy in a Time of Terror*, Derrida and Habermas broach the subject of terrorism after September 11.[33] The editor of the book, Giovanna Borradori notes that there is a close affinity between Habermas's and Derrida's respective philosophies and their styles of writing and answering questions. Habermas's style is dry and 'elegantly traditional [allowing] his thinking to progress from concept to concept'.[34] He starts from the concepts handed down to us from the Enlightenment tradition: democracy, human rights, tolerance, and so on. However, he wants to relate critically to these concepts in order to draw out their full potential. Derrida, too, starts from these concepts handed down to us from our traditions, but he proceeds along 'a longer and winding road that opens unpredictably onto large vistas and narrow canyons'. It is a characteristic of Derrida's deconstruction that the 'extreme sensitivity for subtle facts of language makes Derrida's thought virtually inseparable from the words in which it is expressed'.[35] Thomas McCarthy, on the other hand, is not impressed. In a discussion of Derrida's work, he writes that 'Derrida's discourse . . . lives from the enormous elasticity, not to say vagueness and ambiguity, of his key terms.'[36]

Habermas approaches terrorism in the way he approaches other issues: through immanent critique and rational reconstruction. His critique of Enlightenment concepts and practices is an immanent critique, rather than a break with that tradition. There is already an emancipatory potential, all we have to do is to realise it conceptually and practically. Enlightenment discourse has a 'peculiar self-reference that makes it the vehicle for self-correcting learning processes'.[37] For instance, crimes may be committed in the name of universals – say, 'humanity' – but immanent critique allows us to distinguish true from false uses of universals. Linked to this immanent critique is the rational reconstruction of – often implicit, but unavoidable – universal presuppositions of communicative action and democratic law-making. With regard to terrorism, what is central is a basic distinction between violence and the forceless force of the better argument. Terrorism is measured vis-à-vis free dialogue and the rights and procedures of constitutional democracy. Here, as in his writings on the terrorism of the *Rote Armee Fraktion* in the 1970s, relies on a distinction between violence and the forceless force of the good argument. He does accept the demonstrative violence of, for instance, civil disobedience, though, but only insofar as it functions *as an argument* in public debate.

With the new 'international terrorism', Habermas says, 'we are encountering a *new* phenomenon, which we should not be too quick to assimilate to what we already know.'[38] He proceeds to identify the characteristics that distinguish the terrorism of September 11, bin Laden and al-Qaeda from previous and existing kinds of terrorism and from things that are not terrorism. Habermas does not suggest that the distinctions are clear, and he acknowledges that today's terrorist may be tomorrow's freedom fighter.[39] Yet, the purpose of theorising is to get the distinctions right and to clarify matters through critique and rational reconstruction, and philosophical resolution of paradoxes and ambiguities remain within the realm of the possible.

Derrida, too, is concerned with clarification of concepts and distinctions, yet in a different way than Habermas, reflecting their different assumptions about language and the task of philosophy. This is also clear from the way in which he approaches the interview with Borradori. He starts by *talking about how we talk about* September 11 and terrorism. The way we talk about things – including the concepts and distinctions we use – cannot be distinguished from 'the thing itself' (as if there were such a thing) or from the relations of power permeating language. Therefore, we cannot uncritically accept the discourse handed down to us by tradition or presented to us by the media, even if this discourse will have to be the starting point for the deconstruction. This is the point of Derrida's style of writing and speaking, which can otherwise seem irritating because it appears never to get to the point. Thus, three pages into the interview, Derrida says, 'for the moment we are simply preparing ourselves to say something about it [that is, September 11 and terrorism].'[40] For Derrida, however, the way we talk about things is part of the point. We are never in a position where we are entirely ready to approach, for instance, terrorism in an unmediated fashion or with the correct vocabulary and distinctions. The clarification of concepts and distinctions is not a neutral operation, clearing the ground for a rational problem-solving discourse as Habermas would have it.

Derrida's deconstructive readings put distinctions into question, for instance, the distinction between terrorist and freedom fighter. But, despite Borradori's assertion that '[in] Derrida's mind, it is impossible to draw any distinctions regarding terrorism',[41] Derrida does not give up on distinctions; instead he aims to show their limits. These limits are not only practical limits that can be overcome by the critical refinement of the distinctions, as in Habermas, but internal limits or aporias that both undermine and make possible the distinctions.

The ability to define terms and to have agents act on the basis of those definitions is important:

> Semantic instability, irreducible trouble spots on the borders between concepts, indecision in the very concept of the border: all this must not only be analysed as a speculative disorder, a conceptual chaos and zone of passing turbulences in public or political language. We must also recognize here strategies and relations of force. The dominant power is the one that manages to impose and, thus, to legitimate, indeed to legalize . . . the terminology and thus the interpretation that best suits it in a given situation.[42]

If concepts and distinctions are also political, then the '"philosopher-deconstructor"'[43] must also engage in politics and seek to provide answers. Derrida and Habermas are more or less on the same side when it comes to the answers they give to the international situation today. Derrida does not think that judgments and distinctions are impossible, or that his deconstruction does not affirm anything. If forced to choose between real existing American democracy and the discourse of bin Laden and al-Qaeda, Derrida opts for the former. At least democracy and the rule of law contain a promise that things can get better because they allow for their own contestation.[44] Yet, like Habermas, Derrida also tries to resist the blackmail of 'you are either with us or with the terrorists'. This sort of blackmail rests on the possibility of determining once and for all the meaning of 'democracy' (and 'terrorism'), thus erasing the 'to-come' of 'democracy to-come'. For Derrida, it is not simply a question of taking sides as if there were just two sides and as if those sides were homogeneous.

Habermas, too, is interested in the way communication can be distorted in the service of power, but there is an important difference between him and Derrida here. Habermas seems to think of deconstruction as a kind of ideology critique like critical theory: 'any deconstructive unmasking of the ideologically concealing use of universalistic discourses actually presupposes the critical viewpoints advanced by these same discourses.'[45] Whether the characterisation of deconstruction as a form of ideology critique is meant as a compliment or not, it is mistaken because, unlike Habermas's critical theory, Derridean deconstruction does not work with an idea of transparent, undistorted language that can be opposed to distortions of language. Derrida's critique of the idea of transparent communication is dangerous for Habermas, because it is in language that Habermas locates rationality.

Habermas sees the epistemological questions of how we can know what is true and normatively right as intrinsically linked to the possibility of founding social critique and emancipatory politics. To Habermas, language is potentially transparent, whereas for Derrida it is not. For Habermas, distortions can be dissolved and overcome through immanent critique, rational reconstruction and the removal of practical obstacles to the free and equal public use of reason. For Derrida, there is no insight without blindness, no transparency that is not partly occluded. As a consequence, the clarification of distinctions and concepts never comes to an end, and the struggles for the values of democracy, philosophy and so on do not have an end-point (for instance, a rational consensus or resolution of philosophical paradoxes).

CONCLUSION: LET'S HAVE A 'DISCUSSION'!

Despite the personal rapprochement and some political affinities during recent years, deep differences remain between Derrida and Habermas over the task and nature of philosophy, critique and language. This does not exclude the possibility of strategic alliances between Habermasians and Derrideans, critical theorists and deconstructionists – alliances that are possible because they share certain political and theoretical goals: a critique of the limited role of politics in liberalism, of nationalism and other discourses that take identities as given and homogeneous, and of unilateralism in international relations. In more positive terms, they may pull in the same direction on Europe, egalitarianism, tolerance and multiculturalism, whatever their different ways of doing so.

Given the important differences that remain, one should, of course, avoid eclecticism, the mere lumping together of insights from Derrida's and Habermas's respective works. And incorporating insights from one into the other will merely assimilate one theorist to the other. It would, to use Derridean phraseology, be to suppress the singularity of the voice of the other. However, this does not exclude the possibility that continuing critical exchanges between the two sides will develop their understandings of themselves and one another. Although one of the protagonists – Derrida – is dead and can no longer respond (which is central to the 'ethics of discussion'), this should not discourage the rest of us from engaging in discussion. After all, one of Derrida's points was that no authorial intention can control the effects of a text. Looked at in this way, the meaning of Derrida's texts are neither simply past nor present, but always to-come, because no single reading of them can exhaust their meaning. So, let's have a 'discussion', but let's also keep the quotation marks to remind ourselves that part of the 'discussion' is about just what it means to have a 'discussion'.

NOTES

1. I would like to thank Jonathan Dean, Andreas Antoniades, the editors of this volume, the participants at the Derrida – Negotiating the Legacy conference, Wales, January 2005, and the members of the Staff-Student Seminar in the Department of Politics and Public Administration at the University of Limerick, October 2005 for their comments on earlier versions of the argument presented here.

2. For overview and literature, see Lasse Thomassen (ed.), *The Derrida–Habermas Reader*, Edinburgh: Edinburgh University Press, 2006.

3. Jacques Derrida and Jürgen Habermas, 'February 15, or, what binds Europeans together: plea for a common foreign policy, beginning in core Europe', trans. Max Pensky, in Daniel Levy, Max Pensky and John Torpey (eds), *Old Europe, New Europe, Core Europe: Transatlantic Relations After the Iraq War*, London: Verso, 2005, pp. 3–13 at 3. Here is one similarity between the two thinkers: they are not just philosophers, but also public intellectuals.

4. Jürgen Habermas, *The Philosophical Discourse of Modernity: Twelve Lectures*, trans. Frederick Lawrence, Cambridge, MA: MIT Press, 1987.

5. Jacques Derrida and Michael Wetzel (1987), 'Erwiderungen/Antwort an Apel', *Zeitmitschrift*, 3: 76–85; Jacques Derrida, *Limited Inc*, trans. Samuel Weber, Evanston, IL: Northwestern University Press, 1988, pp. 156–8 (note 9); Jacques Derrida, *Memoires for Paul de Man*, revised edn, trans. C. Lindsay et al., New York: Columbia University Press, 1989, pp. 258–61; and Jacques Derrida, 'Is there a philosophical language?', trans. Peggy Kamuf, in Thomassen (ed.), *The Derrida–Habermas Reader*, pp. 35–45. See also Jacques Derrida, *The Other Heading: Reflections on Today's Europe*, trans. Pascale-Anne Brault and Michael B. Naas, Bloomington, IN: Indiana University Press, pp. 54ff; and Jacques Derrida, *Monolingualism of the Other; or, The Prosthesis of Origin*, trans. Patrick Mensah, Stanford, CA: Stanford University Press, 1998, pp. 2–6.

6. Jacques Derrida, 'Honesty of thought', trans. Marian Hill, in Thomassen (ed.), *The Derrida–Habermas Reader*, pp. 300–6.

7. For instance, Thomas McCarthy, 'The politics of the ineffable', in Michael Kelly (ed.), *Hermeneutics and Critical Theory in Ethics and Politics*, Cambridge, MA: MIT Press, 1990, pp. 146–68.

8. For instance, Geoffrey Bennington, 'Ex-communication', Social and Political Thought Seminar, University of Sussex, 4 March 1996, accessed 19 December 2005 at userwww.service.emory.edu/~gbennin/habermas.doc

9. Christopher Norris, 'Deconstruction, postmodernism and philosophy: Habermas on Derrida', in David Wood (ed.), *Derrida. A Critical Reader*, Oxford: Blackwell, 1992, pp. 167–92.

10. For instance, Richard J. Bernstein, 'An allegory of modernity/postmodernity: Habermas and Derrida', in Thomassen (ed.), *The Derrida–Habermas Reader*, pp. 71–97; and Richard Rorty, 'Habermas, Derrida, and the functions of philosophy', in Thomassen (ed.), *The Derrida–Habermas Reader*, pp. 46–65.

11. For instance, William van Reijen (1994), 'Derrida – Ein unvollendeter Habermas?', *Deutsche Zeitschrift für Philosophie*, 42: 6 1037–44.
12. For instance, Axel Honneth, 'The other of justice: Habermas and the ethical challenge of postmodernism', trans. John Farrell, in Stephen K. White (ed.), *The Cambridge Companion to Habermas*, Cambridge: Cambridge University Press, 1995, pp. 289–323.
13. For instance, Simon Critchley, 'Frankfurt impromptu – remarks on Derrida and Habermas', in Thomassen (ed.), *The Derrida–Habermas Reader*, pp. 98–110.
14. Derrida and Habermas, 'February 15', p. 3.
15. See Jürgen Habermas (with Eduardo Mendieta) (2004), 'America and the World: a conversation with Jürgen Habermas', trans. Jeffrey Craig Miller, *Logos*, 3:3; Jacques Derrida, *Rogues: Two Essays on Reason*, trans. Pascale-Anne Brault and Michael Naas, Stanford, CA: Stanford University Press, 2005; and Jacques Derrida and Lieven De Cauter, 'For a justice to come: an interview with Jacques Derrida', trans. Ortwin de Graef, in Thomassen (ed.), *The Derrida–Habermas Reader*, pp. 259–69. But see also Jacques Derrida, 'Intellectual courage: an interview with Thomas Assheuer', trans. Peter Krapp, *Culture Machine*, 2, 2000.
16. Derrida, 'Honesty of thought', p. 302.
17. Habermas, *The Philosophical Discourse of Modernity*, p. 193.
18. Derrida, 'Intellectual courage'; Jacques Derrida, 'Performative powerlessness – a response to Simon Critchley', in Thomassen (ed.), *The Derrida–Habermas Reader*, pp. 111–14; Derrida, 'Honesty of thought'; Habermas, 'America and the World'; and Jürgen Habermas, 'A last farewell: Derrida's enlightening impact', in Thomassen (ed.), *The Derrida–Habermas Reader*, pp. 307ff.
19. I will not try to explain Habermas's (1929–) and Derrida's (1930–2004) differences with reference to their respective biographies. Despite being born only a year apart, their upbringings – Habermas in Germany before, during and after the Second World War, and Derrida in Algeria as a French-Jewish Algerian – are quite different and no doubt interesting in light of their subsequent work. For Habermas, the War and the Holocaust raised the question of how to defend modernity and Enlightenment; for Derrida, the experiences during the War left him suspicious of any claim to communal self-identity.
20. Habermas, *The Philosophical Discourse of Modernity*, pp. 161–210. Also Jürgen Habermas, 'Philosophy and science as literature?', in Habermas, *Postmetaphysical Thinking: Philosophical Essays*, trans. William Mark Hohengarten, Cambridge: Polity Press, 1992, pp. 205–27.
21. Habermas, *The Philosophical Discourse of Modernity*, pp. 187ff.
22. Ibid. p. 205.
23. Ibid. pp. 209ff.
24. Derrida, *Limited Inc*, p. 157.
25. Derrida, 'Is there a philosophical language?', p. 36.
26. Derrida and Wetzel, 'Erwiderungen/Antwort an Apel', p. 84, my translation.

27. Derrida, 'Is there a philosophical language?', p. 37.
28. Jacques Derrida, 'Force of law: the "mystical foundation of authority" ', trans. Mary Quaintance, in Drucilla Cornell, Michel Rosenfeld, David Gray Carlson (eds), *Deconstruction and the Possibility of Justice*, London: Routledge, 1992, pp. 3–67 at 27.
29. Derrida, 'Is there a philosophical language?', pp. 36ff.
30. Derrida, 'Is there a philosophical language?', p. 42.
31. Habermas, *The Philosophical Discourse of Modernity*, p. 187.
32. Derrida, *Rogues*, pp. 159 and 142.
33. Giovanna Borradori, *Philosophy in a Time of Terror: Dialogues with Jürgen Habermas and Jacques Derrida*, Chicago, IL: University of Chicago Press, 2003.
34. Giovanna Borradori, 'Philosophy in a time of terror', in Borradori, *Philosophy in a Time of Terror*, pp. ix–xiv at xii.
35. Ibid. p. xii.
36. McCarthy, 'The politics of the ineffable', p. 162.
37. Jürgen Habermas, 'Fundamentalism and terror – a dialogue with Jürgen Habermas', in Borradori, *Philosophy in a Time of Terror*, pp. 25–43 at 42.
38. Habermas, 'America and the World'.
39. Habermas, 'Fundamentalism and terror', p. 34.
40. Jacques Derrida, 'Autoimmunity: real and symbolic suicides – a dialogue with Jacques Derrida', in Borradori, *Philosophy in a Time of Terror*, pp. 85–136 at 87.
41. Giovanna Borradori, 'Deconstructing terrorism – Derrida', in Borradori, *Philosophy in a Time of Terror*, pp. 137–72 at 153.
42. Derrida, 'Autoimmunity', p. 105.
43. Ibid. p. 106.
44. Ibid. pp. 113ff.
45. Habermas, 'Fundamentalism and terror', p. 42.

Conclusions: The Im/Possibility of Closure

Madeleine Fagan and Marie Suetsugu

The suspension of the urge to complete an argument, to bring it to closure, comprises an act of resistance against dominant ways of talking and thinking.[1]

Jacques Derrida, *Of Grammatology*

CLOSURE AND OPENNESS

To conclude a collection animated by the theme of negotiation is an impossible undertaking. Any conclusion is a closure, or an attempt at closure, which must necessarily fail. Not only is moving to conclude these diverse contributions premature, we do not want to close down these discussions by offering a final word, and this closure would, in any case, not be possible. Instead, we want to offer a brief reflection on this very difficulty of closure and concluding. Firstly, by drawing on Derrida's 'Afterword' in *Limited Inc*, and on a number of chapters in this book which have been animated by the theme of closure, to inform discussion of the concepts of closure and openness, and secondly through an attempt at avoiding certain closures. To do this, we focus briefly on an example of the negotiation between closure and non-closure in a context outside academia and outside a strict reliance on Derrida's work. Our example is the work of Daniel Barenboim, who founded an orchestra comprised of young Palestinians and Israelis, and the way in which his approach to music reflects some of the key concerns of deconstruction, in particular how it reflects an active negotiation between closure and non-closure, whilst not being directly influenced by Derrida's work.

While the central role of non-closure, or openness, in deconstruction is well rehearsed, one of our concerns is that this important foregrounding might act to obscure the way in which non-closure itself is not a pure self-identical concept, that it may pose its own problems and that the idea of closure, too, has a role to play in deconstruction. There is a danger that deconstruction can be understood as a complete rejection of categories, as negative, open-ended and indeterminate,[2] and we want to foreclose this possibility by emphasising the role of closure. The relationship between closure and openness is as complex as that between any other binary that Derrida addresses. Further, the centrality of this particular pair to deconstruction means that the risk of simplifying and of presenting deconstruction as an unproblematic commitment to openness or rejection of closure is particularly pertinent. As Alex Thomson argues in his chapter, to negotiate with Derrida's legacy must involve facing up to ambivalence.[3] Not just, we argue, by asserting the importance of ambivalence in any analysis and the opportunities and possibilities it may allow, but by highlighting ambivalence in the very concept of openness, and in the relation between distinction and ambivalence, closure and non-closure.

The themes of closure and non-closure have been central to many of the chapters in this book. They are fundamental to any engagement with Derrida's work and to any discussion of what his legacy might be. These chapters are, in themselves, negotiations with these problematic concepts and as such a number of different approaches and emphases have been articulated. These differences are the starting point for our discussion, as well as in themselves an example of the impossibility of closure or stability in meaning and interpretation.[4]

The problematic nature of closure is highlighted by Maja Zehfuss when she examines the consequences of particular closures enacted in discourse surrounding the 'war on terror'. Zehfuss highlights the way in which particular closures are achieved and what the effects of these strategies are. She argues that links made between the 'war on terror' and the Second World War serve to close down debate over what the 'right' thing to do now might be because these links mean that the answer to this question has been established by an understanding of what the 'right' thing to do was in the past.[5] The uncomplicated, black and white representation of this past provides a shorthand that instantly closes down discussion and the possibility of decision. The effect of this closure, of this use of the Second World War, Zehfuss argues, is to shut down the possibility of response.[6]

This commitment to openness in deconstruction also emerges in a number of other contributions to this book. April Biccum, for example, sees Derrida's influence in terms of a foregrounding of ambivalence and instability.[7] Thomson refers to the ultimate horizon of deconstruction as 'an opening to the infinite, to the unpredictable and the incalculable'.[8]

These arguments stem from the central concern with openness which is found in deconstruction. Although we want here to attempt to disabuse the understanding of deconstruction as somehow vague, indistinct, indecisive and relativistic, what this entails is not a denial of the central role of openness within deconstruction. Rather, what we are concerned to explore is what is meant by this commitment to openness and, more importantly, what is not.

What sustains this position in deconstruction is a commitment to the coming of the future, that is, the coming of the absolute other: in Derrida's words, 'It's better to let the future open – this is the axiom of deconstruction'.[9] To the extent that deconstruction is anything more than a diagnosis of the way things happen and becomes a project with a strategy and goal, this goal is informed by a concern with the other. It is openness to the future that binds deconstruction to alterity; non-closure is important because of the other.

However, while openness plays a pivotal role in any understanding of deconstruction, particularly in terms of its affirmation of the other, it is important to stress that this openness is not some kind of indeterminacy or relativism. Derrida is at pains to demonstrate the way in which his thought is not an unconditional rejection of traditional categories or enlightenment values.[10] Deconstruction is not set up against these positions, but rather works within them. It is not, and does not entail, a simple rejection of categories.[11] Rather, as Richard Beardsworth cautions, we need to be attentive to both 'the ethical, the nomadic and the unilaterally deconstructive' and 'construction, law and institution'.[12]

There is a second strand to this discussion of openness, as highlighted by Biccum when she argues that ambivalence, which she aligns with non-closure, happens in discourse. In any attempt at closing there is a certain failure and deconstruction highlights this. Any attempt at framing or delimiting a context in order to provide a completely stable meaning fails; there is, for Derrida, 'an indefinite opening of every context, an essential nontotalization'.[13] There is, in the border of any context, 'a clause of nonclosure'.[14] This failure of complete closure points to the argument we want to make, that closure and non-closure are inextricably linked in Derrida. While there is a commitment to non-closure in deconstruction, this entails aspects of closure.

The idea of a limitless context in Derrida is what renders complete closure impossible: 'However stabilized, complex and overdetermined it may be, there is a context and one that is only relatively *firm*, neither absolutely solid nor entirely closed . . . In it there is a margin of play, of difference, an opening . . .'[15] This is, in a way, determined by the very concept of stability. The idea of complete stability does not work; the idea of an absolute, eternal, intangible, natural stability goes against the concept of stability itself.[16] Stability, by virtue of being stability rather than, say, immutability, is by definition always destabilisable.[17] So the outside of the concept of stabilisation determines the limits of the concept. Destabilisation taints any attempt at stabilisation. Non-closure haunts any attempt at closure.

Beardsworth, in his concern for legislating for non-closure, seems to sideline the argument made, for example, by Biccum, that non-closure happens anyway, that it is a necessary component of any attempt at closure.[18] Difference and singularity, for him, only have their chance through universal mechanisms of law and institution, through a particular type of closure;[19] whereas a focus on the clause of non-closure in every attempt at closure would highlight the ways in which singularity and difference always already resist attempts to shut them down.

A similar argument regarding the interpenetration of closure and non-closure can be made with reference to undecidability, and this perhaps illustrates more clearly the complex relationship between closure and non-closure in our reading of Derrida. Dan Bulley points to this argument in discussing the *need* for decision and thus for closure.[20] Undecidability would be meaningless without decision, and decision is not something which somehow spoils the concept of undecidability, rather it is an integral part of it. Undecidability is, in part, the very demand for a decision. It is not a state of limbo but rather an urgent negotiation in the name of decision. The undecidable, for Derrida, 'has decision as its necessary condition'.[21] The openness of the undecidable and the possibilities it creates for the future are necessarily always already destabilised by decision (and this interruption of openness by the closure of decision is not, we argue below, somehow unproblematically negative in deconstruction). Closure and non-closure, decision and the undecidable, are not pure, clearly defined and distinguishable, self-identical concepts; in the same way as with all distinctions for Derrida 'the outside penetrates and thus determines the inside'.[22] So, while this closure is necessary to the very idea of non-closure, it is also the case that this closure is always flawed, never complete, and that this undoing of the closure is always already happening, that non-closure intervenes whether or not we formulate strategies to enable it.

Not only is pure non-closure impossible but rather non-closure is always enmeshed with closure, closure itself also plays an important substantive role in deconstruction. The alignment of decision with closure comes out in Bulley's chapter, where the problematic closure entailed by any decision or judgement is focused on.[23] As Bulley argues, closure is needed in order to avoid the worst, because decision is needed to do this.[24]

The axiom of deconstruction, to let the future open, is not a rejection of closure. The decision is the condition of possibility of anything happening, and this includes the future. Refusing closure does not let the future open; it is only through closures that this can come about. For example, acts of closure can themselves be resisted only through closures, that is, through decision and engagement, as emphasised by Beardsworth.

This complex relationship between closure and non-closure is played out in the discussions arising in this book. A focus on the critique of closure provided by deconstruction as seen in Biccum and Zehfuss above also animates Beardsworth's chapter, though in a different way. Beardsworth is interested to provide a particular strategy for closing. His concern is that deconstruction fails to affirm alterity precisely because of its commitment to openness. He sees deconstruction as an endeavour to 'promote alterity and difference', but argues that by keeping things open this is endangered: 'by not determining the real in the name of alterity, *contra* other determinations that reduce it to the same, deconstruction risks giving less chance to alterity rather than more'.[25] For Beardsworth, determining the other is what gives it its chance.[26]

Bulley makes a similar point in arguing for particular strategies for closing in his argument that closure is itself important and unavoidable, although this need for closure is something he finds within Derrida, whereas Beardsworth approaches it as a problematic omission within deconstruction. Bulley argues that closures must happen, acknowledges their problematic nature, and suggests that there may be more or less problematic options.[27] What this seems to entail, for him, is to enable the decision with which he is concerned to resist events that close the future to the coming of the other.[28] He too, then, is concerned to provide a strategy for closing in order to promote alterity, although he finds this within deconstruction.

Thomson's argument is positioned against these readings of the possibilities and limits of deconstruction and suggests an alternative way of approaching non-closure in deconstruction. He argues that the refusal to close that Beardsworth identifies in deconstruction is not representative of Derrida's project. He highlights the way in which closure is central to the deconstructive project, that the distinction between 'the finite calculation which would characterise the invention of new forms of sovereignty and the indefinite melancholia of deconstruction in Derrida's hands is a false one'.[29]

The chapters in this book also highlight the way in which non-closure, when understood as indistinction and separated out from closure and decision, poses difficulties of its own. Openness requires that distinctions and categories not be drawn, but a lack of distinction poses its own dangers. It is precisely this indistinction which can allow for violence and domination. Zehfuss suggests, for example, that a lack of categorisation or continuity in representing events means that they can be used to support the most convenient position on different matters.[30] Non-closure can thus, in particular contexts, render critique difficult.

On the other hand, whilst Beardsworth and Bulley focus on strategies for closure, Biccum highlights the way in which the non-closure that Zehfuss is wary of might be exploited as a political strategy. Biccum focuses on ambivalences in the workings of civil society and public discourse, and argues that exposing these ambivalences denies authority.[31] Non-closure thus functions in this chapter as a possibility, although the strategies for intervention in these ambivalent discourses necessitate, once again, some form of closure in terms of decision and engagement.

So non-closure is inextricably linked to closure, closure is inescapable and deconstruction's project is not to refuse it. Further, however, deconstruction also implies that this rejection of closure is not desirable. While a more nuanced understanding of the concepts of openness and undecidability goes some way to refuting the claims that deconstruction is negative, open-ended or indeterminate, some of the contributions to this volume, by foregrounding closure, suggest this as an alternative site for defending the definite and determinable in deconstruction.

What we have tried briefly, then, to draw out of some of the chapters in this collection is the importance of the negotiation that has emerged around the themes of closure and non-closure. Our concern, animated by these contributions, is to emphasise the role of closure within deconstruction, as part of, rather than at the expense of, its commitment to openness.

NEGOTIATING CLOSURES

In attempting the impossible and yet necessary task of concluding the negotiations of the legacy of Derrida, then, we divert attention to someone who may not normally be associated with Derrida: Daniel Barenboim. Barenboim is a pianist/conductor, born in 1942 into a Russian Jewish family in Buenos Aires. He learned the piano from his mother and subsequently from his father, and gave his first official concert when he was only seven years old. He then moved to Israel with his parents in 1952. Two years later, the eleven-year-old Barenboim was hailed as a phenomenon by the great German conductor Wilhelm Furtwängler. Barenboim is now a leading conductor as well as a renowned pianist, and has been Music Director of the Chicago Symphony Orchestra since 1991 and of the Deutsche Staatsoper Berlin since 1992.[32] Those who are not so familiar with classical music may nevertheless recall him in the 1998 film *Hilary and Jackie* where, as the husband of the British cellist Jacqueline du Pré, Barenboim was played by James Frain.

In April and May 2006, Barenboim delivered a series of lectures on BBC Radio 4: the Reith Lectures 2006. The Reith Lectures were inaugurated in 1948 to mark the contribution made by the BBC's first director-general John Reith, who 'maintained that broadcasting should be a public service which enriches the intellectual and cultural life of the nation'.[33] Entitled 'In the beginning was sound', Barenboim's five lectures were given before audiences in London, Chicago, Berlin, a predominantly Palestinian part of Jerusalem and a predominantly Jewish part of the same city. The subject of the lectures was music, of course, but it extended to life and to politics.[34] Indeed, Barenboim is an *engagé* artist: his chance encounter with the Palestinian intellectual Edward Said in the early 1990s led the two to organise the West-Eastern Divan orchestra,[35] a workshop project where young musicians from both Israel and Palestine as well as other Arab countries such as Egypt, Syria, Lebanon, Jordan and Tunisia 'come together to make music on neutral ground with the guidance of some of the world's best musicians'. The workshop has been held annually since 1999, and Barenboim has been continuing the project since Said's death in 2003.[36]

Importantly, Barenboim does not mention Derrida's name in his lectures: the philosophical figure that he says has influenced him is Baruch Spinoza, and we are by no means claiming that the legacy of Derrida can somehow be grouped with the legacy of Spinoza. On the contrary, we consider our attempt a 'diversion' and *therefore* worthwhile, precisely because we argue that Derrida's legacy is not something that is bequeathed monopolistically to the so-called 'Derrideans' (which many of the contributors to this volume may be); neither is it something that is bequeathed only to those in academia (which many of the readers of this volume may be). Rather, the Derridean spirit lives on, in fact has lived on, always, already.

We have quoted above from Barenboim's official website that the West-Eastern Divan orchestra is a forum where Israelis and Arabs 'come together to make music on neutral ground'.[37] This idea may sound completely Utopian, given that there is no 'neutral ground' in reality. Indeed, in his lectures Barenboim calls the orchestra 'our [small] Utopian republic'[38] and admits that '[t]his is not going to solve the problems'.[39] However, not only is 'the West Eastern Divan orchestra . . . not going to bring about peace'[40] as such Utopia is possible only in music, but 'this project is not a project for peace' in the first place, because what is meant by Utopia here is a forum that is full of 'different elements'.[41] As Barenboim says of Bach fugues and Mozart concertos and operas, in music, the other voice, the counterpoint or the accompaniment is often 'subversive'.[42] 'Conflict, difference of opinion, is the very essence of music',[43] and yet 'the two fit together'.[44] The two must fit together, because 'when you play music . . . you have to do two very important things and do them simultaneously. You have to be able to express yourself . . . but at the same time it is imperative that you listen to the other.'[45] Otherwise 'we cannot make music'.[46] Through music, then, we can learn or are forced to learn to make the impossible attempt of including the other without subsuming the other within the self, without collapsing the self and the other into one. Importantly, what is happening here, for Barenboim, is an attempt which may not succeed: 'Music in this case is not an expression of what life is, but an expression of what life could be, or what it could become.' The West-Eastern Divan project is a permanent attempt through which, nevertheless, 'everybody's life has been to some extent changed by these experiences.'[47]

'Music demands permanently, at all times, passion and effort',[48] not only because it requires expressing and listening simultaneously, but also because it necessitates a fight against 'the power of silence'.[49] The very first thing that Barenboim highlights in this series of lectures is the 'permanent constant and unavoidable relation' between sound and silence, that sound does not exist positively on its own, but rather it dies as 'the object [falls] back to the law of gravitation on the ground', unless provided with 'additional energy'.[50] Or, to be more precise, even if the attempt is made to provide additional energy, '[music] is by its very nature ephemeral' and, therefore, it is 'essential in music . . . to be able to start from scratch each time we play something', 'to start from scratch, to start from zero, to take experience from the past and yet think it anew'. It is something, for Barenboim, that is essential 'in music as well as in life'.[51]

Such a view may have a tincture of pessimism, but, if so, it is a constructive and positive one: 'I think this is a very positive thing', Barenboim says. It is constructive in the sense that it enables construction to be made, and action to be taken: 'the impossible, if there is some sense behind it, has not only a feeling of adventure, but a feeling of activity.'[52] It enables you to 'make judgement and make a point of view',[53] which, while being 'absolutely elemental', none the less requires 'courage'.[54] In this regard, Barenboim is cogently critical of 'mechanical repetition' where you repeat and rehearse until 'you feel you know everything that you can know about it', because to him such a search for security is, though very difficult to refuse, 'a pattern of life instead of a way of life'.[55] Moreover, it is linked to 'political correctness' which he understands as 'not to have any responsibility for any judgement'.[56] For Barenboim, then, it is crucial to make judgements, and this can only be done 'from the point of view of one individual.'[57]

In attempting the task of concluding this volume, we have made a decision to offer a brief reading of Barenboim's lectures, from the point of view of two individuals. This is our attempt at closure, and, necessarily, a failed one. Any conclusion is a failed closure, but to conclude negotiations of Derrida's legacy with a reading of something which is not normally associated with Derrida is uncomfortable. Still, we would like to attempt to conclude our conclusion to the negotiations of Derrida's legacy by leaving it to the point of view of another individual, Barenboim: 'ambiguity means that there are many many possibilities, many many ways to go.'[58]

NOTES

1. Jacques Derrida, *Of Grammatology*, trans. by Gayatri Chakravorty Spivak, Baltimore, MD: Johns Hopkins University Press, 1976, p. 9.
2. See, e.g., Zygmunt Bauman, *Postmodern Ethics*, Oxford: Blackwell, 1993, p. 13.
3. Alex Thomson, 'Derrida's Rogues: Islam and the futures of deconstruction', p. 76.
4. This should not be read, though, as suggesting a reading of Derrida whereby texts can mean anything, that their meaning is completely unstable. Derrida argues that there is a 'right track, a better way', in terms of reading and understanding what a text is saying. Jacques Derrida, *Limited Inc*, Evanston, IL: Northwestern University Press, 1988, p. 146.
5. Maja Zehfuss, 'Derrida's memory, war and the politics of ethics', p. 108.
6. Ibid. p. 98.
7. April Biccum, 'Exploiting the ambivalence of a crisis', p. 148.
8. Thomson, 'Derrida's *Rogues*', p. 67.
9. Jacques Derrida, *Echographies of Television*, filmed interviews, Jacques Derrida and Bernard Stiegler, trans. by Jennifer Bajorek, Cambridge: Polity Press, 2002, p. 21.
10. Derrida, *Limited Inc*, pp. 146–152.
11. Ibid. p. 117
12. Richard Beardsworth, 'The future of critical philosophy and world politics', p. 55.
13. Derrida, *Limited Inc*, p. 137.
14. Ibid. p. 152.
15. Ibid. p. 151.
16. Ibid. p. 151.
17. Ibid. p. 151.
18. Beardsworth, 'The future of critical philosophy and world politics', p. 65.
19. Ibid. p. 65.
20. Dan Bulley, 'Ethical assassination?', p. 130.
21. Derrida, *Limited Inc*, p. 116.
22. Ibid.
23. Bulley, 'Ethical assassination?', p. 132.
24. Ibid. p. 132.

25. Beardsworth, 'The future of critical philosophy and world politics', p. 63.
26. Ibid. p. 63.
27. Bulley, 'Ethical assassination?', p. 132.
28. Ibid. p. 133.
29. Thomson, 'Derrida's *Rogues*', p. 76.
30. Maja Zehfuss (2003), 'Forget September 11', *Third World Quarterly*, 24:(3), 513–28, at 520. It should be noted that Zehfuss also points out that any particular or distinct framing also entails violences.
31. April Biccum, 'Exploiting the ambivalence of a crisis', p. 148.
32. 'Biography', in the Daniel Barenboim official website: www.danielbarenboim.com/biography.htm.
33. 'The History of the Reith Lectures', in the BBC Radio 4 Reith Lectures website: www.bbc.co.uk/radio4/reith/reith_history.shtml.
34. The recordings and transcripts of the lectures can be found at the BBC Radio 4 Reith Lectures 2006 website: www.bbc.co.uk/radio4/reith2006/.
35. In Daniel Barenboim, 'Lecture 4: Meeting in Music', BBC Radio 4 Reith Lectures 2006, Barenboim explains how the orchestra earned its name:

    We took the name of our project, the West Eastern Divan, from a poem by Goethe, who was one of the first Germans to be genuinely interested in other cultures. He originally discovered Islam when a German soldier who had been fighting in one of the Spanish campaigns brought back a page of the Koran to show to him. His enthusiasm was so great that he started to learn Arabic at the age of sixty. Later he discovered the great Persian poet Hafiz, and that was the inspiration for his set of poems that deal with the idea of the other, the West Eastern Divan, which was first published nearly two hundred years ago, in 1819 . . . Goethe's poem then became a symbol for the idea behind our experiments in bringing Arab and Israeli musicians together.

36. 'Biography', in the Daniel Barenboim official website.
37. Ibid.
38. Daniel Barenboim, 'Lecture 1: In the Beginning was Sound', BBC Radio 4 Reith Lectures 2006; and Barenboim, 'Lecture 4: Meeting in Music'.
39. Barenboim, 'Lecture 4: Meeting in Music'.
40. Ibid.
41. Barenboim, 'Lecture 1: In the Beginning was Sound'.
42. Barenboim, 'Lecture 1: In the Beginning was Sound'; and Daniel Barenboim, 'Lecture 2: The Neglected Sense', BBC Radio 4 Reith Lectures 2006.
43. Barenboim, 'Lecture 2: The Neglected Sense'.
44. Barenboim, 'Lecture 4: Meeting in Music'.
45. Ibid.
46. Barenboim, 'Lecture 1: In the Beginning was Sound'.
47. Barenboim, 'Lecture 4: Meeting in Music'.
48. Ibid.
49. Barenboim, 'Lecture 1: In the Beginning was Sound'.

50. Ibid.
51. Daniel Barenboim, 'Lecture 5: The Power of Music', BBC Radio 4 Reith Lectures 2006.
52. Barenboim, 'Lecture 1: In the Beginning was Sound'.
53. Ibid.
54. Daniel Barenboim, 'Lecture 3: The Magic of Music', BBC Radio 4 Reith Lectures 2006.
55. Barenboim, 'Lecture 2: The Neglected Sense'.
56. Barenboim, 'Lecture 3: The Magic of Music'.
57. Barenboim, 'Lecture 5: The Power of Music'.
58. Barenboim, 'Lecture 3: The Magic of Music'.

Notes on the Contributors

Josef Teboho Ansorge completed an undergraduate degree in International Relations at the University of Wales Aberystwyth and an MPhil degree in International Relations at the University of Cambridge. His research interests include the politics of political theory, post-structural approaches to International Relations and nineteenth-century German political thought.

Richard Beardsworth is Professor of Modern Philosophy at the American University of Paris. He is the author of works on Derrida and Nietzsche and has written and translated extensively in contemporary critical philosophy. He is presently writing on the current challenges of critical philosophy, world politics and political economy.

April R. Biccum is a lecturer in the Department of Politics and International Relations at Lancaster University. Her research focuses on bringing post-colonial theory into the domain of political theory and the politics of development. A book currently under review offers a critique of development from a postcolonial perspective using the promotional literature of the Department for International Development (DFID) as its case study. She has published on this subject previously in an article entitled 'Interrupting the discourse of development: on a collision course with postcolonial theory', in *Culture, Theory and Critique*, 43:(1), pp. 33–50, and 'Development and the "New" Imperialism: A reinvention of colonial discourse in DFID promotional literature', in *Third World Quarterly*, 26(5), July 2005.

Dan Bulley is a Temporary Lecturer in International Relations at the University of Warwick. His research involves the problematisation of the 'ethical' in foreign policy, looking specifically at UK foreign policy since

1997 and the developing EU foreign policy. He has previously published in the *Review of International Studies*, and he was a guest editor of the edition of *International Politics* entitled 'Ethics and World Politics: Cosmopolitanism and Beyond?'.

Michael Dillon is Professor of Politics at Lancaster University. He is the author and editor of several books on politics and security including: *Dependence and Deterrence* (1983); *Defence Policy Making: A Comparative Analysis* (1984); *The Falklands Politics and War* (1989); *The Political Subject of Violence* (co-ed. with David Campbell, 1993); and *Politics of Security* (1996). He publishes widely in international relations, cultural studies and political theory. Journal essays in the last three years have appeared in *Alternatives*, *Body and Society*, *European Journal of Political Theory*, *Millennium*, *Theory*, *Culture and Society*, and *Theory and Event*. He has three books forthcoming: *Governing Terror* (Palgrave/Macmillan); *Foucault: Politics, Society and War* (Palgrave/Macmillan, co-ed. with Andrew Neal); *The Liberal Way of War* (Routledge, with Julian Reid). He is also co-editor of *The Journal of Cultural Research* (Routledge) and international editor of the Edinburgh/New York University Press political theory series *Taking on the Political*.

Jenny Edkins is Professor of International Politics at the University of Wales Aberystwyth. Her recent publications include *Trauma and the Memory of Politics* (Cambridge University Press, 2003) and, with Micahel J. Shapiro and Veronique Pin-Fat, *Sovereign Lives: Power in Global Politics* (Routledge, 2004).

Christina Howells is Professor of French at the University of Oxford and Fellow of Wadham College. She has published and edited several books on Sartre including *Sartre: The Necessity of Freedom* (1979) and *Sartre: A Companion* (1988), both with Cambridge University Press. She has also published a monograph on Derrida with Polity Press in 1998: *Derrida: Deconstruction from Phenomenology to Ethics*, and most recently a collection of texts with Routledge: *French Women Philosophers, A Contemporary Reader: Subjectivity, Identity, Alterity*.

Christopher Norris is Distinguished Research Professor in Philosophy at Cardiff University. He is the author of more than twenty books to date on various aspects of philosophy and literary theory. Among his latest publications are *Quantum Theory and the Flight from Realism* (2000), *Deconstruction and the 'Unfinished Project of Modernity'* (2001) and *Language, Logic and Epistemology: A Modal-Realist Approach* (2004).

Lasse Thomassen is Lecturer in Politics in the Department of Politics and Public Administration at the University of Limerick . He is the editor of *The Derrida–Habermas Reader* (Edinburgh University Press, 2006) and, with Lars Tønder, *Radical Democracy: Politics between Abundance and Lack* (Manchester University Press, 2005). He is currently working on a research monograph on Deconstructing Habermas, to be published with Routledge.

Alex Thomson is Lecturer at the Department of English Literature at the University of Glasgow. He is the author of *Democracy and Deconstruction: Derrida's 'Politics of Friendship'* (Continuum, 2005) and of *Adorno: A guide for the perplexed* (Continuum, forthcoming), as well as of essays and book chapters on deconstruction and critical theory.

Daniel Watt is Research and Publications Assistant at the Centre for Performance Research (CPR), University of Wales Aberystwyth, and is co-editing the CPR anniversary publication *A Performance Cosmology* and books on Meyerhold and Kantor. He holds an MA in Philosophy and Literature from the University of Warwick and his DPhil thesis (University of Sussex) examined 'The future of the fragment: transformations of writing in the work of Blanchot, Beckett, Coetzee, Derrida and Jabès'. His research interests include fragmentary writing, ethics and literature, and philosophical and literary influences on theatre and performance in the twentieth century. He has contributed to *The Oxford Literary Review* and *Wormwood: Writings about Fantasy, Supernatural and Decadent Literature*.

Maja Zehfuss is Lecturer in International Relations at the University of Warwick. She is the author of *Constructivism in International Relations: The Politics of Reality* (Cambridge University Press, 2002). Her second book *Wounds of Memory: German Memories of the Second World War and the Question of War Today* is currently under review, also with Cambridge University Press.

Index